T0129089

PRAISE FOR
SHORTCUT

"A thrilling book, intellectually exciting and engagingly written."

—*Booklist*

"A cogent look at one of the conceptual bedrocks of language."

—*Kirkus Reviews*

"John Pollack is the William Safire of his generation. In *Shortcut,* he blends his encyclopedic knowledge, hard-earned experience in politics, and deep love of words to craft a book that consistently rewards the reader with keen insights into the wonders of how language shapes our thinking."

—Jake Siewert, global head of corporate communications
for Goldman Sachs

"As a historian, I have been professionally trained *not* to use analogies. But as John Pollack demonstrates in this eye-opening, mind-blowing, puzzle-solving book, comparisons and analogies infuse our thinking, infect our decisions, and inflect our efforts at persuasion. Once you lower your guard to Pollack's clever forays, you will never undervalue the power of analogical reasoning again—or ignore the risks of using comparisons too sloppily."

—Jack Rakove, professor of history and political science at
Stanford University, and winner of the Pulitzer Prize

"In the battle for public opinion, the best analogy usually wins. *Shortcut* shows us how—and why. It makes you think before you speak, literally. This is a great book, particularly for people who care about communicating effectively."

—Loretta Ucelli, White House communications director for
President Bill Clinton

"Like a hot knife through warm butter, Pollack's clean prose cuts to the heart of the matter: we communicate, think, learn, and discover through analogies. Filled with captivating and entertaining examples, from falling apples to toppling dominos, the book teaches us how to best use analogies to win hearts, convince minds, and just have fun. Sure to float your boat."

—Scott Page, director of the Center for the Study of Complex Systems
at the University of Michigan

"Pollack takes us on a fascinating journey through the shortcuts of the mind, revealing the immense power of analogy as a psychological device affecting our lives in intricate ways."

—Daniela Schiller, PhD, neuroscientist at the Icahn School of Medicine
at Mount Sinai

"Our minds work like supercomputers, processing impossibly vast amounts of information, creating patterns and parallels to make sense of all the data. *Shortcut* reveals how, through analogies (like the one in the previous sentence!), we understand our world, and, ultimately, ourselves. A fascinating read."

—David Zweig, author of *Invisibles: The Power of Anonymous Work in an Age of Relentless Self-Promotion*

"Pollack offers up an unparalleled feast of analogies, digging deep into his extensive experience as a writer to show why analogy is important, how it's constructed, and what makes it effective. *Shortcut* is to analogies what *The Joy of Cooking* is to brisket."

—Benjamin Bergen, director of the Language and Cognition Lab at the University of California, San Diego, and author of *Louder Than Words*

"Anyone who has ever tried to find the right analogy to win an argument, to settle a dispute, to persuade squabblers to compromise—or who wants to avoid making things worse by using the wrong analogy—should read this insightful book!"

—Suzanne R. Butler, PhD, JD, member of the National Academy of Arbitrators

Also by John Pollack

The Pun Also Rises
Cork Boat

SHORTCUT

· · · · · · · · · · · · · · · · · · · ·

How Analogies Reveal Connections, Spark
Innovation, and Sell Our Greatest Ideas

JOHN POLLACK

AVERY
an imprint of Penguin Random House
New York

AVERY

An imprint of Penguin Random House LLC
375 Hudson Street
New York, New York 10014

The Library of Congress has catalogued the hardcover edition as follows:

Pollack, John.
Shortcut: how analogies reveal connections, spark innovation, and sell our greatest ideas / John Pollack.
p.   cm.
ISBN 978-1-592-40849-8
1. English language—Business English.   2. Creative thinking.   3. Business communication.
4. Analogy.   5. Sociolinguistics.   I. Title.
PE1479.B87P65   2014   2014009895
808'.032—dc23

ISBN 978-1-592-40947-1 (paperback)

Designed by Spring Hoteling

146119709

To my mom and dad,
who show me what is possible

CONTENTS

There is a tide in the affairs of men,
Which, taken at the flood, leads on to fortune;
Omitted, all the voyage of their life
Is bound in shallows and in miseries.
On such a full sea are we now afloat;
And we must take the current when it serves,
Or lose our ventures.

William Shakespeare, Julius Caesar, Act 4, Scene 3

INTRODUCTION

....

BOARDING THE SHIP OF STATE

I tried to look confident but, sitting awkwardly on a yellow couch in the West Wing of the White House, I couldn't get comfortable. Across the room, behind a big wooden desk, sat the chief speechwriter for the president of the United States, scrutinizing my résumé.

Decades earlier, perhaps during the Johnson years, the couch on which I sat had begun its life as a handsome piece of furniture. But after bearing the brunt of many administrations and more than a few crises, its springs were spent. If I leaned back, I'd be swallowed by cushions. If I scooched forward, I might end up on the floor. On edge, I waited.

Only a day earlier, I had been sitting in my fifth-floor walk-up apartment in Dupont Circle—unshaven, unemployed, and uncertain about my future. The call from the White House had caught me by surprise. While I had worked for several years as a speechwriter on Capitol Hill and had twice applied to become a presidential speechwriter, I hadn't been selected. Now one of the president's speechwriters was moving on, and there was an opening. Would I come in for an interview?

When the chief speechwriter, Terry Edmonds, finally looked up, he pushed his glasses to the top of his head. "Your writing is good," he said. "I have no doubt you can do the job. But you have a lot of other . . ." He paused, searching for the right word. "You have a lot of other . . . projects. What is this *cork boat?*" The way he said those words, I knew it wasn't just a question but something of a challenge.

He was asking about the last line on my résumé: *Currently building the world's first cork boat.* I explained that I was saving a hundred thousand wine-bottle corks to build a boat modeled after a Viking ship, which I planned to take on a voyage through French wine country. Building the boat had been a boyhood dream, and I was determined to see it through.

As Edmonds' eyes narrowed, I could feel my last chance to work at the White House ebbing away. But at that moment, as both my career and I teetered on the edge of that couch, an analogy sprang to mind.

"Sir, building a cork boat is a lot like writing a good speech. . . ."

Edmonds' head tilted; his eyebrows rose. It was too late to retreat. "In both cases," I explained, "you take a jumble of small things—corks or words—that don't do much on their own. But if you assemble them carefully, and put them into just the right order, they'll carry you on the most amazing journey."

And then I shut up.

For a long moment, Edmonds stared at me. Then a grin spread across his face, and he shook his head in grudging admiration—not for my nautical ambitions, but for my escape. He got the analogy, and I got the job.

A dozen years later, when I set out to write this book, I intended to explore the subtle yet powerful role of analogy in persuasion. Because while they often operate unnoticed, analogies aren't accidents, they're arguments—arguments that, like icebergs, conceal most of their mass and power beneath the surface. In many arguments, whoever has the best analogy wins.

But as my research progressed, it became clear that analogies do more than just persuade; they also play a catalytic role in innovation and decision making—often with dramatic consequences. From the bloody Chicago slaughterhouse that inspired Henry Ford's first moving assembly line, to the "domino theory" that led America into the Vietnam War, to the "bicycle for the mind" that Steve Jobs envisioned as a Macintosh computer, analogies have played a dynamic role in shaping the world around us.

Despite analogy's importance, many people have only a vague sense of its definition. In broad terms, an analogy is simply a comparison that asserts a parallel—explicit or implicit—between two distinct things, based on the perception of a shared property or relation. In everyday use, analogies actually appear in many forms. Some of these include metaphors, similes, political slogans, legal arguments, marketing taglines, mathematical formulas, biblical parables, logos, TV ads, euphemisms, proverbs, fables, and sports clichés.

Wearing such disguises, analogies can play a much bigger role than most people recognize. Not just because analogies make arguments, but because they often trigger emotions that override the circuits of reason, and sometimes at a subconscious level. All day every day, in fact, we make or evaluate one analogy after the other, because such comparisons are the only practical way to sort a flood of incoming data, place it within the context of our experience, and make decisions accordingly.

The investor Warren Buffett, known for his rich use of analogy, has noted that "You never know who's swimming naked until the tide goes out." In other words, when times are good, it's easy to look good; when times are hard, weaknesses that were hidden beneath the surface are suddenly exposed. The same could be said for analogies themselves: We never know what assumptions, deceptions, or brilliant insights they might be hiding until we look beneath their surface.

Despite the ubiquity and impact of analogical thinking, most people are unaware of just how much this core process influences their decision making. Such lack of awareness comes at a cost. Evidence suggests that people who tend to overlook or underestimate analogy's influence often find themselves struggling to make their arguments or achieve their goals. The converse is also true. Those who construct the clearest, most resonant and apt analogies are usually the most successful in reaching the outcomes they seek.

The ideas in this book draw from the observations, insights, and work of many people, including psychologists, inventors, business leaders, linguists, advertisers, political strategists, legal scholars, neuroscientists, and the world's best pickpocket. A caveat is in order, however. Readers hoping for an exploration of analogy in literature and poetry will not find it in these pages. As rich as those mines are, one could spend a lifetime excavating the metaphors and similes of Shakespeare alone—and many scholars have. This book has a different purpose: helping readers use analogies more effectively to innovate and persuade, and helping them get better at spotting analogies that may sound persuasive but are actually deceptive, faulty, or even dangerous.

Throughout history and across cultures, analogies have animated many of the greatest debates and sparked brilliant discoveries. Similarly, poor analogies have misled many people, companies, and nations into dead ends and disasters. But now, in this age of compounding global challenges, the analogies we embrace—good and bad—will likely produce more serious and lasting consequences. It's in this context that I hope *Shortcut* helps readers become more adept with analogy, enabling them to sidestep its pitfalls and put its power to good and noble use.

SHORTCUT

SHORTCUT

CHAPTER 1

....

APPLES TO ORANGES

How Our Analogical Instinct Fuels Thought

A confident, square-jawed man is skippering a sailboat when a critical piece of hardware fails, causing the sail to start flapping. As the boat loses headway, the man calmly strips the belt from a spare life vest and uses it to reattach the flapping sail to the boat's long, rigid boom. Filling with wind, the big sail—once again stiff—carries the boat onward through waters that part like a V.

The entire incident, depicted in a TV ad, takes less than thirty seconds. And while the analogy between a flapping sail and the ad's subject—erectile dysfunction—is never explicitly stated by the ad's matter-of-fact narrator, the implicit parallel is clear. Even the name of the advertised drug, Viagra, rhymes with Niagara—an awesome physical wonder whose surging white water is at once natural, powerful, and unstoppable. Coincidence? Hardly.

The utility of the imagery and name depend on the audience's ability, even instinct, to analogize. At its core, this instinct is not just the human urge to seek and compare patterns but to infer abstract concepts from one domain and apply them to another. Unlike other animals (many of which are also able to compare superficial patterns), people can identify and compare domains that have nothing to do with each other except for a common, abstract intellectual scaffolding that we ourselves construct.

Intrinsically, sailing and erectile dysfunction have nothing to do with each other. But once stripped of their particulars, both domains can be said to share—within the context of the ad—two common ideas. First, hard is better than soft. Second, controlling a situation is better than a situation controlling you.

Subtle but strong, the ad suggests a firm congruence between two unrelated domains: Just as a confident captain maintains control of his vessel no matter what, so, too, can the average Joe control *his* vessel in the stormy seas of love. While the analogy is not explicitly stated, it is nevertheless clear. Given the barest minimum of cultural knowledge, our minds process the sailing analogy unconsciously and instantaneously.

This is also what we do with the overwhelming majority of data we encounter in daily life. As Leonard Mlodinow notes in *Subliminal: How Your Unconscious Mind Rules Your Behavior*, about 95 percent of all thought is unconscious. This is because our senses send our brains roughly eleven million bits of information per second—vastly more than our conscious processing capacity, which maxes out at an estimated fifty bits per second. "So if your conscious mind were left to process all that incoming information," Mlodinow writes, "your brain would freeze like an overtaxed computer."

But the unconscious brain isn't just discarding all that extra incoming data; it's sorting through it for pattern, contextual relevance, utility, and urgency. A lot of the information we process has to do with keeping the body's many systems running smoothly, no matter what surroundings or activity we may be experiencing at the moment. Much as an apartment building's maintenance team works behind the scenes to keep the furnace, air-conditioning, plumbing, and electrical systems in good order without bothering the tenants, the mind runs most bodily functions without conscious oversight—most of the time. Only when a task is particularly taxing, uncomfortable, or urgent does the unconscious call up the head office for direction and additional resources.

LOG OR CROCODILE?

Such analogical thinking is as old as humanity. Indeed, without it, we wouldn't be here. Imagine our human ancestors, millions of years ago in East Africa, stopping in the midday heat to drink at a stream. Presumably, those who could more quickly and accurately detect differences in obscure or incomplete patterns—such as the knobby brown snout of a submerged crocodile versus a knotty brown protrusion of a submerged log—would have done better detecting danger and therefore enjoyed a significant advantage in the struggle for survival. Those who were unable to spot the difference, fill in the missing visual gaps, and infer their potential impact became the crocodile's lunch.

As noted, we humans aren't the only animals capable of pattern recognition or the quick reactions that follow. Widespread pattern recognition is the reason that camouflage is so common in nature, as animals have adapted to blend in with their surroundings. Other creatures have adopted the opposite strategy, mimicking the appearance of an unappealing or threatening alternative for those who might otherwise eat them. But while many other animals are adept at such comparison, evidence suggests that only humans are capable of using deep analogical thought to identify and exploit conceptual similarities that go beyond the superficial.

As researchers have explored the function of analogy in human thought, they have found that analogy may lie in the core of all decision making. Psychologists Douglas Hofstadter and Emmanuel Sander, authors of *Surfaces and Essences: Analogy as the Fuel and Fire of Thinking*, are leading experts in the study of analogy. They argue that whether we're ordering food in a new restaurant, looking both ways before crossing a busy street, or deciding that an approaching golden retriever is less threatening than the rottweiler we saw earlier, we're making a series of analogies with past experiences that we've already categorized for easy reference.

Such analogizing is so common that we aren't necessarily conscious that we're doing it. And even when incoming data demands higher-order decision making, the unconscious does a lot of screening and organizing before passing on an executive summary for conscious evaluation. To get a better sense of this, think about how the White House processes, evaluates, and filters the thousands of calls, letters, and e-mails from people constantly clamoring for the president's attention. Only a small subset of messages ever reaches the Oval Office for the president's consideration and potential executive action. Yet some, especially those concerning key legislation or urgent matters of national security, receive priority routing.

Other messages, such as letters from struggling citizens, might be less urgent but still important. And while all the letters the president ends up reading tell stories that are unique in their specifics, they are typically representative examples—analogs—of hundreds or thousands just like them. In actuality, all those other letters "just like" them are not identical in every detail. But they share the same gist, and it is in that context that the president makes the intuitive, analogical leap to grasp the deeper truths they reveal about a bigger social, economic, or political narrative.

Effectively, this is how the brain works. Every day, all of us are constantly evaluating a flood of incoming data—sight, sound, touch, smell—for their relevance and utility in a wide range of cause-and-effect narratives, which we then use to inform our decision making.

"If one never trusted a single analogy, how could one understand anything in this world? What, other than one's past, can one rely on in grounding decisions that one makes when facing a new situation?" Hofstadter and Sander write. "And of course all situations *are* in fact new, from the largest and most abstract ones down to the tiniest and most concrete ones."

ANALOGIES ARE MODELS

In essence, analogies are a type of model that can take virtually limitless forms, well beyond the verbal realm. For example, people use mathematics to help model the future in abstract terms—numbers and processes—that enable them to predict supply and demand in a particular market, explore the ramifications of different retirement plans, or estimate how fast climate change might increase sea levels.

On a simpler level, envision a child's model train set. However idealized, the image that comes to mind is an analogy of the actual working railroad that inspired it, and serves as a catalyst for imaginary journeys and adventures. Similarly, a bathroom air freshener's pine scent is supposed to be analogous to the smell of a coniferous forest, just as some industrially produced breakfast syrup—derived from corn—is supposed to taste like real maple syrup. As such, these analogies, whether direct or subtle, are intended to trigger a set of positive sensations, thoughts, and emotions.

In an entirely different context, we interpret Ansel Adams' iconic photographs of Yosemite to be analogies of the landscape they depict, and accept the recorded words of Dr. Martin Luther King Jr. as the actual voice of the late civil rights leader himself. Were humans to lack this analogical instinct, all that we encounter would fail to trigger the rich networks of ideas, memories, and emotions that endow our experiences with contextual meaning and potential utility.

THINK OUTSIDE THE BUBBLE

The word *analogy* traces its linguistic roots to the Greek *analogia*, a mathematical term meaning proportion, or equality of ratios. Over the centuries, though, the word has taken on much broader, richer meaning. In 1843, John Stuart Mill wrote that there is no word "which is used more loosely, or in a greater variety of senses, than Analogy." The *Oxford English Dictionary* suggests he may be correct: Some meanings it cites for *analogy* include correspondence, equivalency or likeness of relations, resemblance of form or function, agreement between things, similarity, and the process of reasoning from parallel cases under the assumption that if things have some similar attributes, their other attributes will also be similar.

To some, such a definition of *analogy* may seem too elastic. Admittedly, like a rubber band stretched too far, every definition eventually reaches a breaking point. But while a standardized test question such as "Race cars are to the Indy 500 as _____ are to the Kentucky Derby" is certainly one type of analogy, it is just that—one type. Fixated on such a narrow definition, though, many people often fail to recognize analogy's true role in our thinking, language, and decision making.

Even ordinary, everyday speech is filled with subtle analogies. Consider the sentence "The stock market skyrocketed today as traders, relieved to see Congress break months of gridlock, embraced news of a bipartisan budget plan." On its face, this is a straightforward sentence. But look again, and at least four analogies become apparent. The words *stock market* originally referred to a gathering place to trade livestock. The word *skyrocket* originally referred to a rocket shooting into the sky. The word *gridlock*—originally coined in the 1970s to describe traffic so bad that it brought the flow of vehicles in a city's street grid to a standstill—traces its own root components to the Middle English *griddle* (a flat forerunner of the ridged waffle iron) as well as the Old English *loc*, meaning bolt, fastening, barrier, or enclosure. Finally, traders can't physically "embrace" news unless they're hugging their computers or, perhaps, a copy of *The Wall Street Journal*. Neither do members of Congress "break" gridlock in any literal sense. But through a process of analogical extension, we have enriched these words—and many others such as *understand* and *backstab*—to encompass much more than the physical actions they once connoted.

This makes sense, for we can describe something new only in terms of things we already understand. That's why we constantly adapt old words to new uses and update their meaning. Otherwise, how could one ever *sail* through school with *flying colors*? Or use a *mouse* to *drag* a *folder* across a computer's *desktop* and drop it into the *trash*? In an age when few people sail, let alone fly pennants from their ship's halyards, and when laptops and wireless Internet access free us from the confines of an office, we hardly ever think of such words in terms of their antecedents. That's because all of them have become analogies whose new, expanded meanings are entirely familiar and natural.

Most idioms and clichés, in fact, have lost their original, literal meaning. When we take a rain check, spill the beans, become a whistle-blower, sow our wild oats, judge a book by its cover, lose our marbles, or decide that it's high time we got the hell out of Dodge, we are using analogies whose origins rarely enter our consciousness.

Yet these all remain useful phrases, because they offer a convenient shorthand to distill common but complex ideas, and communicate them quickly. For example, what do we actually mean when we say, "It's not over until the fat lady sings?" The cliché certainly encompasses a wide range of situations beyond the classic, operatic finale from which it is derived. In its most general sense, the phrase suggests that the final outcome of a contest or struggle has yet to be determined, no matter how likely one outcome may appear. But it can also serve as a beleaguered protagonist's declaration of determination to prevail, even as time runs short. Alternatively, it can signal a speaker's knowledge of a pending reversal in fortune, perhaps through a secret plan or trick play, or simply their hope for a timely stroke of good luck, however unlikely that might be.

Closely examined, such idioms reveal that even familiar or mundane analogies can trigger networks of ideas that radiate outward, much as a pebble tossed into a pond creates concentric ripples, which in turn create still more patterns when they themselves encounter obstacles.

ANALOGIES CAMOUFLAGE ARGUMENTS

Given this rippling chain reaction of association, the analogies we encounter can dramatically alter the way we think. Sometimes even one-word analogies, which sound innocuous enough, camouflage entire arguments. Think about how many politicians, journalists, economists, and business leaders describe the economy as a commercial "ecosystem." Implicitly, this description asserts an analogy between a complex web of relationships and interactions in the economic world with a complex web of relationships and interactions in the natural world.

This parallel implies that markets, like ecosystems, are entirely natural, balanced, and self-regulating, with little need for human oversight or intervention. Another analogy describes the economy as a specific type of ecosystem: a jungle. To many in the world of business, such an analogy would suggest steaming, primordial, and untamed danger—hardly a reassuring thought for those seeking to save for retirement in their 401(k) plans. As Princeton economist and historian Tim Leonard argues, a more accurate analogy for the economy might be that of a garden whose careful cultivation—intervening to encourage desired growth and to eliminate weeds and pests—improves the harvest.

It is not surprising that most people fail to pay close attention to the many subtle analogies they encounter, let alone the corresponding implications. In the thousands of thoughts we have every day, we just don't have the time to examine every analogy. And from an evolutionary standpoint, that's positive, at least on average. If we couldn't quickly and accurately analogize to extract the essence of a situation, we'd have a hard time getting through most days, let alone a lifetime.

AS EASY AS ABC

Research suggests that even one-year-old children can make basic perceptual analogies. By the age of four, most can understand abstract analogies such as "bird is to nest as dog is to doghouse"—that is, each animal lives in its own, special kind of home. Grasping analogies is a slow process at first, but as we begin categorizing what we encounter and steadily enriching those categories as circumstances demand, our understanding of the world expands and accelerates.

A prototypical progression might be how we expand our concept of "mother." Starting as infants with our own mother, we gradually expand the concept to encompass the mothers of our playmates, then mothers of animals, then mothers of our own parents and other adults, and eventually such abstractions as mother ship, motherboard, and Mother Earth. We keep broadening concepts through the analogical process because it is not only helpful but also a necessity, and necessity is the mother of invention.

Research suggests that it is this ability to make and manipulate increasingly abstract mental representations that explains humanity's ascent to dominance in a world of stronger, faster, sharper-toothed competitors. And much of this ability correlates with a gradual, evolutionary increase in the size of the human braincase; ancient skulls seem to increase in volume in concert with an archeological record of technological advancement. One area of the prefrontal cortex called Brodmann Area 10 seems to play an important role in organizing sensory input and putting plans into action. As this and other areas grew, there was more room for more connections between more neurons, which enabled greater free association and a correspondingly better ability to make analogies.

Over time, this increasing cognitive fluidity enabled people to grasp and exploit increasingly abstract insights. Roughly 35,000 years ago, in Southern Africa, someone carved twenty-nine notches into the tibia of a baboon, an artifact known today as the Lebombo bone, named for the mountains in which it was unearthed in the early 1970s. Given that the number of notches matches the number of phases of the moon, and that modern Bushmen use similar tally sticks as calendars, scholars believe this to be an ancient tool used to track the passage of time, possibly in correspondence with a woman's menstrual cycle.

The Lebombo bone suggests that ancient people had not only a conceptual awareness of time but also the ability to translate observations about the orbit of the moon into a linear two-dimensional analog of time. In short, these early astronomers had the capacity to represent natural phenomena abstractly and to analyze long-term patterns for cause and effect, at least in terms of menstruation and fertility.

In Europe, contemporaries of the Lebombo bone's creator were painting cave walls with images of the animals they hunted, and carving stone figurines of animals and people. And although these artistic depictions are significantly different from their subjects in form, material, and scale, we can still recognize them easily because most are analogs of familiar, modern descendants.

While the deeper spiritual meaning or purpose of such paintings and carvings may be forever lost to history, they still tell an important story. Their existence reveals that early humans had developed the ability to create and manipulate symbolic representations of living beings. This, in turn, suggests an ability to see themselves and the animals in their world as objects within larger systems. Such observational detachment likely helped people make decisions that improved their chances for survival. Even the decision to worship a totem might have endowed a worshipper with greater determination to prevail—an invaluable psychological resource in challenging times.

Such prehistoric representational art eventually evolved into writing, as Mesopotamian and Egyptian scribes began developing various pictographic scripts that over time became increasingly abstract. Then, about 3,700 years ago, an unknown scribe (or scribes) in what is today the Sinai Desert recognized that, among the seven hundred Egyptian hieroglyphs then in common use, nearly all comprised a limited number of sounds.

Seeking a more flexible, convenient way to represent ideas than these traditional, cumbersome pictograms, these scribes distilled the most common sounds into twenty-two symbols, which today we call letters. Each of these letters was an abstract, visual analog derived from a hieroglyph, or part of a hieroglyph, whose specific meaning was abandoned when its phonetic value was pressed into service.

This intellectual breakthrough produced the world's first phonetic alphabet, which modern scholars call North Semitic. Its logic of one symbol representing one sound—rather than one symbol for every word, syllable, or concept—made writing simple to learn and easy to use, not just for a few highly trained scribes but for a relatively broad population.

FINDING OUR WAY

For the first time in human history, people had a practical way to write down ideas of infinite complexity and transmit them over time. This meant that people could accumulate and distribute knowledge with unprecedented ease, which accelerated learning, exploration, trade, economic growth, and scientific progress. As one of history's most innovative tools, the North Semitic alphabet was so practical that it was adopted and adapted for thousands of years to come, evolving into alphabets that included Phoenician, Greek, Hebrew, Arabic, Latin, English, Persian, Russian, and the scripts of Ethiopia and the Indian subcontinent, including Sanskrit.

Another ancient example of the analogical instinct at work finds expression in the navigational feats of early seafarers who, beginning about 5,000 years ago, began sailing east from Southern Asia into the vast reaches of the Pacific, eventually populating thousands of far-flung islands. In retrospect, their navigational achievements are especially impressive because currents or accidental drift cannot account for the settlement of certain islands or archipelagos, including those of Easter Island, New Zealand, and Hawaii.

So how did these sailors navigate? Long before the invention of the compass and sextant, these aboriginal voyagers invented a range of tools to guide their canoes to isolated atolls in a vast and unforgiving sea. Among others, these included woven "swell charts" to track progress in relation to wave patterns, miniature celestial maps carved inside of gourds, and corresponding "wind compasses" that correlated prevailing winds with the migration of stars. Given the navigational challenges of such long voyages, during which small errors could have mortal consequences, a strong analogical instinct was critical. Only those who honed it were likely to survive and pass on their knowledge to successive generations.

Even today, with all the latest technology, many of us still rely on the analogical instinct to navigate. When we use Google Maps on an iPhone, for example, we track our movement, represented as a pulsating blue dot on a map, which is a two-dimensional analog of three-dimensional geography. As we move, we compare this dot with corresponding clues from our actual, physical surroundings, such as street signs, highway exits, landmark buildings, parks, rivers, and other natural features. Google's Street View feature makes this process especially easy. If we were incapable of analogical reasoning, such digital maps—or any printed map—would be useless.

This is why, when we complain about a bad map, we're really complaining about the disappointing quality of a given analogy. Over time, maps generally become better, as cartographers update their charts, using more accurate and detailed information. A good example is the evolution of maps of what is today the state of Michigan, the geographic borders of which are defined almost entirely by the coastlines of the Great Lakes. Originally, these maps were largely conjecture, based on verbal descriptions by natives and the crude observations of European fur traders who plied the waters in large birch-bark canoes. Later, explorers and trained surveyors took more accurate measure of the geography, and today satellites provide more detailed information yet—all of which yield progressively more accurate two-dimensional analogs of the actual geography.

In the end, a map's accuracy matters only to the level of detail that its users need to guide navigation. Today, when native Michiganders are asked where they're from, many will use their right hand as a map, holding it up as if swearing an oath, and point out their hometown's "location" with their other hand. Why? Because Michigan's Lower Peninsula bears a striking resemblance to a mitten. People who live in Cheboygan, just south of the Straits of Mackinac (which separate the Upper and Lower Peninsulas), might say they're from the "Tip of the Mitt." Similarly, residents of Bad Axe, about one hundred miles north of Detroit, live in the "Thumb."

In a second, handy coincidence of geography and physiology, Michigan's Upper Peninsula is also shaped like a mitten, but for the left hand, this one extended as if offering a handshake rather than taking an oath. Once it is explained, even those who have never visited the Great Lakes State understand the geographic analogy, because their mind—visualizing a comparison between those hands and a map of Michigan—makes the conceptual leap.

But *how* does the mind actually make that leap? How does it identify the intrinsic essence of something, whether that something is an object, a situation, a living thing, or even just an idea? And how does one person make an analogy that triggers the intended associations in the mind of another, especially when most of the assumptions or implications of any given analogy are never explicitly mentioned?

LOST IN TRANSLATION

Benjamin Bergen is a neuroscientist at the University of California, San Diego, and an expert in how the brain translates perception into meaning. As he notes in his book *Louder Than Words: The New Science of How the Mind Makes Meaning*, symbols and words don't have any intrinsic meaning except that which we assign to them. For example, the words *dog*, *chien*, *sag*, and *perro* all refer to the same animal, respectively, in English, French, Farsi, and Spanish. Indeed, the diverse vocabularies of more than six thousand languages attest to the arbitrary nature of such linguistic labels. "Simply identifying and arranging symbols in some language, even if those symbols represent something in the real world, isn't enough to make meaning," Bergen writes.

Rather, much of the meaning we assign to things—whether they're physical objects or abstract ideas—flows out of our own direct, accumulated experience with them. According to Bergen, one of the core aspects of human cognition is not just that we know superficial qualities of cartoon things, but that we intuit about their less apparent qualities, too. This ability to identify something's intrinsic properties can be exceptionally useful, even vital.

What would your reaction be if a potential business partner pulled out a long contract with lots of fine print, uncapped a pen, and suggested you sign it on the spot? Chances are, based on rudimentary knowledge of contracts and their potential for complexity, you'd defer signing until your lawyer could review the document and suggest any necessary changes.

Alternatively, imagine that you are walking through a city at night, when you begin to suspect that a stranger across the street is following you. You might seek refuge in the nearest crowded, well-lit place, pull out your phone to call 911, or begin thinking of ways to defend yourself. After all, we've seen analogous situations unfold hundreds of time on TV and in the movies—and they often don't end well.

But what's amazing about the human mind, as opposed to the minds of other animals who also possess a fight-or-flight instinct, is that people can imagine things that are entirely novel, nonexistent, or utterly impossible. As Bergen notes, when people are instructed to think of a flying pig, most can easily imagine one in their minds, even though such a creature is completely fictional.

Some people might envision one with two feathered wings attached to their front shoulders, much like a Renaissance angel. Others might envision a pig wearing a caped superhero outfit, leaping tall barns in a single bound. Still others might recall Miss Piggy, the Muppet, gracefully airborne in the arms of guest star Rudolf Nureyev in *Swine Lake*, or picture a wild boar sitting in the cockpit of an F-16 fighter jet, sporting a pair of Ray-Bans. In short, when presented with the words *flying pig*, the actual image we construct in our mind's eye depends on an infinitely rich array of inputs and experiences that vary from person to person.

Bergen marshals significant new laboratory and neurological evidence to support the embodied simulation hypothesis—a theory suggesting that we understand the words we encounter by actually simulating, in our minds, the experience the language describes. Envision a dolphin leaping from the ocean. Imagine the smell of brewing coffee on a cold winter morning. Hear the sound of a high school marching band in a Fourth of July parade. Recall the exhaustion you felt climbing a long flight of stairs, helping a friend move into a new apartment.

Now, depending on your personal experience, some of these words may evoke more vivid mental imagery than others, but to speakers of English, all will trigger the firing of neurons that, to one degree or another, echo patterns created by these actual experiences in our lives, or secondary knowledge of such experiences. According to Bergen's research and that of others, this is because we are using much of the same basic equipment in the brain to *imagine* a leaping dolphin as we do when we actually *see* a leaping dolphin. Similarly, if you are told to think about the actual motions you make in opening your front door, your brain will fire many of the same neurons as it does when you actually *do* open your door, except that in the imagined scenario, the brain inhibits the actual execution of those motions.

GETTING A GRIP ON REALITY

Surprisingly, this process of embodied simulation also seems to occur when we're thinking about abstract concepts such as reality, rejection, interest rates, joy, time, or even the very notion of idea. Building on the seminal work of linguist George Lakoff and philosopher Mark Johnson, Bergen argues that our brains manipulate such concepts by ascribing physical, perceptual, or spatial properties to them, as when we say:

She's losing her *grip* on reality.

Repeated rejection had left him *bitter*.

When the lab tests came back negative, his spirits *rose*.

The instant she agreed to marry me, I was *filled* with joy.

As his manager announced the annual sales quota, the salesman thought: "That *stinks!*"

Much as we might slip a bridle and reins onto a horse to help direct it as we choose, we harness abstract concepts by endowing them with qualities we perceive in the physical world—volume, taste, direction, quantity, and smell, among others—to help manage them more easily in our minds.

In their classic 1980 book, *Metaphors We Live By*, Lakoff and Johnson explore the ways in which we conceptually lasso time, a neat linguistic rope trick that gives us some rudimentary control over the idea of time but, alas, not time itself.

Often, we endow time with substance and quantity—"We're *running out of time*. There just *aren't enough hours* to get the job done." We also put time in a physical location, either in front of or behind us— "When I leave for vacation, I'm going to *put this whole year behind me*. That's why I'm really *looking forward to my time off*." Sometimes we think about time itself as moving—"He was supposed to be the future of the Democratic Party, but *time passed him by*." Or "As she waited for the bus to arrive, *time really started to drag*." Or "For a moment, when he saw her walk into the room, *time stood still*."

We also give time the power of agency—"I can't be sure at the moment, but *time will tell*." Or "She was very beautiful in her twenties, but *time took its toll*."

Apparently, this capacity to understand language—even language that is abstract—comes from the way we have adapted old perceptual systems to new and powerful uses. As Bergen sums it up, "Evolution has cobbled together a new machine from old parts it had lying around in the junkyard of the brain."

A $60 MILLION MASTERPIECE

In the dark early hours of August 8, 1963, an intrepid gang of robbers hot-wired a six-volt battery to a railroad signal not far from the town of Leighton Buzzard, some forty miles north of London. Shortly, the engineer of an approaching mail train, spotting the red light ahead, slowed his train to a halt and sent one of his crew down the track, on foot, to investigate. Within minutes, the gang overpowered the train's crew and, in less than twenty minutes, made off with the equivalent of more than $60 million in cash.

Years later, Bruce Reynolds, the mastermind of what quickly became known as the Great Train Robbery, described the spectacular heist as "my Sistine Chapel." To some, the comparison with Michelangelo's masterpiece might seem as audacious as the theft itself. Yet whether one agrees with Reynolds' analogy, we understand the point he's trying to make. Still, how is it that we are able to make the conceptual leap from a twentieth-century British train robbery to a sixteenth-century Vatican chapel, and grasp the parallels? Analogy researchers believe this happens through a process called structure mapping.

First advanced in the early 1990s by Dedre Gentner, a psychology professor at Northwestern University who directs the university's cognitive science program, structure mapping describes how we map knowledge from a conceptual base (such as the Sistine Chapel) onto a target (the Great Train Robbery) in a way that preserves the structure of relevant relationships within each, while discarding what we consider to be irrelevant differences. Evidence suggests that we tend to map this knowledge according to higher-order relations—the highest order we can identify.

In this case, based on our knowledge of the creativity, planning, and extraordinary skill that went into creating the Sistine Chapel, we infer that similarly elevated levels of creativity, planning, and skill were required to successfully intercept and rob a Royal Mail train loaded with 120 bags of cash and get away with the loot.

In processing Reynolds' analogy, we intuitively disregard all the obvious differences between train robbery and Renaissance art. Reynolds, in asserting their equivalence, implies an associated, higher-order relation: the parallel between Michelangelo (the genius who conceived and painted the Sistine Chapel) and himself (the genius who conceived and led the robbery).

Like the Sistine Chapel, the Great Train Robbery stands in a class of its own in its audacity and execution. This in turn implies an even more abstract, higher-level relation between the two domains: Those who admire Michelangelo as an artistic genius should admire Bruce Reynolds as an artistic genius, too. Those who would paint the competing masterpieces with a different moral brush are missing the point; art is art after all, so give the artist his due.

Even for those whose sense of morality constrains them from accepting the equivalence of art and robbery, some might still concede the basic point that both Michelangelo's and Reynolds' most famous works were arguably the best in their respective categories. It's the same idea, in principle, as calling a pricey vacuum cleaner the Rolls-Royce of vacuums, or describing a generous health insurance policy as a Cadillac plan.

But any given analogy's "truth" is intrinsically subjective. Was the American occupation of Iraq a modern Vietnam? Is hip-hop the new jazz? Is Washington just Hollywood for ugly people? Argue away—there are no right or wrong answers, at least not by any purely objective standard.

Once we pay conscious attention to the words we use and the way most people talk, it quickly becomes apparent what a central role analogy plays and the many forms it can take, including that of metaphor, simile, allegory, idiom, parable, aphorism, cliché, euphemism, and proverb. Without people's analogical instinct, none of these rhetorical devices would be possible, let alone useful.

Even the ways we describe basic concepts in our lives are analogical in nature—life is a journey, time is money, the body is a machine, the mind is a computer, and love is a roller coaster. We accept these because we perceive that the paired concepts, however different in actuality, are indeed alike in important ways.

While a member of the Yanomami tribe who has lived his entire life in the Amazon rain forest without exposure to money, machines, computers, or roller coasters might not understand these culturally dependent analogies, those of us who live and work in modern, technological societies grasp their meanings almost intuitively. And in grasping these intended meanings, we embrace their "obvious" truths and dismiss their myriad dissimilarities.

QUICK TO JUDGE

Daniel Kahneman is a psychologist whose research into human decision making earned him a share of the 2002 Nobel Prize in Economics. In his 2011 book, *Thinking, Fast and Slow*, Kahneman argues that, conceptually, two mental systems drive the way people think. What he calls System 1 works quickly, intuitively, and emotionally. System 2 works more slowly, logically, and deliberately—and often only to justify the impulsive decisions of System 1. Both systems operate within every person's mind, although some people tend to favor one over the other.

Just as most people will generally exert the least amount of energy necessary to complete a given physical task, such as taking an elevator instead of climbing stairs, a similar "general law of least effort" also applies to people's cognitive efforts. Research suggests that this tendency might be due to the fact that challenging mental activity appears to require more of the body's basic fuel, glucose. When we avoid hard thinking, we save mental energy, literally. Bluntly, we're programmed to be lazy, and are inclined to follow the path of least resistance.

Usually, such quick thinking works to our advantage. Much as computers use algorithms to compress digital data, people's minds seek efficient ways to compress mental data. One tactic we use is to record information outside our brains in numbers, written words, images, and recorded sound. Another tactic, this one internal, is remembering stories. And many analogies are just that—compressed stories. Fables, which owe their instructive power to the analogical instinct, illustrate this well. Aesop's "The Boy Who Cried Wolf" has been shortened to the analogical expression "crying wolf." In another fable, "The Fox and the Grapes," a fox becomes frustrated because he cannot reach clusters of juicy grapes that, however tantalizing, hang just out of reach. Giving up, the fox declares they looked sour anyway—a sentiment that generations have distilled into the expression "sour grapes."

We may take these quick analogies for granted, but the ideas they convey are actually quite complex. And the degree to which an analogy is or is not "accurate" in a given circumstance is irrelevant; it is the feelings and ideas they evoke that make them so powerful.

This may be one reason that effective analogies, which are essentially compressed and spring-loaded stories, often enable people to seize the high ground in an argument. In offering a coherent narrative, they allow their creators to deftly sidestep the quicksand of competing "facts" and more closely approach the intellectual and emotional core of their argument.

THE STIGMA OF A TOILET SEAT

But when narratives conflict, we're forced to evaluate competing analogies and judge them in relation to each other. In late 1957, for example, the Ford Motor Company introduced a new line of cars intended to appeal to upwardly mobile drivers. The car, whose initial clay model reportedly drew a standing ovation from Ford executives, was billed as "the revolutionary car of the future." In a complimentary preview of the car, *The New York Times* likened its horizontal taillights to "the graceful wingspread of a sea gull" and suggested that the car's vertical front grille gave it a "distinctive continental flair."

Analogical descriptions were necessary, because the car would be strikingly different in appearance from all other cars on the market, and Ford withheld all images of the car until its official launch. The analogy between the taillights and seagulls was especially apt, because it was both visually accurate and emotionally evocative. Seagulls are extraordinarily graceful in flight. Whether they're swooping across the blue sky or floating in place with the slightest of effort, they rarely need to flap their wings. More than a few weekend sunbathers, lying on a beach and dreading their return to work on Monday, have gazed upon a gull's freedom with a certain envy. It's no coincidence that the cliché "free as a bird" captures that very emotion. Given such a wealth of positive associations, who wouldn't want a car that evoked feelings of soaring grace and freedom?

Thanks to a masterful public relations campaign, Ford built up such excitement for this new car that, on the day it was released, some three million people flocked to dealerships to get their first look at the oddly named Edsel. But their reactions were, on the whole, dramatically less enthusiastic than that of *The New York Times*. Quickly, people began lampooning its front grille as a horse collar and a toilet seat, among other unflattering descriptions. Compared to associations with a seagull soaring in the ocean breeze, those evoked by a working draft horse and a toilet seat are more earthbound. As a consequence, Ford found itself on the defensive, insisting that the car really *was* attractive.

Compounding Ford's problems, *Consumer Reports* criticized the Edsel's quality. Also, between the time it was conceived and launched, a recession had undermined the purchasing power of its target market. Given this, it would be inaccurate to attribute the Edsel's dismal reception solely to public descriptions of the front grille. But all the millions of dollars that Ford poured into advertising and marketing the car couldn't overcome the public's unflattering analogies.

The public's descriptions of the Edsel offer three instructive insights into the analogical instinct. First, one can only describe or explain something new in an effective way by using concepts with which an audience is already somewhat familiar. In the late 1820s, it was common to call a steam-powered locomotive an iron horse because this novel, powerful machine was starting to replace the horses that initially pulled railcars along tracks. Similarly, all the sooty smoke from the Industrial Revolution, combined with fog, gave rise to the word *smog*. In the case of Ford's new automobile, its unconventional design left everyone who saw it searching for a way to describe it.

Second, the more familiar we are with the subject matter of a given analogy, the easier the analogy is to grasp and the more likely it is to resonate. As such, "toilet seat" would likely beat out "horse collar" as a descriptor because, by the 1950s, affluent suburban Americans—this car's target market—were much more familiar with toilet seats than with equine farm equipment.

Third, due to the way our minds perform embodied simulation, an explicit visual analogy will generally communicate an idea more quickly and effectively than a vague, abstract description. This is because specific images, especially of something familiar, will trigger bigger and more resonant networks of associated images, ideas, and emotions. People in the Western world often associate toilet seats with defecation, which can in turn trigger one of the oldest and strongest human emotions—disgust. Compare that to the emotional power of "continental flair." Well, what exactly *is* continental flair? Certainly, with enough time and cultural literacy, one could articulate what the critic probably meant by that description, but to communicate the subtleties of such an aesthetic sensibility would require a lot more effort by critic and reader alike. That's why describing something as specific and familiar as a toilet seat is the stickier analogy.

Although it is highly unlikely that anyone in 1957 puzzled their way through this battle of analogies with such conscious deliberation, they didn't have to; most people took one look at the car and rendered a quick verdict—it stank. The toilet seat grille just happened to symbolize their gut reaction to the car as a whole.

Entirely apart from its unpopular design and the analogies used to describe it, the name Edsel didn't help the car's sales either. Originally, Ford had code-named the project the E-Car—the *E* stood for *Experimental*—and researched and rejected thousands of possible names. Then, in a meeting of the company's executive committee, Ford's chairman of the board Ernest Breech suggested naming it after the late Edsel Ford, who was Henry Ford's son and had served as the company's president before his death in 1943.

"He was brown-nosing Mr. Ford," the Edsel's former public relations director, C. Gayle Warnock, told *The Washington Post* in 2007. "I knew nobody would like that name," he said. "When they did interviews and asked about Edsel, people always said, 'Did you say pretzel?'"

Edsel had never been a popular name in the United States, and was not even among the top 1,000 when the car was launched. To compound problems, its phonetic similarity to a cheap, common snack didn't communicate the upward mobility that Ford intended the car to symbolize. In a curious twist, some etymologists trace the origin of the word pretzel to the medieval Latin description of an indigenous, looping German pastry known as folded arms. The snack's name makes total sense: Cross your arms over your chest, and you'll discover they actually do resemble a traditional pretzel. Ironically, in the mid twentieth century, "crossed arms" turned out to describe the body language of thousands of skeptical customers enduring an Edsel dealer's sales pitch.

Whatever the cause, Edsel sales lagged from the start. Having projected to sell 200,000 the first year, Ford sold only 63,100 in the 1958 model year, and fewer than 45,000 the next. Even a desperate promotional effort, in which people who test-drove an Edsel were offered the chance to win a pony, failed to stir up sales. Optimistically, Ford had purchased a thousand ponies and shipped them throughout the country, where Edsel dealers tethered them outside their showrooms. And while the contest did attract some families whose kids begged their parents to win them a pony, both dealers and "lucky" winners soon came to appreciate why cars had replaced horses in the first place; it wasn't just a matter of feeding the ponies, it was cleaning up after them. Soon, dealers were shipping the animals back to Detroit.

In late 1959, limping into its third year of dismal sales—a paltry 2,486 cars—Ford canceled production and shut down the entire Edsel division. The Edsel, which cost the company more than $2.7 billion in today's dollars, was such a colossal, spectacular, and public failure that its name quickly became an analogy itself, a synonym for any big new product so overwhelmingly and immediately unpopular that people refuse to purchase it.

Generally, nobody wants to take the blame for failure, especially a big one. As President John F. Kennedy famously noted after the 1961 Bay of Pigs fiasco, "Victory has a thousand fathers; defeat is an orphan." But in the case of the Edsel, chief designer Roy Brown Jr. took the fall. Despite going on to help design a number of highly successful vehicles, such as Ford's Econoline van, he was always remembered for his most unpopular effort, the car whose design he defended until his death in 2013 at the age of ninety-six.

"A lot of people said, 'Hey, it's Roy Brown's fault,' " Brown told an interviewer, years after the Edsel debacle. "I did what I was told and I did a good job of it." Nevertheless, he lamented, "There are people that have toilet-seat minds." Such is the analogical instinct.

CHAPTER 2

....

THREE STRIKES AND YOU'RE OUT

How Analogies Shape Outcomes

On a summer evening in 1992, eighteen-year-old Kimber Reynolds was walking out of a Fresno restaurant when two men pulled up on a motorcycle and tried to grab her purse. When she resisted, one of them yanked a .357 Magnum from his waistband, put it to her ear, and pulled the trigger. As she collapsed to the pavement, the assailants roared off. Kimber died the next day.

Police soon tracked down the two men, both of whom were convicted felons. Cornered, one tried to shoot his way out but was killed. Officers captured the second one alive. Kimber's father, Mike, distraught with anger and grief yet determined to prevent other families from suffering such a brutal tragedy, made a vow: to see that such dangerous, career criminals were locked up once and for all. Nothing could bring his beloved daughter back, but perhaps her memory could end up saving others.

It was a noble and worthy goal, but one that was soon stymied amid the politics and bureaucracy of Sacramento. Frustrated by the state legislature's inaction on mandatory sentencing for repeat offenders, Mike Reynolds began collecting signatures to put the issue directly onto the California ballot. His campaign slogan? "Three Strikes and You're Out." And in 1994, two years after his daughter's death, seven in ten voters cast ballots to impose mandatory sentences of twenty-five years to life on third-time felons.

Californians weren't alone in embracing three-strikes sentencing. Responding to justifiable public anger with recidivist criminals, politicians around the country—both Democrats and Republicans—roared with indignation. As Mario Cuomo, then governor of New York, put it: "In baseball, it's three strikes and you're out. In dealing with violent crime, it should be: three strikes and you're in—permanently."

It's easy to see the argument's appeal. Locking up violent criminals is both a laudable and necessary function of government, and the public was rightfully outraged at a system that let rapists and killers go free. However, the rush to impose three-strikes laws was based on a deeply flawed analogy. In baseball, a batter's third strike is qualitatively different from the first two. Even with two strikes, a batter has the right to keep swinging at pitches indefinitely, as long as his bat connects with the ball and as long as nobody from the opposing team catches the resulting pop-up. So in this case, a foul ball that might constitute a first or second strike doesn't count as a third.

Still, on a superficial level, the three-strikes analogy resonated deeply with people's sense of justice. Why? Because it tapped into deep cultural associations relating to baseball, rules, fairness, and individual accountability. Michael Mandelbaum, a professor of American foreign policy at Johns Hopkins University School of Advanced International Studies, is also an avid sports fan and the author of *The Meaning of Sports: Why Americans Watch Baseball, Football, and Basketball and What They See When They Do*. Part of baseball's appeal, he argues, flows from Americans' sense of nostalgia, our celebration of individualism, and a cultural affinity for rules that facilitate competition.

Much more so than competitors in football and basketball, baseball players are held individually accountable for their actions. Reams of statistics assign either credit or blame to individuals for specific successes or failures, creating what he calls a "stark moral universe."

"Baseball is therefore a realm of complete transparency and total responsibility," Mandelbaum writes. It's a sport whose rules are accepted as universal, transparent, and binding. "Everything that every player does is accounted for and everything accounted for is either good or bad, right or wrong. Toward the supreme goal of winning baseball games, every act counts as either a debit or a credit. Nothing is overlooked and there is no middle ground."

Over time, about half of all US states passed three-strikes laws. Cumulatively, this had major unforeseen consequences. Yes, mandatory sentencing laws did lead to the lengthy incarceration of more violent criminals. But the laws snagged tens of thousands of nonviolent offenders, too. Soon, people were being sentenced to life in prison for third offenses that included shoplifting videotapes, passing bad checks, or breaking into a parked car to steal a handful of change from the cup holder. As a result, the nation's prison population more than quintupled.

Can one attribute the widespread passage of three-strikes laws to the popularity of baseball? Not entirely. The emotional and political impetus came from the anger and frustration associated with rising crime. But baseball did legitimize three strikes as a standard of criminal justice. And in a decade when the public's appetite for serious policy debate had been reduced to little more than sound bites, "three strikes and you're out" served as a moral call to action that both simplified and sold the idea of definitive justice. If the baseball analogy didn't really hold up well under close scrutiny, the public wasn't paying close attention—inattention that cost them dearly for decades to come. The United States now boasts the highest prison population in the world, with 2.3 million people behind bars—nearly a quarter of all prisoners, globally. The cost to taxpayers? As much as $75 billion every year.

HIDING SAND ON A BEACH

In the early years of World War II, German air defenses, guided by radar, were shooting down Allied bombers at an alarming rate. On any major mission, the Royal Air Force might have lost dozens of aircraft and hundreds of airmen. Britain's bomber command, while grimly realistic about the costs of war, determined that the cumulative toll was unsustainable, and set out to develop countermeasures.

Tasked with this challenge, a physicist named R. V. Jones, the head of scientific intelligence at the British Air Ministry, struggled to devise a new approach to protecting Allied aircraft. Installing jamming equipment on Allied aircraft might thwart the Germans' ground-based radar, but such jammers could themselves be used as a homing beacon by enemy fighter planes. Another approach would be to construct aircraft out of materials invisible to radar, but given available technology, cloaking the radar-reflecting qualities of metal engines seemed an insurmountable challenge.

Then Jones had an epiphany, one that came to mind in the form of an analogy. Where do you hide a grain of sand? You put it on a beach.

Code-named Window, the concept was elegantly simple: Send in a few intrepid British pilots to drop tons of short, paper-thin metallic strips that, fluttering downward, would reflect and multiply the German radar signals. If the strips were of the right dimensions relative to the type of radar waves the Germans used, they would create the appearance—electronically, at least—of an enormous wave of incoming bombers. Paint them black, and they wouldn't even show up in the searchlights the Germans used to sweep the night sky.

Scattering these clouds of tinfoil, a small number of Allied planes could, Jones theorized, trick the Germans into misdirecting both their antiaircraft guns and fighter interceptors against a harmless mirage. Meanwhile, significant groups of real Allied aircraft could slip in to attack true targets elsewhere, free of most German countermeasures, and retreat unscathed before the Luftwaffe discovered the subterfuge. Alternatively, subsequent waves of Allied bombers flying through the metallic cloud would be able to "hide" more effectively from radar during nighttime raids, as confused German ground controllers struggled to distinguish enemy aircraft from the surrounding electronic chaff.

The plan had its risks. What if the air intakes of Allied bombers sucked in the strips, clogging their own engines? Worse, what if the Germans figured out the technique and deployed it against Allied air defenses in return, exposing Britain to even greater devastation? Debate raged among Britain's military leaders, but eventually a Danish spy—eavesdropping on two Luftwaffe women talking aboard a train—sent word that the Germans were already aware of chaff's potential as camouflage. At a critical meeting to decide the matter, Prime Minister Winston Churchill listened to the pros and cons and made a decision. "Very well," he said, "let us open the Window!"

The impact of Window was immediate. Comparing loss rates on bombing raids with and without chaff, the Allies saved an estimated seventy-eight aircraft on a single night over Hamburg, and forty-nine on a raid over Essen. Conversely, the Germans suffered horrific casualties of up to 50,000 people, mostly civilians, in Hamburg alone.

Meanwhile, British pilots released flocks of carrier pigeons into the sky over France with questionnaires strapped to their legs; those who encountered the birds were asked to write down what intelligence they could offer before sending the pigeons, questionnaires complete, back on their way. Fortuitously, one pigeon was discovered by a sympathetic French janitor who just happened to work in a German radar station at Croix-Caluyau, near the Belgian border. When the exhausted bird arrived back at its English dovecote, it brought news of the "beach" Jones had created in the sky. Apparently, German radar operators had spent an entire night struggling to intercept seven hundred Allied "bombers," but failed to locate a single one. According to the janitor, the frustrated German station commander had fumed he "would rather be attacked by a hundred bombers than submit to that torrent of paper again!"

While the Germans eventually developed tactical countermeasures that reduced the effectiveness of the aerial camouflage, Allied bombers were able to press their advantage for weeks, seriously degrading Germany's industrial capacity and thereby shortening the war.

DOMINO THEORY

In April of 1954, as Vietnamese communists besieged the French garrison at Dien Bien Phu, a reporter asked US President Dwight D. Eisenhower about the strategic importance of Indochina. Eisenhower answered with an analogy: "You have a row of dominoes set up, you knock over the first one, and what will happen to the last one is a certainty that it will go over very quickly." If the communists were not defeated in Vietnam, their victory could lead to the sequential toppling of neighboring Laos, Cambodia, Thailand, Malaysia, Indonesia, and eventually even Japan.

As a leader, Eisenhower had certain strengths, but eloquence generally wasn't one of them. And the domino analogy wasn't even his idea, originally. The previous year, in a meeting of the Joint Chiefs of Staff, Admiral Arthur Radford had advocated the use of nuclear weapons to relieve the French forces. The goal, he said, was to prevent Indochina and Southeast Asia from toppling before the communists "like a row of dominoes." Eisenhower rejected the recommendation to go nuclear but embraced the analogy.

At once succinct, visual, and easy to grasp, the domino analogy was a more accessible, kinetic explanation than diplomat George Kennan's technocratic "containment." And while the underlying fear of successive communist takeovers certainly wasn't new, the domino analogy put that foreign policy challenge into everyday language that anyone could grasp. A few weeks after Eisenhower's seemingly off-handed explanation, Secretary of State John Foster Dulles referred to the "so-called 'Domino Theory,'" and the phrase took on a life of its own, going on to drive US foreign policy in Southeast Asia for the next two decades. Under successive presidents, the analogy's hold on the American imagination continued to draw the nation deeper and deeper into the quagmire of Vietnam, which eventually cost taxpayers the equivalent of more than $686 billion, killed 58,252 American soldiers, and claimed the lives of some two million Vietnamese.

There was one problem with Eisenhower's domino analogy, though: It was wrong. Even after the last Americans were evacuated by helicopter from the roof of the US embassy in Saigon—a humiliating defeat televised around the world—Vietnam's neighboring countries didn't topple like dominoes before a communist onslaught. In the decades since, several Southeast Asian nations have actually emerged as some of the world's fastest-growing market economies. And even as Vietnam's government remains nominally communist, the country thrives on capitalism, with native millionaires driving Bentleys, and a rising middle class eating Dunkin' Donuts and KFC.

MOUSE ON A DESKTOP

Sometimes the popular embrace of a simple analogy can have extraordinarily positive effects. For the first forty years of computing, one company dominated the market: IBM. Since the 1930s, IBM had funded academic research, collaborated to build early prototypes, and, in 1953, marketed the first commercially successful computer. By the late 1970s, IBM's computer business employed tens of thousands of employees and was spending millions of dollars on research and making billions in sales.

Given all its advantages, who could ever challenge this behemoth? Two idealistic computer geeks named Steve Jobs and Steve Wozniak. From a suburban garage, they launched Apple Computer in 1977 to bring computing to the masses—not through the existing, giant mainframe computers that required users to learn programming skills and visit computer centers, but through simple, portable, personal computers that people could both afford and use at home. Apple's early models, which still required users to type in technical commands, drew praise from other hobbyists and early adopters, and their growing popularity soon made Apple one of the fastest-growing companies in American history.

In 1981, IBM, which had initially dismissed the personal computer market, introduced its own PC for business users and quickly took control of the growing market. By 1983, it was selling nearly three times the number of personal computers as Apple and controlled 26 percent of the PC market—dominance that led *Business-Week* to run a cover proclaiming PERSONAL COMPUTERS: AND THE WINNER IS . . . IBM.

But Jobs and his team were about to launch a counterattack. Driven by a determination to build something that he said would "make a dent in the universe," Apple had been developing a new computer, the Macintosh, whose interface would not be driven by typing arcane commands at a blinking green cursor but by manipulating graphic icons representing an environment that almost all office workers were already familiar with: a desk. Collaborating with a small, relatively unknown software start-up called Microsoft, Apple transformed the Mac's screen into a virtual "desktop" featuring documents, folders, a clipboard, scissors, paste, and even a trash can. Blank documents looked like white paper, which one could "stack" and "overlap," virtually. The trash can "bulged" until it was "emptied." Choices appeared on "menus" and in "windows." And nearly every operation was quick and easy to execute, because all a user had to do was "point" and click. In making this simple analogy between a horizontal, physical desktop and a vertical, virtual "desktop," Apple transformed the computer into an intuitively simple tool that just about anyone could learn to use—not in weeks but in minutes.

Jobs talked about all this at a design conference, while the Mac was approaching completion. "The main thing in our design is that we have to make things intuitively obvious," he said. "People know how to deal with a desktop intuitively. If you walk into an office, there are papers on the desk. The one on top is the most important. People know how to switch priority. Part of the reason we model our computers on metaphors like the desktop is that we can leverage this experience that people already have."

As many tech historians have noted, Apple didn't invent the computer mouse, nor the graphical user interface that enabled users to "click" virtual "buttons" on the screen in front of them. Far from it— those innovations had been conceived by computer pioneer Douglas Engelbart at the Stanford Research Institute and advanced by researchers at Xerox's Palo Alto Research Center (Xerox PARC). But upper management at Xerox failed to recognize the mass-market implications of their research team's pioneering work and, for $100,000 in Apple stock, gave Jobs and one of his top engineers an inside look at the underlying technology—and the right to mimic it.

From the moment Jobs saw the technology at work, he recognized its tremendous potential. According to one of the Xerox PARC engineers who first demonstrated a prototype of the graphical user interface for Jobs, "He watched for about a minute and started jumping around the room, shouting, 'Why aren't you doing anything with this? This is the greatest thing. This is revolutionary!'"

Within days, Jobs began pushing his team (and hired consultants) to develop a cheaper, simpler, more robust mouse, as well as the other hardware and software necessary to deliver the accessible and affordable computer he envisioned. But Xerox, with a big head start, was the first to market with a computer using the novel interface. Fortunately for Apple, that machine, the Xerox Star, turned out to be painfully slow; just saving a file could take minutes. It also retailed for a whopping $16,595 and, not long after its 1981 launch, Xerox's costly clunker disappeared from the market altogether.

Even so, another fierce competitor was already at work. Bill Gates, whose firm Jobs had hired to help develop the software for the Mac's consumer-friendly applications, also recognized the virtual desktop's commercial potential. In secret, even as his team continued to code and polish Apple's easy-to-use programs, it started developing similar software to run on IBM PCs and PC clones.

When Jobs found out about Microsoft's parallel effort a few months before the January 1984 launch of the Mac, he summoned Gates to Cupertino for an angry dressing-down. In a conference room at Apple headquarters, Gates confirmed that yes, Microsoft was indeed launching a graphical user interface called Windows that would be similar in look and feel to Apple's design. He also pointed out that, due to a seemingly innocuous clause in its contract, Microsoft had the clear legal right to do so. According to Jobs' biographer, Walter Isaacson, Jobs was apoplectic. "You're ripping us off!" Jobs yelled. "I trusted you, and now you're stealing from us!"

The skinny, bespectacled Gates seemed unfazed by the tirade. "Well, Steve," he responded coolly, "I think there's more than one way of looking at it. I think it's more like we both had this rich neighbor named Xerox and I broke into his house to steal the TV set and found out that you had already stolen it."

Jobs could only fume and hope that the Mac's head start would be enough to reestablish Apple's lead in the personal computer market. And a few months later, following the Mac's public introduction with a spectacular ad during the 1984 Super Bowl, it looked like this might happen. For the first time, millions of people suddenly discovered not just that they *could* use a computer but that they wanted one of their own, too. Unfortunately, as much as people loved the Mac, it was an expensive machine. Jobs had originally set out to build a $1,000 computer, but design improvements had driven up the cost. And when Apple CEO John Sculley insisted on factoring in marketing costs, the Mac was priced at $2,495.

Sculley's pricing decision, which Jobs protested, hurt sales. But it was Jobs—visionary, egotistical, and abrasive—who was forced out of the company first, in 1985. And with the help of Microsoft Windows, released in the fall of that same year, IBM roared back. But in a sense, it was too late for Big Blue. Over the ensuing years, in the face of rising competition from Hewlett-Packard, Dell, Gateway, and other companies whose PCs also ran Microsoft Windows, IBM never again dominated the PC market. Rather, it was Gates who emerged triumphant and took computing to the masses, albeit in a less elegant form than Jobs had attempted.

Despite Jobs' ouster and Apple's ensuing struggles, the desktop analogy continued to flourish and spread. Over the course of the following three decades, it would not just enable and facilitate the daily work of billions of people around the world but reshape the way people interacted with digital devices generally, and therefore with each other. In the broadest sense, the genie Jobs had released—democratic access to computing power—was out of the bottle forever, and the information age had truly begun.

· · · · ·

Together, the preceding examples of analogies in action—three strikes, sand on a beach, falling dominoes, and the virtual desktop—highlight just a few of the ways that analogies can affect outcomes, not just by engaging, motivating, or persuading people, but by generating or inhibiting useful insights. This capacity to evoke comparison, assert equivalency, reveal potential, and make implicit arguments makes analogy an exceptionally powerful tool.

Why is analogy so powerful? One reason is the way it structures our thoughts. Think of a hungry lobster that, spotting supper, passes through a sunken trap's one-way funnel only to find itself a prisoner, soon to be supper itself. Similarly, we, too, often swallow an analogy's subtle premise, unaware of the associated implications until it's too late. By then, the argument is already lost and—like the lobster—we're boiling mad and unable to do much about it. In fact, the analogies we accept don't influence just the outcomes of any given argument but *how* we actually argue.

ARGUMENT IS WAR

How often do we seek to win an argument? Every time we engage in one. How often do we actually win? Less often. Usually, as in formal debates, we stake out a position, summon evidence to support it, and try to attack or undermine that of our opponent. But more often than not, these arguments end in stalemate; even when we "win," the victory is often only rhetorical. Alternatively, the person with more power or authority "wins" by virtue of their status. But consider the analogy "argument is war," which George Lakoff and Mark Johnson examine in *Metaphors We Live By*. As they note, "argument is war" likens two things that are fundamentally different. Argument involves an exchange of conflicting ideas; the other involves a systematic infliction of violence.

In accepting the premise of "argument is war," as most of us are apt to do on some level, we've swallowed the bait, and the trap is sprung. As a consequence, the premise structures not just the way we talk about arguments but also the way we actually argue and the actions that follow from it. To illustrate, Lakoff and Johnson cite the following sentences (italics are original):

"Your claims are *indefensible*."

"He *attacked every weak point* in my argument."

"His criticisms were *right on target*."

"I *demolished* his argument."

"You disagree? Okay, *shoot!*"

"He *shot down* all of my arguments."

We are so accustomed to the idea of "argument is war" that few people even notice that the war metaphor is there, let alone compressing ideas, imposing assumptions, establishing a point of view, and shaping possible outcomes. According to Lakoff and Johnson, metaphors create realities in people's minds that become guides for action. Since those actions tend to reinforce the metaphor that inspired them, metaphors often become self-fulfilling prophecies.

Sadly, the US government's respective "wars" on poverty, drugs, and terror illustrate this all too effectively. Presumably, by likening the pursuit of any large policy goal to an actual war, those who declare the war are signaling the moral imperative of their cause, the profound danger of a declared enemy, the stakes for society as a whole, and their willingness to expend almost anything in pursuit of victory.

Once we've swallowed the premise of a war on X, though, we're trapped within its limitations. Setting aside the question of war's moral dimensions—opinions will vary—let's identify some of the analogy's basic implications. First, who exactly is the enemy? In a war on poverty, what constitutes "poor" and who sets that threshold? Are we talking Appalachia working-class poor or beggar-in-Bangladesh poor? Perhaps the true enemy is really unemployment? How about income inequality? Or is the enemy hiding among complex root causes, such as illiteracy, single-parent households, and childhood malnutrition?

A similar challenge emerges when we seek to define the enemy in America's war on drugs. Is the enemy that disaffected high school student smoking a bong at a party? Inner-city drug dealers selling crack? The foreign kingpins who ship heroin to our shores? Wall Street traders doing a line of coke out in the Hamptons? Or is the enemy actually the drugs themselves? If so, which drugs and in what quantity? Alternatively, is the real enemy addiction itself?

Clearly, it is hard to fight a war, let alone "win" it, when people can't even agree on who or what constitutes the enemy. Which brings us to the war on terror. Who is the enemy? And how does one define a terrorist? Certainly, the 9/11 hijackers were terrorists, as their attacks killed thousands of people in dramatic fashion and, as millions watched on TV, inspired true terror.

But what about the fugitive Joanne Chesimard, a member of the so-called Black Liberation Army who was convicted of murdering a New Jersey state trooper in 1973, only to escape from prison in 1979 and flee to Cuba, where she has lived ever since? In 2013, on the fortieth anniversary of the trooper's murder, the Federal Bureau of Investigation added Chesimard—aka Assata Shakur—to its list of "Most Wanted Terrorists." According to the FBI, she merited inclusion on the list because she is "a supreme terror" and "a danger to the American government."

By any measure, it is highly offensive that an escaped murderer should enjoy retirement in the Caribbean while the victim's family must forever suffer the loss of their loved one. But is Chesimard a supreme terror? A danger to the US government? In the context of planes crashing into the World Trade Center, or pressure-cooker bombs exploding at the Boston Marathon, declaring Chesimard a "terrorist" smacks of hyperbole. While nobody likes to see a murderer escape justice, one could argue that adding her to the "Most Wanted Terrorists" list actually does a disservice to law enforcement officers everywhere. Because while most are rightfully vigilant—police work can be dangerous—few if any are "terrorized" by an aging fugitive who's been hiding out in Cuba for the past three decades.

Naming Chesimard to the FBI list raises another issue. Given that the government regularly uses drone strikes to kill those it defines as enemies in the war on terror—even, occasionally, American citizens—does Chesimard's inclusion on the list suggest that a drone strike is warranted in Havana, too? By the logic of the government's war on terror, yes. War is war, after all. Enemies are enemies. Victory at all costs. And who ever declares war intending to achieve anything but victory?

The definition of victory in all these wars—on poverty, drugs, and terror—isn't just some rhetorical challenge; it flows directly from the choice of war as the governing analogy. Analogies, like mule trains, can carry a lot of baggage. And when such baggage is examined carefully, it often includes things a careless analogizer never intended to bring along in the first place.

Within the context of the war on poverty, does the persistence of poverty at any level fifty years later suggest defeat, an endless battle, or stalemate? Similarly, is a state ballot initiative that legalizes medical marijuana the moral equivalent of surrender in the nation's war on drugs? And in a democracy where government contractors scan millions of innocent citizens' e-mails and phone records, and where air travelers must regularly submit to radiologic strip searches in so-called naked scanners—is this really "victory" in the war on terror? If so, who's winning?

When those bombs went off at the Boston Marathon (itself an analogy of ancient origin), the people of Massachusetts responded with stoic bravery. So was this attack and the brave public response it evoked a defeat? If so, for whom? Or was it a victory with casualties? Again, such questions and answers, which are imposed when we make the analogy to war, have serious implications for policy makers and citizens alike.

Andrew Bacevich is a graduate of West Point who fought in Vietnam. Following a long army career, from which he retired as a colonel, he became a professor of history and international relations at Boston University. In 2007, his son, also a soldier, was killed in Iraq. Subsequently, Bacevich was invited to testify before the Senate Foreign Relations Committee.

"The mystical war against communism finds its counterpart in the mystical war on terrorism," he told the committee. "As in the 1960s so too today: mystification breeds misunderstanding and misjudgment. It prevents us from seeing things as they are. As a direct result, it leads us to exaggerate the importance of places like Afghanistan and indeed to exaggerate the jihadist threat, which falls well short of being existential."

Ironically, the US Congress never declared war on Iraq or Afghanistan. Rather, the nation's leaders declared war on terror. The declaration, while unofficial, was nonetheless real and binding. Because what politician, having declared "war" on any given issue, is ever willing to admit defeat? If they have the power to do so, many will keep spending other people's money—and sometimes blood—to save face, save their agenda, and save their own job. Not because they necessarily think "victory" is still possible but because the war analogy they initially embraced does not sanction retreat, surrender, or even compromise.

"For political reasons, the Obama administration may have banished the phrase Global War on Terror," Bacevich concluded, "yet by whatever name the larger enterprise continues. The president who vows to 'change the way Washington works' has not yet exhibited the imagination needed to conceive of an alternative to the project that his predecessor began."

It is important to emphasize that regardless of the language used to describe them, the goals of all these wars—to redress or even prevent the terrible consequences of terrorism, drug abuse, and poverty—are laudable. Who doesn't want to live in a safe, healthy, prosperous nation? But as emotionally satisfying as declaring war might initially seem, it tends to narrow your options and trigger a cascade of problematic implications. Often it means writing a blank check for something you don't end up wanting.

In 2013, thousands of lives and hundreds of billions of dollars later, President Obama delivered a speech at the National Defense University in which he seemed to struggle with the analogy that had, after 9/11, led the United States into a financial and political quagmire. He described the fight against al-Qaeda, the Taliban, and their associated forces as "a just war, a war waged proportionally, in last resort and in self-defense."

But he also noted that "America is at a crossroads. We must define the nature and scope of this struggle, or else it will define us. We have to be mindful of James Madison's warning that 'no nation could pre-serve its freedom in the midst of continual warfare.'

"Looking beyond Afghanistan," he added, "we must define our effort not as a boundless global war on terror but rather as a series of persistent, targeted efforts to dismantle specific networks of violent extremists that threaten America."

Critics were quick to pounce on what they saw as a retreat from a war defined as such. "The president's speech today will be viewed by terrorists as a victory," said Republican Senator Saxby Chambliss of Georgia. Maybe so. But it also represents an American escape from a bad analogy of its own construction, and that escape is a victory, too.

THROWING THE LONG BOMB

In his insightful book *Words That Work: It's Not What You Say, It's What People Hear*, the political strategist Frank Luntz notes that too many leaders, virtually all of them male, tend to reduce almost any subject to a sports analogy. Think about how many managers tell their teams to "keep your eye on the ball" and "swing for the fences" so the company can "win in the marketplace."

And just as Americans describe business in terms of sports, we of-ten speak of sports in terms of war, especially when talking about foot-ball. As Michael Mandelbaum notes in *The Meaning of Sports*, "War involves the organized, deliberate use of force to attain a goal, often the control of territory. So does football." Offensive linemen "battle in the trenches" to give the quarterback, often called a "field general," the time to throw "bullet" passes and "march" his team downfield. If he's got a "cannon of an arm," he might even "throw a bomb."

Meanwhile, the defense launches an all-out "blitz," from the Ger-man *blitzkrieg*, meaning lightning war, hoping to "sack" the quarter-back and force the offense to "surrender" the ball. Games that go into overtime can end in "sudden death." In this same martial spirit, the bitterly competitive gridiron rivalry between Ohio State and Michigan coaches Woody Hayes and Bo Schembechler is remembered as the Ten-Year War. For more than a century, the Kansas-Missouri game has been known as the Border War, and the Utah-BYU rivalry is the Holy War.

BUSINESS AS WAR

The nineteenth-century Prussian soldier and military theorist Carl von Clausewitz famously wrote that "war is a continuation of politics by other means." Looking at the titles in the business section of any major bookstore, one might also conclude that modern business is just a continuation of war by other means. A brief sampling includes:

The Art of War for Executives: Ancient Knowledge for Today's Business Professional

Business Wargaming: Securing Corporate Value

The War for Talent

Sun Tzu Strategies for Selling: How to Use The Art of War *to Build Lifelong Customer Relationships*

Recruit or Die: How Any Business Can Beat the Big Guys in the War for Young Talent

The list goes on. Battling for customers, fighting for territory, defeating the competition, taking aim at a rival's product, and strategizing for victory are all familiar phrases in the business world. The analogy between war and business is so deeply ingrained that most people don't even question it, let alone challenge its profound implications.

Wars between states authorize organizations and individuals to commit morally reprehensible acts that, if committed by individuals without state authorization, would lead to severe social ostracism and punishment. In a similar way, the business-is-war analogy tends to free corporations to commit morally questionable or even shameful acts that may be necessary for the company's "victory" but which inflict significant collateral damage. Examples might be coal-fired power plants using the sky as an open sewer, fast-food chains offering "free" toys that beguile children into a lifetime of unhealthy eating habits, or agribusiness giants marketing pesticides that may cause birth defects at the beginning of life and dementia at the end. In such cases, the short-term profits are privatized while the long-term costs are borne largely by the public.

War dehumanizes and often decouples individual and collective actions on behalf of the greater cause from individual or collective moral accountability. As a governing analogy, business-is-war can have the same effect because most corporate decision makers are insulated from significant accountability to anyone but their most aggressive board members. Given this, some may feel largely absolved of personal responsibility for the negative economic, environmental, and human tolls that this war analogy—and their actions—exact.

THE LIPSTICK ECONOMY

In a commercial society, all this talk of war tends to alienate female audiences, many of whom control their household's spending, according to Frank Luntz. "There's altogether too much allusion to 'battles' and 'charging' and 'fighting' in our lexicon—and it's a context most women simply don't appreciate," he writes. "Cola wars, beer wars, and burger wars are entertainment to men . . . and noise to women."

This may be one reason the National Football League, which in recent years has been working hard to cultivate a growing female audience, now discourages the use of war analogies to describe its games. According to a 2009 report in *The Washington Post*, "The NFL no longer endorses using military terminology to describe its contests." And at NFL Films, which long glorified the image of football as warfare, writers and crews have been instructed to remove all allusions to war from its new productions. "I don't think you will ever see those references coming back," NFL Films president Steve Sabol told the *Post*. "They won't be back in our scripts, certainly not in my lifetime."

Shifting analogies seems to be working. According to *Advertising Age*, 55 percent of American women report watching regular-season football, and the gender gap between men and women watching the Super Bowl has narrowed to 54–46. Roughly 51 million women watched the 2012 Super Bowl, more than the *total* audience of 39 million that tuned in for that year's Academy Awards.

FROM MADISON AVENUE TO MAIN STREET

For advertisers spending millions to capture the attention and business of viewers, this is critical data. Just like the NFL, which retreated from war analogies as its demographics shifted, other advertisers pay close attention to analogies, too. That is because analogies often play a starring role in advertising. The 10 Best Super Bowl Ads of All Time, as compiled by CNBC in 2012, all depend to one degree or another on analogies. In 2003, Budweiser Clydesdales played football, with a zebra as referee. In 2000, E*Trade spoofed an *ER* episode, in which a patient—presumably an E*Trade investor—was rushed into the emergency room with "money coming out the wazoo." In 1996, Pepsi ran a spot in which a Coca-Cola deliveryman, after restocking a refrigerated case at a convenience store, is caught on security camera trying to sneak a Pepsi, only to have the entire shelf of his rival's product collapse onto the floor. Throughout the ad, the late Hank Williams is singing "Your cheatin' heart will make you weep . . ." None of these ads would work, let alone make us chuckle, without appealing to our analogical instinct.

A BEAR IN THE WOODS

Analogies drive politics, too, and get results. A great example is President Reagan's artful "Bear" ad. In this 1984 reelection spot, a large grizzly bear ambles through wilderness as the laconic voice of a matter-of-fact narrator intones: "There is a bear in the woods. For some people, the bear is easy to see. Others don't see it at all. Some people say the bear is tame. Others say it's vicious and dangerous. Since no one can really be sure who's right, isn't it smart to be as strong as the bear? If there is a bear?"

As the narrator begins to pose these rhetorical questions, the grizzly approaches a hunter standing resolutely atop a ridge, a rifle slung on his back. While the hunter never reaches for his gun, the bear pauses, then begins to back off. At that point, a picture of the president appears on the screen, along with the text PRESIDENT REAGAN—PREPARED FOR PEACE.

The analogy between the grizzly and the so-called Russian Bear—a nickname for the Soviet Union—is never explicitly stated, but the message still comes through. The elegance of the ad lies in the subtle way it acknowledges a wide range of viewpoints and does so more neutrally than most political ads ever do. The narrator even concedes that there is debate over who's right. But the actual bear on the screen, and the armed hunter confronting it, make the message clear: Better safe than sorry, and President Reagan is the strong leader who will protect the United States from the Soviet menace.

A REVOLVING DOOR

Entering the closing stretch of the 1988 race for president, Vice President George H. W. Bush was locked in a tight race with Massachusetts governor Michael Dukakis. A month before Election Day, Bush's campaign started airing an attack ad that depicted prisoners circulating through what looked like a revolving prison door. A narrator suggested that Dukakis, as governor of Massachusetts, had a "revolving-door prison policy" that "gave weekend furloughs to first-degree murderers not eligible for parole" who—out on the streets again—committed other crimes.

The ad capitalized on, but did not mention, the infamous case of Willie Horton. Horton, an African American, was a convicted murderer who had been released on a forty-eight-hour furlough from a Massachusetts prison and ended up kidnapping a couple, torturing the husband, and raping the wife. The crime had made headlines and was also the subject of a slashing, anti-Dukakis ad paid for by a conservative political action committee.

For millions of white suburban voters afraid of rising crime, the revolving-door analogy resonated instantly. It didn't matter that nearly all of the "convicts" walking in and out through that revolving door were white; that was simply the Bush campaign's inoculation against anticipated accusations of racism. Fundamentally, the ad drew its emotive power from a deep well of fear and its ability to distill several complex policy debates—sentencing, prison reform, public safety—into a single, unsettling analogy.

In the ad, the prisoners rotate in and out of prison through the revolving door, not even pausing for a moment inside before walking right out again, presumably to commit more crimes. Out on the campaign trail, a hapless Dukakis was slow to address the questions these ads raised in people's minds. Though he and his proxies eventually mustered a raft of logical arguments and statistics to rebut Bush's analogy, that revolving door kept spinning in voters' minds.

Opening up a wide lead, Bush beat Dukakis in an electoral college landslide. When pollsters for CBS News and *The New York Times* later asked voters which ads had made the biggest impression on them, "Revolving Door" was ranked as the newly elected president's number one spot.

WHICHEVER WAY THE WIND BLOWS

Although Bush was president for only one term, he paved the way for his son George W. Bush's subsequent political ascent. And while W was admittedly a communicator of limited rhetorical ability, he put analogy to effective use, too. Having squeaked into the White House in 2000 with a minority of the popular vote but a majority of Supreme Court votes, Bush the younger found himself in another close campaign four years later, this time against Senator John Kerry of Massachusetts.

In a clever TV spot designed to undermine any public perceptions of Kerry as a decisive leader, the Bush campaign showed Kerry wind-surfing back and forth across Nantucket Harbor. As Kerry tacked, a narrator highlighted votes that suggested the senator was both for and against a number of policy positions. Set to a friendly waltz, the humorous ad fanned public perceptions of Kerry as an indecisive flip-flopper, a concern amplified by a Kerry gaffe in which he said he voted for $87 billion in Iraq war funding "before I voted against it."

While ads accusing candidates of flip-flopping on issues were nothing new in American politics, the image of Kerry tacking back and forth on his Windsurfer made its point through analogy. "In which direction would John Kerry lead?" the narrator asked. "Whichever way the wind blows." The image stuck. In concert with a cynical, mendacious attack questioning his service as a Swift Boat captain in Vietnam, the Windsurfer ad torpedoed Kerry's credibility as a decisive leader, and his campaign never recovered.

DON'T THINK OF AN ELEPHANT

Given the intrinsic power of analogies, it is important to manage their impact, positive or negative. And to do this effectively, we need to understand the underlying mechanics of how they work. Effective, persuasive analogies frame situations and arguments, often so subtly that we don't even realize there *is* a frame, let alone one that might not work in our favor. Such conceptual frames, like picture frames, include some ideas, images, and emotions and exclude others. By setting a frame, a person or organization can, for better or worse, exert remarkable influence on the direction of their own thinking and that of others.

In *Don't Think of an Elephant*, George Lakoff explores the issue of framing thoroughly. He begins with an instruction: "Don't think of an elephant! Whatever you do, do *not* think of an elephant." Of course, once we are instructed *not* to think of an elephant, it becomes hard—impossible, actually—to chase the elephant from our mind. At least, it's hard until we stop thinking about the instruction altogether and allow our mind to move on to other topics. But as soon as the instruction floats back into consciousness, there's that elephant again, looming large. And not just an elephant, but a wide range of associated ideas an elephant might trigger, such as other exotic animals—perhaps lions or hippos—images of Africa, thoughts about the circus or even of the GOP.

"Every word, like *elephant*, evokes a frame, which can be an image or other kinds of knowledge," Lakoff writes. That's why it is important to control the frame, however subtle or oblique it may be, rather than be controlled by it. Lakoff examines an analogy that President George W. Bush made during his 2004 State of the Union address, in which he dismissed international criticism of the US war in Iraq by arguing that the conflict was necessary to win the war on terror. In the speech, Bush proclaimed that "America will never seek a permission slip to defend the security of our people."

As Lakoff notes, Bush could have said, "We won't ask permission." Instead, by using the analogy of a *permission slip*, he framed the issue in terms that would likely trigger stronger, more negative emotional associations that endured in people's memories of childhood rules and restrictions. Through structure mapping, we correlate the role of the United States to that of a young student who must appeal to their teacher for permission to do anything outside the classroom, even going down the hall to use the toilet.

But is seeking diplomatic consensus to avoid or end a war actually analogous to a child asking their teacher for permission to use the toilet? Not at all. Yet, once this analogy has been stated, the debate has been framed. Those who would reject a unilateral, my-way-or-the-highway approach to foreign policy suddenly find themselves battling not just political opposition but people's deeply ingrained resentment of childhood's seemingly petty regulations and restrictions. On an even subtler level, the idea of not asking for a permission slip also frames the issue in terms of sidestepping bureaucratic paperwork, and who likes bureaucracy or paperwork?

Much as this permission-slip analogy establishes a subtle but powerful frame, so too did all the other examples we examined earlier, whether they drew upon people's feelings about baseball, the artistry of the Sistine Chapel, ambivalence about a toilet seat, familiarity with a desktop, or the danger of a bear in the woods. Stripping away the particulars of each, how do these analogies function so effectively? Essentially, they meet five criteria:

1. Use the familiar to explain something less familiar.
2. Highlight similarities and obscure differences.
3. Identify useful abstractions.
4. Tell a coherent story.
5. Resonate emotionally.

To see how this works in greater detail, let's reconsider the way Bruce Reynolds, master thief, described the Great Train Robbery as his Sistine Chapel. First, Reynolds exploits the public's basic familiarity with the famous chapel in Vatican City, which after Leonardo da Vinci's *Mona Lisa* is perhaps the best-known work of Renaissance art in the world. Millions of people, even those who aren't art connoisseurs, would likely share the cultural opinion that the paintings in the chapel represent "great art" (as compared to a smaller subset of people who might feel the same way about Jackson Pollock's drip paintings, or Marcel Duchamp's upturned urinal).

Second, Reynolds' analogy highlights, through implication, similarities between the heist and the chapel—both took meticulous planning and masterful execution. After all, stopping a train and stealing the equivalent of $60 million—and doing so without guns—does require a certain artistry. At the same time, the analogy obscures important differences. By invoking the image of a holy sanctuary, Reynolds triggers a host of associations in the audience's mind—God, faith, morality, and forgiveness, among others—that camouflage the fact that he's describing an action few would consider morally commendable, even if the artistry involved in robbing that train was admirable.

Third, the analogy offers a subtle but useful abstraction: Genius is genius and art is art, no matter what the medium. The logic? If we believe that genius and artistry can transcend genre, we must concede that Reynolds, whose artful, ingenious theft netted millions, is an artist.

Fourth, the analogy offers a coherent narrative. Calling the Great Train Robbery his Sistine Chapel offers the audience a simple story that, at least on its surface, makes sense: Just as Michelangelo was called by God, the pope, and history to create his greatest work, so too was Bruce Reynolds called by destiny to pull off the greatest robbery in history. And if the Sistine Chapel endures as an expression of genius, so too must the Great Train Robbery. Yes, robbing the train was wrong. But the public perceived it as a largely victimless crime, committed by renegades who were nothing if not audacious. And who but the most audacious in history ever create great art? Ergo, according to this narrative, Reynolds is an audacious genius, master of his chosen endeavor, and an artist to be admired in posterity.

Is this narrative accurate? Well, that depends on one's perspective. But within the structure of the chosen analogy, Reynolds' argument rings true. The frame it establishes is succinct and subtle, and it's all the more powerful for that.

Fifth, the analogy resonates emotionally. To many people, mere mention of the Sistine Chapel brings an image to mind, perhaps the finger of Adam reaching out toward the finger of God, or perhaps just that of a lesser chapel with which they are personally familiar. Generally speaking, chapels are considered beautiful, and beauty is an idea that tends to evoke positive emotions. Such positive emotions, in turn, reinforce the argument that Reynolds is making—that there's little difference between his work and that of a great artist.

JUMPING TO CONCLUSIONS

As frames, analogies encourage and sometimes even force our thoughts in certain directions. And like the Colorado River cutting through the sandstone of the Grand Canyon, these mental currents begin carving channels of thought that make it harder and harder to change course. Why is this?

Recall how Daniel Kahneman, in *Thinking Fast and Slow*, explains the dual systems that govern the way we think. System 1 works quickly, intuitively, and emotionally as we jump to conclusions. By contrast, System 2—the province of doubt, deliberation, and logic—works relatively slowly. According to Kahneman, "Jumping to conclusions is efficient if the conclusions are likely to be correct and the costs of an occasional mistake are acceptable, and if the jump saves much time and effort."

A good analogy serves as an intellectual springboard that helps us jump to conclusions. And once we're in midair, flying through assumptions that reinforce our preconceptions and preferences, we're well on our way to a phenomenon known as confirmation bias. When we encounter a statement and seek to understand it, we evaluate it by first assuming it is true and exploring the implications that result. We don't even *consider* dismissing the statement as untrue unless enough of its implications don't add up. And *consider* is the operative word. Studies suggest that most people seek out only information that confirms the beliefs they currently hold and often dismiss any contradictory evidence they encounter.

Think of the revolving prison door that Bush the elder used to define Dukakis, his opponent. It resonated, intellectually and emotionally, with people who already believed that Democrats were soft on crime. Similarly, the public's embrace of Apple's virtual desktop analogy grew in large part from a familiarity with, and confidence in, manipulating objects on a physical desktop. Having accepted Apple's abstraction that the two were nearly identical, most people dismissed any differences as irrelevant. What people really want is coherence, and they will often engage in contorted intellectual gymnastics to preserve it.

Drew Westen is an Emory University psychologist and the author of *The Political Brain: The Role of Emotion in Deciding the Fate of the Nation*. He notes that we make judgments constrained by two influences that often compete with each other. The first is the set of cognitive constraints imposed by the availability of relevant information. The second is the set of emotional constraints imposed by how a given conclusion would make us feel. Often, the latter wins out.

The battle between fact and feeling commonly takes place beyond our awareness, as our subconscious searches out evidence that makes us feel good about what we already think. As Westen writes, "Our brains have a remarkable capacity to find their way toward convenient truths—even if they're not all that true." In other words, we jump to conclusions, recruit arguments to support them, and then organize these arguments into the most coherent possible story. Ultimately, it is the consistency of the story, not its completeness, that helps make it effective. As spring-loaded stories, effective analogies work in much the same way by offering an incomplete but coherent narrative that bolsters an emotionally satisfying conclusion.

IS A DNA SAMPLE THE FINGERPRINT OF THE TWENTY-FIRST CENTURY?

The intellectual or emotional satisfaction that any given analogy delivers, though, often varies from person to person. So does what constitutes "jumping" to a conclusion. One person's analogy—which in their mind may constitute a clear, logical, step-by-step argument—is another person's illogical and maddening leap. The 2013 decision by the US Supreme Court in *Maryland v. King* illustrates this conflict well.

This case traces its origins to 2003, when a masked gunman broke into a woman's home in Salisbury, Maryland, raped her, and escaped. The case went unsolved for six years, until police—after arresting a man for menacing a group of people with a shotgun—swabbed the man's cheek for a DNA sample. Running it through the FBI's national DNA database, authorities discovered that the genetic code of the suspect in custody matched that of the Salisbury rapist. Unless the rapist was a family member of the man in custody (therefore sharing a significant overlap in genetic code), there was only one chance in 100 trillion that the police had identified the wrong man. The suspect, Alonzo Jay King Jr., was later charged, convicted, and imprisoned for the rape.

King's lawyers appealed, arguing that police collection of the DNA sample had constituted an unreasonable search under the US Constitution's Fourth Amendment, which states: "The right of the people to be secure in their persons, houses, papers, and effects, against unreasonable searches and seizures, shall not be violated, and no Warrants shall issue, but upon probable cause, supported by Oath or affirmation, and particularly describing the place to be searched, and the persons or things to be seized."

King's lawyers argued that, since police had no probable cause to suspect King of a six-year-old rape by an unknown assailant, taking his DNA upon arrest was a violation of his Fourth Amendment rights, and therefore, evidence of the crime-scene DNA match should not have been permitted at trial. Since the evidence in question was central to King's conviction, they requested that his guilty verdict be set aside. After countervailing reversals in two state courts put Maryland's DNA collection statute in limbo, the US Supreme Court agreed to hear the case, one that Justice Samuel Alito called "perhaps the most important criminal procedure case that this Court has heard in decades."

Like many of the amendments that make up the Constitution's Bill of Rights, the Fourth Amendment is the intellectual offspring of English common law, which limited the English monarch's authority to enter people's homes without a lawful warrant. As Sir Edward Coke, a prominent jurist of the seventeenth century, argued, "The house of every one is to him as his castle and fortress, as well for his defence against injury and violence as for his repose." Or, as the analogy was soon famously condensed: "A man's house is his castle." To intrude lawfully therefore required not just suspicion of wrongdoing but official paperwork to back up specific accusations, and a knock at the door before resorting to forceful entry.

In the modern era, issues related to government searches of a citizen's personal sphere—not just physical property but also their digital property and genetic code—have only become more complex. Due to the government's increasing technological capabilities, such as the National Security Agency's surreptitious monitoring of millions of Americans' phone records, its sweeping collection of citizens' online metadata, its scanning of every envelope passing through the US mail, and the rise of inexpensive DNA testing, legal debates over the Fourth Amendment are intensifying.

In the case of *Maryland v. King*, the oral arguments were especially spirited. US Deputy Solicitor General Michael Dreeben opened his argument by asserting that people who are arrested for serious crimes "are on the gateway into the criminal justice system" and therefore sacrifice some of the Fourth Amendment rights accorded to free citizens.

As such, he said, police are legally permitted to search an arrestee—naked, if necessary—and inventory his or her property, whether or not it is connected with a crime. Most arrestees, he added, are "repeat customers in the criminal justice system" and cited statistics indicating that more than 70 percent of those taken into custody have prior arrest records.

Chief Justice John Roberts interrupted. "Yes, but that doesn't mean, for example, that you can go into their house without a warrant." Unfazed, Dreeben made an analogy. "Taking a DNA sample is not of that character," he said. "It is far more like taking a fingerprint."

And from that point on in the verbal jousting between the justices and the attorneys for both sides, one question kept coming up again and again in various forms: Is taking a DNA sample from someone arrested for a serious crime the same thing as taking his or her fingerprints?

Under sharp questioning, Dreeben insisted that the two were in fact analogous, with one exception: Taking a DNA sample "is far more accurate."

Justice Elena Kagan interjected: "If this were like fingerprints, I think that you would have quite a good case. But, as I've been reading about this, it seems as though the technology is not the same as the fingerprint technology; and, because the technology is different, it is used differently." Fingerprints are checked rapidly, she noted, while DNA analysis can take weeks or months—a fact that undermined Maryland's assertion that DNA samples served primarily as a means to identify arrestees.

Later, Justice Alito weighed in: "But why isn't this the fingerprinting of the twenty-first century? What is the difference?" he asked. Given that it is permissible to take fingerprints from anyone who is arrested, Alito asked, "Why is it not permissible to take a DNA sample from anybody who is arrested?"

King's attorney, Kannon K. Shanmugam, said they were different on three counts. First, DNA contains far more personal information than that contained in a person's fingerprints. Second, taking fingerprints "does not constitute a search" because people leave their fingerprints in public places; by contrast, the DNA from King came from a swab inserted into his mouth. Third, the primary purpose of fingerprinting is to "identify an individual who is being taken into the criminal justice system." Contrary to the claims of Maryland police, who took months to process King's DNA, the primary purpose of taking a DNA sample—and searching for a match in the FBI's database of forensic evidence from unsolved crimes—was to fish for evidence not related to King's identity but rather to past, unspecified crimes.

"Maryland searched my client without a warrant, in order to investigate crimes for which there was no suspicion," Shanmugam said. "It is settled law that warrantless, suspicionless searches are presumptively unconstitutional."

Except when the Supreme Court rules otherwise. In a 5–4 decision that found conservative and liberal justices on both sides, the majority found that the police had followed Maryland law in collecting the DNA sample and that this search and statute fell under the uncontested "right on the part of the Government, always recognized under English and American law, to search the person of the accused when legally arrested."

The majority went on to note that "the most direct historical analogue to the DNA technology used to identify respondent is the familiar practice of fingerprinting arrestees." Citing a 1932 ruling by Judge Augustus N. Hand in *United States v. Kelly*, the justices noted that routine fingerprinting did not violate the Fourth Amendment because it was a customary part of processing suspects who'd been taken into custody.

"Finger printing seems to be no more than an extension of methods of identification long used in dealing with persons under arrest for real or supposed violations of the criminal laws," Hand had written in an excerpt included in the majority decision. "It is known to be a very certain means devised by modern science to reach the desired end, and has become especially important in a time when increased population and vast aggregations of people in urban centers have rendered the notoriety of the individual in the community no longer a ready means of identification."

Writing for the majority in *Maryland v. King*, Justice Anthony Kennedy concluded that "DNA identification of arrestees is a reasonable search that can be considered part of a routine booking procedure. When officers make an arrest supported by probable cause to hold for a serious offense and they bring the suspect to the station to be detained in custody, taking and analyzing a cheek swab of the arrestee's DNA is, like fingerprinting and photographing, a legitimate police booking procedure that is reasonable under the Fourth Amendment."

Justice Antonin Scalia, joined in dissent by Justices Ruth Bader Ginsburg, Sonia Sotomayor, and Kagan, excoriated the majority's reasoning. "The Fourth Amendment forbids searching a person for evidence of a crime when there is no basis for believing the person is guilty of the crime or in possession of incriminating evidence," he wrote. "That prohibition is categorical and without exception; it lies at the very heart of the Fourth Amendment." Innocent people, he said, will pay the price.

"Today's judgment will, to be sure, have the beneficial effect of solving more crimes; then again, so would the taking of DNA samples from anyone who flies on an airplane . . . applies for a driver's license, or attends a public school," Scalia concluded. "Perhaps the construction of such a genetic panopticon is wise. But I doubt that the proud men who wrote the charter of our liberties would have been so eager to open their mouths for royal inspection."

OPEN UP AND SAY "AHHH . . ."

A quick inspection of the DNA-as-fingerprint analogy reveals that it won the day by achieving the five requirements of all effective analogies. First, it exploited the audience's knowledge of something familiar—

taking the fingerprints of an arrestee—to help explain something less familiar, taking a DNA sample from an arrestee.

Second, it highlighted similarities between source and target, and obscured differences. Just as fingerprinting was novel a century ago, DNA sampling is relatively novel today. And just as fingerprinting can be used to establish or verify a person's identity and link them to crime scenes, so can DNA. Finally, both fingerprinting and rubbing a Q-tip inside of someone's cheek for a DNA sample are considered minimally invasive procedures—especially since arrestees can, under certain circumstances, be legally strip-searched.

At the same time, the analogy obscured the distinctly different ways in which fingerprints and DNA are analyzed and the purposes they typically serve. Fingerprints lend themselves to quick analysis to help police establish someone's identity, and advances in the FBI's computerized database have reduced the typical search to less than half an hour. If suspects present false ID or offer an alias upon arrest, and if they have a previous arrest record, their fingerprints can help police determine their true identity. Analyzing DNA, by contrast, typically takes weeks or months, depending on the availability of lab resources and the bureaucratic backlog. As a result, DNA is rarely used to identify a suspect per se, but rather to connect that suspect to a specific crime or to exonerate them from guilt.

In his minority dissent, Scalia cites evidence suggesting that the Maryland authorities were not seeking King's identity when they took his DNA. In fact, the Maryland statute at issue in the case identifies five purposes for which DNA samples may be tested, and identifying an arrestee is not among them. Rather, the record indicates that authorities used King's DNA to search for matches with forensic evidence from unsolved crimes, and thereby discovered the rape. As Scalia wrote, "King was not identified by his association with the sample; rather, the sample was identified by its association with King."

Third, the analogy established an abstraction that was extremely useful for those arguing that DNA sampling of arrestees is justified:

DNA is just a "modern" fingerprint. And since taking fingerprints from an arrestee has always been considered legally acceptable since its adoption about a century ago, taking a DNA sample should be legally acceptable, too. Under this logic, authorities are simply substituting one biological identifier for another, and a more accurate one at that.

Fourth, the DNA-as-fingerprint analogy offers a plausibly coherent narrative. If, under close scrutiny, that analogy is incomplete or requires us to dismiss certain differences as irrelevant or unimportant, that's the nature of analogy; no two situations are identical in every particular. For five justices, who like all people are prone to confirmation bias, the analogy worked well enough.

Fifth, the DNA-as-fingerprint analogy resonated emotionally, at least with a majority of the Court. While Justice Scalia's dissent reveals thinly veiled feelings of incredulity, frustration, and even scorn for the analogy, the majority found it to be reasonable and fair. Yes, someone arrested for a serious crime still enjoys certain protections under the Fourth Amendment, but these protections must be weighed against the State's reasonable interests in identifying such arrestees, assessing the risks they pose, and processing them appropriately under the law. Therefore, since taking fingerprints has been determined to be reasonable and fair, taking a DNA sample would also seem to be reasonable and fair.

Right or wrong, embracing the DNA-as-fingerprint analogy might also have served another emotional purpose for the majority: It offered a reasonable justification to uphold the conviction of a known rapist and therefore spare themselves the sense of revulsion that would likely be associated with a vote to overturn King's conviction and its cascading effect on cases all across the country.

As the late Supreme Court Justice Oliver Wendell Holmes Jr. once noted, "It is the merit of the common law, that it decides the case first and determines the principle afterwards." In short, the DNA-as-fingerprint analogy leveraged a powerful, if unspoken, antipathy toward the alternative—handcuffing police in their basic duties while letting violent criminals go free. If the goal is justice, it is the judge's job to find a way to render it, at least within the limits of the law. The DNA-as-fingerprint analogy artfully enables that.

JUDGMENT CALLS

The use of analogy is central to adjudication in the legal tradition of the United States and to other common law systems around the world, all of which trace their roots to England. While courts are instructed to reach judgments based on federal and state constitutions, statutes, regulations, ordinances, and common law—in that order, as applicable—jurists often draw heavily from precedent, the decisions that emerged from similar cases that came before. The content may change from case to case, but analogy always fuels the inquiry and affects the outcome.

The use of analogy also comes into play in the European civil law system, whose judges ignore precedent and make rulings by considering how codified legislative rules, often quite abstract, apply to the specific facts of each case. Although this may appear more "logical" and less arbitrary than the common law system, civil law judges must also tap the analogical instinct to determine how the code applies to a set of facts. That is, they must strip any given case of superficial details in order to compare its deeper, abstract structure with the law.

Religious judgments also draw heavily from analogy, both in formal religious courts and more informal situations. After all, what use would the Ten Commandments be if one were to interpret them only literally? If so, the prohibition against coveting thy neighbor's wife would not apply to a quick, clandestine liaison with your coworker's girlfriend during the office Christmas party.

"It is tempting to think that with deductive reasoning, we can come up with truth," writes Harvard law professor Cass Sunstein in a *Harvard Law Review* article entitled "On Analogical Reasoning." "But what is the relationship between analogical thinking and truth? Use of analogies produces principled consistency, at best, and truth not at all. The response is that sometimes there may be no criteria for truth in law except for our considered judgments about particular cases, once those judgments have been made to cohere with each other." That's why courts of law, after considering incomplete, inaccurate, and often conflicting evidence, end up rendering verdicts, not verities.

Is gay marriage like straight marriage? Is searching someone's personal e-mail account the same as searching their home office? Is banning civilian use of modern, military-style assault weapons akin to restricting an eighteenth-century frontiersman's access to muskets? Do the Ku Klux Klan's public cross-burnings constitute free speech? Is the cluster of cells that constitute a woman's newly fertilized egg a person? And for the purposes of political speech, are corporations people, too?

The answers to these questions all hinge, to a large degree, on how people evaluate the analogies that frame each respective argument and the coherence they're able to achieve, given all the emotional, political, religious, legal, or other constraints they're striving to satisfy. Go deep enough, and one hundred percent coherence is never possible. But as Sunstein notes, "The process of reasoning by analogy is not science, and it cannot be anchored in anything other than what human beings actually believe."

SAFE AT HOME

Sometimes, people only learn this the hard way. In 2004, California voters reconsidered the state's Three Strikes law. After a decade of mounting costs and concerns about the law—one man was sentenced to twenty-five years to life for stealing a slice of pizza—voters went to the polls to vote on a proposition that would limit what constituted a "third strike." The measure failed, narrowly.

Eight years later, though, with the state's coffers empty and its prisons overflowing, reformers took another swing at the issue. Sentiment, apparently, had shifted. Tired of paying nearly $150 million annually to hold more than 3,000 nonviolent offenders in state prisons, Californians overwhelmingly passed the Three Strikes Reform Act of 2012, which ended mandatory life terms for most nonviolent repeat offenders and permitted authorities to reconsider the sentences of many prisoners currently serving long terms.

This shift became politically feasible not only because voters had grown deeply concerned about anecdotal cases of gross injustice and the state's mounting debt but also because the proposition didn't force them to abandon the baseball analogy, reverse their support for law enforcement, or renounce any of their core values on accountability and justice. Rather, the proposition extended and enriched the original analogy by empowering judges to differentiate between the legal equivalent of balls and strikes.

All of these examples, from baseball terminology to virtual desktops to grizzly bears to genetic fingerprints, illustrate just a few of the ways that seemingly inconsequential analogies make a big impact. This isn't to argue that analogies always determine outcomes but rather that they can shape outcomes in significant ways.

CHAPTER 3

....

THE MODEL T-BONE

How Analogies Spark Innovation

In 1439, torrential rains deluged central Germany and flooded the city of Mainz, which stands at the confluence of the Main and Rhine Rivers. The damage was so severe that it forced the city to postpone the display of its holy relics, which merchants had hoped would attract religious pilgrims passing through the region. For a local, middle-aged metalsmith named Johannes Gutenberg, the delay could not have come at a worse time. Having borrowed money to produce polished metal mirrors designed to capture "holy light" reflected from the relics, Gutenberg had not only lost his anticipated market but also any way to pay back creditors. Soon taken to court for nonpayment of debts, he was forced to reveal his assets, which included a stockpile of materials for a new technology he had been secretly developing: a printing press with movable type.

The idea for the invention was sparked by two conceptual analogies. First, Gutenberg lived in the capital of Germany's principal wine-producing region, where local vintners used vertical, hand-operated screw-driven presses to squeeze juice from grapes in bulk—labor-saving technology that allowed them to vastly scale up their operations. Similarly, local papermakers used screw-driven presses to expel water from a sodden mash of linen, hemp, or cotton fibers to manufacture sheets of paper. And in an insight that Gutenberg later described as "coming like a ray of light," he recognized that such presses could be adapted to perform what was essentially the same process but with a radically different purpose and outcome. Rather than pressing liquid out of paper, he envisioned pressing liquid—ink, specifically—into it.

While this idea may seem painfully obvious to modern readers, it wasn't in early fifteenth-century Europe. While Chinese and Korean scribes had experimented with movable type over the previous three centuries (to print paper money, among other purposes), their efforts had never caught on, and Gutenberg was unaware of their efforts. Ever since the emergence of the world's first phonetic alphabet more than 3,000 years earlier, scribes in the West had been hand-copying every document and book, letter by excruciating letter. This laborious process made written material very expensive, which effectively restricted literacy to a privileged elite and limited the exchange of information.

But it was a second analogy Gutenberg recognized that was even more revolutionary. His father, a goldsmith, had worked with the local mint to evaluate the quality of coins, which were all individually hand-struck by local craftsmen and therefore varied slightly in form and relief. What if, Gutenberg wondered, he were to truly standardize such interchangeable tokens and replace their imagery with letters?

Conceptually, a coin's raised image was no different than that of a letter; in fact, many coins of the day actually bore some letters, too. And just as coins in the right combination could be used to purchase any number of distinct items, letters in the right combination could be used to spell any number of distinct words. They were, for practical purposes, interchangeable. And if Gutenberg could figure out how to manufacture such precise letters in bulk, he could then arrange them in his modified press—and, better yet, perpetually rearrange them—to produce any document in unlimited multiples.

Potentially, the invention Gutenberg envisioned could enable one man to do the work of hundreds, even thousands, of scribes. As such, his idea had great commercial potential, and Gutenberg didn't want to reveal it prematurely—certainly not to creditors from his failed mirror business. Fortunately, those creditors couldn't divine the purpose of the materials he had been stockpiling, and when Gutenberg eventually prevailed in the lawsuit, he was saved from any more awkward inquiries into his activities.

Actually transforming his idea into reality, though, ended up taking another decade—time that eventually outstripped Gutenberg's own capital and compelled him to once again recruit investors. But eventually he succeeded. And when Gutenberg got his first commercial press up and running around 1450, many people immediately grasped its revolutionary potential. Not everyone considered it positive, though. When Johann Fust, one of Gutenberg's primary investors, first arrived in Paris to showcase and sell a dozen Gutenberg Bibles, the city's traditional booksellers had him hauled before a judge because "so many identical books could only exist with the help of the devil."

But then as now, the marketplace prevailed, and the most immediate impact of Gutenberg's invention was on business, banking, and government, as large institutions across Europe quickly embraced the technology. His press and those of imitators quickly brought the cost of printing down so much that it helped spark the rapid diffusion of knowledge, the rise of widespread literacy, and the dramatic acceleration of European intellectual and economic progress. Sadly, the father of the most important invention since the wheel was not among those who prospered. Soon embroiled in a lawsuit with Fust, Gutenberg went bankrupt—a pauper among prints—and struggled financially for many years after.

$$\cdot \ \cdot \ \cdot \ \cdot \ \cdot$$

While especially profound in its economic and intellectual impact, the analogical instinct that fueled Gutenberg's inventive success is evident throughout the annals of innovation and in a wide range of fields. In fact, it is the ability to conceive and exploit key analogies that has inspired and continues to advance many of the world's most important scientific discoveries, inventions, and breakthrough business processes.

As noted earlier, the most persuasive analogies achieve five things:

1. Use the familiar to explain something less familiar.
2. Highlight similarities and obscure differences.
3. Identify useful abstractions.
4. Tell a coherent story.
5. Resonate emotionally.

These criteria also hold true in the case of analogies that spark meaningful discovery and innovation—breakthroughs that persuade people to embrace a novel perspective, technology, model, or approach. While the role of emotional resonance may seem less apparent in this arena, such resonance often finds expression in a sense of satisfaction or even thrill, as discoverers—through their analogies—reveal simpler, more elegant explanations or solutions. Even so, such explanations sometimes take time to win over broader audiences, perhaps because, as George Bernard Shaw wrote, "All great truths begin as blasphemies." Nothing illustrates this better than the struggle to reveal Earth's place among the planets and its relationship to the Sun, or—centuries later—Darwin's theory of natural selection.

SPINNING THE TRUTH

In the decades after Gutenberg's death in 1468, a young astronomer was coming of age in what is today Poland. Born into a prominent, well-to-do family of merchants, Nicolaus Copernicus received a first-rate education in church schools and later at universities in Krakow and Bologna, where he studied astronomy and mathematics.

At the time, the prevailing conception of the universe was one that had dominated Western thought ever since it was outlined by the Greek astronomer Ptolemy in the second century. It was a model that put Earth at the center of the universe, with the Sun, stars, and planets rotating about it in a series of nested, concentric orbits. But the Ptolemaic model wasn't quite as simple as it first seemed. To account for the fact that the planets sometimes appeared to slow down, speed up, and slip backward and forward in their orbits through the night sky, ancient astronomers suggested that each planet also followed its own "epicycles"—much smaller loops that decorated the arc of their general orbits.

To understand this in modern terms, think of how passengers aboard a turning Ferris wheel always remain upright. This is because individual passenger gondolas rotate around their own axles, even as they continue to orbit the Ferris wheel's central axle. In the Ptolemaic planetary model, the planets looped like gondolas through their own epicycles as they orbited Earth. It was this apparently irregular motion that inspired the ancient Greeks to call planets wandering stars. Similarly, the Babylonians called the planets wandering sheep.

But as those sheep wandered the night sky, Copernicus compared their movement to tables of astronomical calculations and began to suspect that Ptolemy's model of planetary motion might be wrong. Yes, it offered a crude explanation of the heavens, but it was also highly complicated and not entirely accurate. Might there be a better, simpler explanation?

From Virgil's epic poem the *Aeneid*, Copernicus recalled the line "Forth from the harbor we sail, and the land and the cities slip backward." That shift in perspective, describing the land moving away from the ship instead of vice versa, offered an illuminating analogy. As Copernicus later wrote, "When a ship is floating calmly along, the sailors see its motion mirrored in everything outside, while on the other hand they suppose that they are stationary, together with everything on board. In the same way, the motion of the earth can unquestionably produce the impression that the entire universe is rotating."

Much as Albert Einstein would, four centuries later, when he imagined himself riding a beam of light to explore his ideas of relativity, Copernicus imagined the conceptual implications if one were to place the Sun, rather than Earth, at the center of the universe. According to this model, the stars and planets—including Earth—orbited the Sun. While this reconception of the universal order demoted Earth in the celestial hierarchy, it also did away with many of Ptolemy's complicated epicycles and offered a much simpler model to explain the heavens.

For nearly three decades, Copernicus continued his observations and took notes for his opus, *On the Revolutions of the Heavenly Spheres*. Finally, on his deathbed in 1543, he published the book. Despite Copernicus' fear that his theory, which ran contrary to Church doctrine, would incur a backlash, the pope and his doctrinal enforcers largely ignored the book. But the printing press, at the time still a relatively new technology, enabled Copernicus' revolutionary idea to spread across Europe. And as detailed margin annotations in hundreds of surviving copies indicate, astronomers across the continent found it fascinating.

ALL MODELS ARE WRONG, BUT . . .

Centuries later, the eminent mathematician George E. P. Box would famously write that "all models are wrong, but some are useful." And the Copernican model *was* wrong in big ways: The Sun was neither stationary nor the center of the entire universe. Orbits weren't circular. Epicycles were a misguided illusion. Nonetheless, Copernicus' counterintuitive idea, that Earth and the other planets orbited the Sun, was not only correct but also extremely useful. Astronomers across Europe embraced the idea, which was so *revolutionary* that it shifted the meaning of the word itself.

Apart from its explanatory scientific value, Copernicus' heliocentric model also upended all notions of humanity's location and significance in the universe. As a consequence, it began to undermine the prevailing religious dogma and the Church's corresponding institutional authority. Eventually, nearly three-quarters of a century after Copernicus' death, the Church banned his book and prohibited people from defending his ideas. After all, if one religious tenet were disproved, what others might be called into question?

The Italian astronomer and mathematician Galileo Galilei protested. He had developed a powerful telescope, and the observations he was making supported Copernicus' heliocentric model. Pushing back, Church officials defended the notion of a central, stationary Earth. They argued that if one were to drop a rock from a tower, it always fell at the base of the tower, proving that Earth was stationary, not moving through space around the Sun. Were Earth moving, they argued, the rock would fall at some distance from the tower.

Galileo disproved their hypothesis with a simple experiment, based on analogy. Instead of dropping the rock from a tower, which his opponents supposed to be fixed in space, he dropped a rock from atop the mast of a ship in motion. As Galileo predicted, the rock landed at the base of the mast. Just as tower and mast are analogous, he concluded, so too are ship and Earth, both moving through space. Flummoxed by his logic, the Church put Galileo on trial, found him guilty of heresy, and placed him under house arrest for the last nine years of his life.

ESCAPING THE LONG ARM OF THE LAW

Galileo, an Italian, had been effectively silenced. But one of his contemporaries, the German astronomer and mathematician Johannes Kepler, worked much farther from Rome and consequently enjoyed greater freedom to pursue his research. He too was guided by analogy. "My aim in this is to show that the celestial machine is to be likened not to a divine organism but rather to a clockwork," he wrote, ". . . insofar as nearly all the manifold movements are carried out by means of a single, quite simple magnetic force."

But what was this mysterious force? Eventually, Kepler made an analogy between light and what we now call gravity, reasoning that just as light from the Sun grew weaker with distance while still casting its glow on Earth and the other planets, the force controlling the planetary orbits must exert diminishing influence in a similar way.

Building on the work of Copernicus, Galileo, and others, Kepler analyzed years of careful observations from which he derived three laws of planetary motion. The first law stated that the planets all moved in slightly elliptical orbits with the Sun at one focus—an important insight that corrected Copernicus' erroneous belief in circular orbits around the Sun.

Kepler's second law was derived from his observation that a planet's speed varied during its orbit, moving faster as it approached the Sun and slower as it moved away. The law states that an imaginary line drawn from the center of the Sun to the center of a planet will—as the planet moves—sweep out equal areas within the orbital plane in equal intervals of time.

Together, Kepler's first two laws explained why the planets are not executing epicycles as Ptolemy and Copernicus had thought. Rather, planets only *appear* to move "backward" and "forward" relative to Earth, because in an elliptical orbit around the Sun, their speed varies depending on where they are in that orbit. Earth, subject to similar variations in orbital speed, sometimes appears to pass its fellow planets, while at other times the planets appear to overtake Earth.

In his third law, Kepler identified a formula describing the relationship between the time it takes a planet to orbit the Sun and the dimensions of its orbit. Later, lamenting how long it took him to figure out these laws, Kepler summed up his work with another analogy: "I have cleared the Augean stables of astronomy of cycles and spirals, and left behind me only a single cartful of dung."

Nearly five centuries later, psychology professor Dedre Gentner and other analogy researchers examined how Kepler actually developed his ideas, aided by Kepler's explicit and extensive writings about his own process of discovery. "He was a highly creative thinker, whose work spans and contributes to a period of immense change in scientific theory," according to Gentner and a team who published a study entitled "Analogy and Creativity in the Works of Johannes Kepler." "His writings teem with analogies, ranging from playful to serious, and from local comparisons to large extended analogies that evolved over decades and that were central to his discoveries."

Notably, the mathematical equations Kepler formulated were also a type of analogy. Much like word analogies, mathematical equations strip away superficial externalities and distill the relationships they describe to their symbolic and quantitative essence. As such, equations allow people to better understand and describe a wide range of phenomena, from the orbits of satellites to the behavior of financial markets, and exploit the resulting insights. Like the parallel handrails of an Andean rope bridge that gracefully links two sides of a deep and forbidding chasm, the equal sign links two or more ideas—expressed as mathematical abstractions—that may span distinct and seemingly distant realms. The elegantly simple $E=mc^2$ is an excellent example. The formula is the expression of a relationship that exists in the universe regardless of human existence. Albert Einstein was merely the first to recognize the relationship, distill it into abstract symbols, and explain how they describe physical reality.

The eighteenth-century philosopher Immanuel Kant once noted that while mathematical analogies address a quantitative relationship, philosophical analogies address a qualitative relationship. And both types of insight can be useful, depending on the circumstances. In the preface to the 1787 edition of his book *Critique of Pure Reason*, he praises Copernicus for the ability to reverse his perceptions of whether the heavenly bodies revolved around the spectator or the spectator revolved around the heavenly bodies. Despite the fact that the Polish astronomer's model had flaws, he still ran intellectual circles around his contemporaries.

ANALOGIES AND THE ADJACENT POSSIBLE

In *Where Good Ideas Come From: The Natural History of Innovation*, Steven Johnson writes about "the adjacent possible." As he describes it, the adjacent possible "is a kind of shadow future, hovering on the edges of the present state of things, a map of all the ways in which the present can reinvent itself."

While the number of basic components that can be recombined or reconfigured to make something new is limited, the more one explores the boundaries of possibility, the more options become possible as each new combination generates additional components to work with. Like LEGOs, which can snap together in myriad combinations, such combinations eventually yield new structures that are limited only by the pieces at hand and the builder's imagination. Both history and human culture, Johnson writes, reflect the gradual yet relentless probing of the possibilities that lie just across the frontier of what most people consider possible. This is why small steps forward happen all the time—many of them missteps—and why great leaps of progress are relatively rare.

SURVIVAL OF THE FITTEST

Not coincidentally, this is also how evolution works. In 1831, when the naturalist Charles Darwin set sail aboard HMS *Beagle* for what turned out to be a five-year voyage of research and discovery, he took along a newly published book, the first volume of Charles Lyell's groundbreaking *Principles of Geology, Being an Attempt to Explain the Former Changes of the Earth's Surface, by Reference to Causes Now in Operation.*

In a society in which few scientists were willing to challenge religious doctrine of a 6,000-year-old Earth that God had created in just six days, Lyell turned out to be something of a polite radical. He was the first to argue that given enough time, natural forces can, little by little, change a landscape dramatically. By implication, he surmised, the planet was much older than conventional wisdom suggested. Lyell's ideas had a big impact on Darwin's thinking about the extraordinarily rich diversity of life he was encountering on his journey, how such life-forms might have originally developed, and the mechanisms by which they might still be evolving.

Fundamentally, Darwin recognized a potential analogy between geological and biological processes—specifically, the cumulative impact of small, gradual changes over extremely long periods. He reasoned that if a modest, meandering stream could, by eroding grains of sand one by one, eventually carve a mighty canyon, perhaps small random changes in a plant or animal could influence their relative reproduction and survival rates over successive generations, and thus gradually alter both form and function to yield new species. And if the eighteenth-century cleric and scholar Robert Malthus was correct in his assertions that rapid growth in human populations inevitably sparks competition for limited resources, this same dynamic might govern all species.

A third analogy that influenced Darwin's thinking, and one that he spent considerable time researching after the *Beagle* returned to England, was the parallel between people's deliberate breeding of plants and animals to reinforce and reproduce more desirable traits, and the role of what he called natural selection in the wild. Darwin himself took up pigeon breeding—at the time a gentleman's hobby—to demonstrate that diverse breeds did not descend from distinct origins, as many of his contemporaries (including Lyell) thought, but from a common ancestral source: the wild rock dove. Meanwhile, seeking broader empirical evidence of his emerging theory, Darwin continued to gather parallel examples from other breeders and botanists and naturalists around the world. Some of the evidence he considered was a little close to home; he noted that just as overly inbred flowers often produced offspring of degraded quality, inbreeding in his own family—cousins marrying cousins—might be the cause of suspiciously similar illnesses and decreasing fertility in recent generations.

In 1859, learning that another naturalist, Alfred Russel Wallace, was about to publish similar ideas about the natural evolution of life, Darwin rushed his own book into print: *On the Origin of Species by Means of Natural Selection, or the Preservation of Favoured Races in the Struggle for Life*. In the book, Darwin describes a perpetual and ubiquitous struggle for existence in which many plants and animals inevitably perish while others, through the luck of a random but advantageous variation in traits, survive. As such, he wrote, "Any being, if it vary however slightly in any manner profitable to itself, under the complex and sometimes varying conditions of life, will have a better chance of surviving, and thus be *naturally selected*. From the strong principle of inheritance, any selected variety will tend to propagate its new and modified form."

Quickly selling out its first print run of almost 1,200 copies, *On the Origin of Species* changed the way scientists viewed the evolution of life on Earth, giving them a lens through which to examine not just biological prehistory but also the current relationships between species, as well as ongoing adaptations to environmental challenges and opportunities.

Darwin's fundamental analogy between deliberate breeding and natural selection illustrates the five criteria of effective analogies especially well. First, it used something familiar, breeding in agriculture, to explain something less familiar, change in nature.

Second, Darwin's analogy highlighted similarities between agriculture and nature—gradual, incremental change over time—and obscured differences such as potential gaps in the natural record of evolution.

Third, the analogy identified a useful abstraction—the process through which beneficial adaptations enabled those inheriting them to survive and reproduce at higher rates, while those without them tended to suffer or die out altogether.

Fourth, it offered a coherent story that explained the origins of biological diversity on Earth, and did so simply. If the theory's epic sweep omitted detail, that didn't matter—the basic narrative was simple, consistent, and fundamentally complete.

Fifth, due to its simplicity and profound explanatory power, Darwin's analogy was emotionally satisfying to the growing number of people who embraced logic and the advances in scientific knowledge that logic yielded.

Admittedly, Darwin's explanation of evolution angered many who were invested in defending a literal interpretation of the Bible. But scientific evidence has only continued to reveal the brilliance of his theory. Because in an even larger sense, it has equipped people in many fields with a systematic approach to examine and explain gradual change in virtually any complex system. The "survival of the fittest" offers a lens that reveals why, for example, businesses that don't adapt to changing markets fail, or specific cultural traits enable certain immigrant groups to outcompete others.

Darwin's theory of natural selection is almost always described as a historic scientific breakthrough, one that suddenly empowered people to understand the world around them in radically different ways. But this "suddenness" is deceptive. Darwin, like most other great scientists, arrived at his big idea only after years of study and thought. As noted by Steven Johnson, such aha moments are almost always the product of gradual, iterative explorations or improvements that have finally reached a tipping point of utility, efficacy, or impact. In this sense, meaningful innovation is possible only to the degree that we improve upon—or break from—the past. Throughout history, example after example suggests that people's success in this endeavor often depends on the efficacy of the analogies they identify to expand upon existing perceptions of the adjacent possible.

OF BIRDS, BALLOONS, AND BICYCLES

The history of human flight illustrates this quite beautifully. For thousands of years, those who dreamed of flying like a bird had modeled their craft after the birds they saw flapping through the sky. From the Greek myth of Icarus, whose wings of wax and feathers supposedly melted when he flew too close to the Sun, to Leonardo da Vinci's 1505 design for a flapping flying machine, which never got off the ground, birds were the analog that every would-be birdman attempted to emulate. And in choosing the beating wing as their model, all attempts at feathered, flapping contraptions by various clergy, locksmiths, astrologers, and aristocrats invariably ended in spectacular failure.

Then, on a cold November day in 1782, a young Frenchman named Joseph Montgolfier was warming himself by the hearth and contemplating his country's recent failed assault on the British fortress at Gibraltar, which guards maritime passage into and out of the Mediterranean at Spain's southern tip. After years of siege by thousands of allied French and Spanish forces, a starving, outnumbered but determined British garrison had repelled a final grand attack from both land and sea—a humiliating defeat for England's continental foes. As Montgolfier, who was a diffident lawyer with a keen interest in science, mathematics, and engineering, watched the hot smoke and sparks rise into the chimney, an idea came suddenly to mind: Could the seemingly impregnable fortress be captured from the air?

Scavenging some thin strips of wood, Montgolfier quickly fashioned a light, boxy frame and covered it with silk taffeta, leaving an opening at the bottom. Then he lit some paper underneath and watched in amazement as his contraption, filling with hot air, rose to the ceiling. Thrilled with his discovery, Montgolfier seized a quill and paper and dashed off a letter to his younger brother Étienne, a Paris architect. Summoning him back to their family home in Southern France, Montgolfier wrote, "Get in a supply of taffeta and of cordage, quickly, and you will see one of the most astonishing sights in the world."

Over the course of the next seven months, the two developed and tested a series of larger and larger balloons, then conducted a spectacular public demonstration in Paris with three live passengers: a sheep, a duck, and a rooster. To put Montgolfier's achievement into modern terms, he had suddenly enlarged the adjacent possible by adding a third spatial dimension to conventional military tactics, by demonstrating the feasibility of flight and, by extension, the possibility of aerial attack. By mid-November, not quite a year after Joseph Montgolfier's fireside inspiration, the two brothers sent up their biggest balloon yet—this one with human pilots. To great public acclaim, it traveled five miles in twenty-five minutes. As Benjamin Franklin, then an American emissary to France, wrote, "The invention of the balloon appears to be a discovery of great importance and what may possibly give a new turn to human affairs."

Inspired, other inventors quickly set out to build their own lighter-than-air flying machines. But as they soon discovered, all balloons had a major problem that hindered their practical use: They were all but impossible to steer. When, in 1785, Jean-Pierre Blanchard and a wealthy American surgeon named John Jeffries used a hydrogen balloon to make the first successful flight across the English Channel, they barely made it. Although favorable winds eventually saved the day, the flapping wings Blanchard had designed for propulsion were absolutely useless and eventually had to be jettisoned in a desperate attempt to stay aloft, along with most of their clothes and even the contents of their bladders.

Their harrowing but successful crossing was big news. One who heard of it was an eleven-year-old English boy named George Cayley. Born into a wealthy, aristocratic family in Yorkshire, George was already showing an interest in all things mechanical, from the horse-drawn plows that furrowed his family's estates to the latest steam engines to the intricately geared watches of a friendly local watch-maker. Educated throughout his teenage years by a series of iconoclastic tutors, Cayley was inspired by the era's pioneering aviators and intrigued by the possibilities of human flight. Doodles in one of his schoolboy notebooks show a balloon with geared, crank-driven propellers, as well as diagrams of airflow across what is clearly a wing—the first known depiction of aerodynamic "lift" in history. Meanwhile, Cayley started experimenting with small whirligigs made from sticks, corks, and feathers—novel flying toys that, inspired by the era's "balloonacy," were soaring in popularity.

On the death of his father in 1792, the twenty-two-year-old Cayley inherited the Baronetcy of Brompton and began using the estate's considerable resources to fund his aviation research. Using the large open stairwell of his stately home as a test facility, Cayley began launching small model aircraft of his own design—dropping them from the third floor—in an attempt to understand the physics of how something heavier than air, such as a bird, actually flew. One sketch, which Cayley scratched into a silver medallion in 1799, depicts a flying machine with cambered wings and a tail, and a diagram of the primary forces of air across a moving, inclined plane—the root of the word *airplane*. But while Cayley was steadily working his way toward a better understanding of basic aerodynamic principles, his notebooks of the time also reveal the same fixation that had grounded his predecessors since the dawn of history—a series of man-powered flying machines with flapping wings.

And then one day, perhaps while watching seagulls soaring off the nearby coast, their wings outstretched in effortless balance, Cayley had an epiphany: Heavier-than-air flight didn't necessarily depend on flapping but rather on the flow of air across a fixed wing. Birds offered a good model for human flight, but only if one looked at the right aspects of the bird-airplane analogy and ignored the rest. Flapping, he realized, was largely for propulsion and control, not for the actual lift that kept birds aloft. So inspired, and taking advantage of the ample weaponry from Brompton Hall's gun room, Cayley began shooting birds of all types— crows, gulls, herons, rooks, and even owls. Carefully studying the curvature of their wings, the ratio of surface area to a bird's total weight, and the design of their bodies and tails, he then built a series of large kites and model gliders that flew with greater and greater success—an early example of what modern researchers call biomimicry.

Integrating his rigorous measurements and observations with recent breakthroughs in fluid dynamics, Cayley began to break the chains of the erroneous analogy between flapping and flight. And by 1809, when he penned a three-part article entitled "On Aerial Navigation," Cayley had identified the basic principles governing heavier-than-air flight—lift, gravity, thrust, and drag. In that article, he also identified the basic features that would be necessary to get a powered, heavier-than-air flying machine aloft and safely down again: rigid, fabric-covered wings with a curved cross section that's known today as an airfoil, navigational rudders, propellers of some sort, and a yet-to-be-invented internal combustion engine.

Achieving practical, powered, heavier-than-air flight was just a matter of time, Cayley believed. "I feel perfectly confident," he wrote, "that this noble art will soon be brought home to man's general convenience, and that we shall be able to transport ourselves and families, and their goods and chattels, more securely by air than by water." The air, he analogized, was effectively "an uninterrupted, navigable ocean that comes to the threshold of every man's door."

Unfortunately, the limits of contemporary engine technology prevented Cayley from building the powered aircraft he imagined. And for the next several decades, he worked on aviation only intermittently, instead focusing his creative energies on other interests and inventions, including the railroad cowcatcher, seat belts, automatic railroad signals, breech-loading guns, a self-righting lifeboat, and a forerunner of modern caterpillar treads. Late in life, he returned to his youthful obsession with flight and began working on translating his earlier theories into reality. And in 1853, he coaxed a reluctant coachman to climb aboard a large fabric-covered glider that, when launched from a tall hill, ended up soaring for some three hundred yards before bumping down to a hard landing. When Cayley, then seventy-nine, rushed up to congratulate his test pilot on the first significant manned glider flight in human history, he found him shaken and upset, with a broken leg. "Please, Sir George," the coachman said. "I wish to give notice—I was hired to drive, and not to fly!"

At the time, Cayley's aeronautical breakthrough was little noted, in part because he neglected to publish illustrations of his glider. Additionally, while the pioneering flight had demonstrated the truth of some underlying aeronautical theories, Cayley's rudimentary glider still had no practical use. Following his death four years later, the aircraft slowly disintegrated, largely forgotten, in one of his barns.

BREAKING AWAY

One of the underappreciated innovations on Cayley's pioneering glider was the use of tension-spoke wheels, which he had designed as strong, lightweight substitutes for the heavy, rigid compression-spoke wheels then commonly in use. Cayley reasoned that such lightweight wheels—another departure from birds' anatomical limitations—might enable a manned glider to gain enough speed for takeoff. Modern, wire-spoke bicycle wheels, which emerged in the 1870s, took the same form. And as historians have noted, it is no coincidence that it was two bicycle makers—the Wright brothers—who would eventually expand upon Cayley's aeronautical insights to design, build, and fly the world's first successful airplane in 1903.

Like Cayley, Wilbur and Orville Wright had played with toy whirligigs as children, loved flying kites, and had shown an early aptitude for mechanics. As teens in Dayton, Ohio, they had launched their own printing business. Then in 1892, caught up in the bicycle craze sweeping the United States, they opened their own bike repair and rental business and were soon designing and manufacturing their own models.

As the decade progressed, Wilbur and Orville started reading more and more newspaper articles about the quest for heavier-than-air flight. These included accounts of the German glider designer Otto Lilienthal, who died after an 1896 crash; the experimental aircraft of Samuel Langley; and the research of Octave Chanute, a prominent civil engineer launching experimental gliders from the sand dunes overlooking Lake Michigan. Such daring attempts captured their imagination, and they started talking about designing a flying machine of their own.

In the spring of 1899, Wilbur penned what would become one of the most famously prescient letters in the history of invention, writing to the Smithsonian Institution requesting any information available on human flight. "I have been interested in the problem of mechanical and human flight ever since as a boy I constructed a number of bats [helicopters] of various sizes after the style of Cayley's and Pénaud's machines," he wrote. "My observations since have only convinced me more firmly that human flight is possible and practicable."

The inquiry marked the formal beginning of one of the most extraordinary success stories in the annals of invention. In short order, the two bicycle mechanics reviewed existing research—and there wasn't much—to decide what seemed correct and what didn't. And although it might not have been apparent to outsiders, the Wright brothers' background in the bicycle business gave them a significant advantage as they tackled the challenges of flight. Not just because of their excellent, hands-on mechanical skills, but because the fundamental challenge of riding a bicycle was similar to that which they would need to overcome in flying an airplane—how to control a light-weight, unstable machine in three dimensions, especially one that would fall to Earth as soon as it lost forward momentum.

A bicycle rider, the brothers knew from experience, changed direction not only by turning the handlebars but also by subtly banking the machine itself. Flying a plane would likely require a similar choreography of direction and balance, as a pilot changed direction by turning the plane's shiplike "rudder" and tipping the entire aircraft, all while maintaining control in potentially gusty winds.

This analogy ran contrary to conventional wisdom, which dictated that a successful airplane would need to remain level at all times. Such would-be aviators competing to become the first to fly conceived of an airplane as more akin to a carriage in the sky, one that would be driven like a four-wheeled vehicle on the ground. Unlike a bicycle rider, the driver of a carriage sits passively, only occasionally using the reins to relay instructions to the horses ahead. Nascent automobiles functioned in an analogous way: Remaining horizontal was good, while tilting was dangerous. Within the confines of this intellectual model, to bank a vehicle was to court catastrophe, especially so in the air. As a consequence, most of the Wrights' competitors were obsessed with designing aircraft of such intrinsic stability that their wings would never dip. In the process, they neglected to develop systems that could offer a pilot constant, nuanced control—systems that would eventually prove essential to powered aircraft.

Intuitively and correctly, the Wright brothers set out to build a lightweight craft with wings so flexible that their surfaces could be twisted to alter airflow, and thus change direction, while still maintaining their structural integrity. Frustrated by the excessive weight and complexity of the metal gears and shafts that might accomplish the task, Wilbur was alone in the bicycle shop one day when a customer came in seeking an inner tube. Wilbur retrieved one from the shelf and pulled the tube from its long, narrow box. Chatting with the customer, he began idly twisting the empty carton by its ends, in opposite directions. Suddenly, he realized that the box—stiff even as he twisted it—was analogous to a set of parallel wings. Gears and shafts would not be necessary; if they stacked the wings for strength, separated by struts, the brothers could achieve the desired control through ropes or wires.

Between 1899 and 1903, the Wright brothers overcame many doubts, frustrations, and technical challenges. They tested their emerging theories of aerodynamics using a small wind tunnel they built in the back of their Dayton shop. In the process, they identified key errors in existing aerodynamic data and invented the first modern propeller, later testing models and full-scale gliders on annual trips to the windswept beaches of North Carolina's Outer Banks.

In the fall of 1903, they returned to their isolated proving grounds on the beach at Kill Devil Hills and began refining their craft in a wooden shed they had erected as a hangar-workshop, a rickety structure they braced against the fierce gusts with two-by-fours driven into the sand. Likening their daily setbacks and breakthroughs to the ups and downs of the stock market, they sensed that they were getting close. One nagging problem was their twelve-horsepower engine, which vibrated so much it kept loosening the nuts that secured the bicycle gears they had adapted to multiply engine speed for the chain-driven propellers. A little bicycle tire cement finally fixed the nuts in place. "Stock went up like a sky rocket, and is now at the highest figure in history," Orville wrote. "Unless something else breaks in the meantime, we feel confident of success."

They awoke on December 17 with great anticipation. Around ten thirty that morning, they positioned the asymmetrical, seven-hundred-pound biplane at one end of a sixty-foot wooden track they nicknamed the Grand Junction Railroad. The Wright Flyer incorporated everything they had figured out over the past four and a half years. As on a bicycle, one major control system—to warp the wing to balance and turn the plane—was operated by shifting one's hips left or right. The rudders were operated by pedals. Another adaptation from the bicycle was the lightweight wire bracing, akin to bicycle spokes, which gave the wings strength even as they twisted.

With Orville lying prone at the controls, Wilbur and an assistant fired the engine. As the propellers reached full speed, they released the tether holding the craft in check, and the plane began rattling down the track into a cold, stiff wind. With a man running alongside either wingtip to keep it steady, the Flyer picked up speed.

Forty feet down the track, the machine lifted clear of its launch dolly and rose into the air. At that very moment, a member of the local lifesaving station—a man who had never before operated a camera—did as he was instructed and snapped a photo that would become famous the world over, a bleak yet glorious image of history's first airplane, ascendant.

Twelve seconds and 120 feet along the beach, the Flyer bumped down again, skidding to a halt in the sand. It was the first of four flights that day, the longest of which lasted almost a minute and spanned half a mile. In the afternoon, after a gust of wind wrecked the machine beyond repair, Wilbur and Orville walked the four miles back to the fishing village of Kitty Hawk, lugging the bulky camera that bore proof of their triumph. Exhausted but exultant, they sent a telegram to their father in Dayton: "Success four flights Thursday morning all against twenty-one mile wind started from level with engine power alone average speed through air thirty-one miles longest 57 seconds inform press home Christmas."

The plane's inaugural flight represented a triumph not only for the Wrights but also for anyone who had ever looked into the sky and longed to fly. And when the Associated Press reported the news, many people were as shocked by *who* had achieved the breakthrough as by the actual flight itself. Two amateurs—two bicycle makers, no less—had beaten out the most famous aeronautical engineers in the world, including prominent Europeans and a well-funded team led by the great Samuel Langley, secretary of the Smithsonian Institution.

At the time, few observers recognized what had given the Wright brothers the intellectual edge. In retrospect, it was the way they recognized and exploited better analogies. Because, as odd as it seems, controlling their airplane *was* like controlling a bicycle, at least in principle. Wilbur's idle twist of inner-tube box did inspire parallel wings that torqued, which in turn enabled the brothers to control the aircraft. And after thousands of years in which would-be aviators tried to flap their way into history, reimagining propellers as spinning, vertical wings to generate perpendicular "lift" was ingenious, too.

While it would be overly simplistic to attribute the Wrights' success solely to the power of the analogies that guided them, it is clear that these analogies were fundamental to their success. And this is the crux of exploiting the power of analogies in any endeavor: identifying not just a basic analogy but also which of its specific aspects are relevant, useful, and "true" in a given circumstance and which are irrelevant or misleading.

Yes, there is often an element of serendipity involved in innovative breakthroughs, because big ideas are never born through Immaculate Conception. Rather, breakthroughs are the rambunctious progeny of many other ideas, jostling one another in a crowded intellectual environment, where greater diversity, accumulating insights, and chance encounters expand the range of possible combinations. And it is only by making analogies that we connect ideas from one realm to another in a way that is relevant or useful, revealing the adjacent possible.

Notably, the word *breakthrough* originally referred to breaking through a physical barrier, which created a shortcut from one side to another. Today, breakthroughs come in many forms besides the physical. Still, they all bear a sense of the original in that they bestow upon us the ability to see through or beyond what had been barriers, even if those barriers were only emotional or conceptual. And what we "see" are new possibilities.

BREAK ALL THEIR LEGS

The Wright brothers weren't the only ones exploiting useful analogies at the dawn of the twentieth century. In 1907, a young, knockabout machinist named Bill Klann was working at a Detroit ice company when a New York stock market scandal sparked a run on the nation's banks. When Klann went to cash his paycheck, it bounced—his employer, like so many across the country, had gone bust. Newly married and desperate for work, he went to talk with a man he knew about possible openings at a four-year-old automobile manufacturer called the Ford Motor Company. It wasn't a conversation Klann likely looked forward to; a couple of years earlier, he had already worked nights at Ford as a part-timer but had quit in search of higher pay and better hours.

The manager Klann spoke with, Ed Martin—the fifth person hired at Ford—was reluctant at first. Would Klann just up and quit again when a better offer came along? But with the company growing and skilled machinists in great demand, Martin made Klann an offer: As long as he promised not to quit again, he could have a job working on cylinder blocks. It was hard, dirty work and paid less than Klann had been making at the ice company. Still, it would be steady work and, unlike the ice company with its bad checks, Ford paid its workers in gold. Klann took the job.

Though only twenty-three, Klann already had nearly a decade of hands-on work experience. In addition to his mechanical work for the ice company, Klann had filled oil lamps for a streetcar company, apprenticed with a blacksmith, and worked at an optical equipment manufacturer, a tent-and-awning maker, a machine shop, breweries, and a shipbuilder—all the while taking correspondence courses in drafting, pattern making, foundry work, and machine shop practice.

As a jack-of-all-trades with a special aptitude for building and fixing heavy machinery, Klann quickly distinguished himself as a talented problem solver in the Ford operation. After a few years, he was put on salary and assigned a special project: Speed up production of engines for the Model T. The company had recently set what seemed like an impossible goal—to produce two hundred engines per day—but nobody really knew how that could be achieved, at least not economically. Even at Ford, which put a premium on efficiency, the assembly process was slow and labor-intensive, with workers fetching parts from multiple bins, ferrying them around on hand trucks, and struggling to coordinate a complex manufacturing process in a sprawling, multistory factory.

Sometime in the early months of 1913, Klann was in Chicago and took the opportunity to tour the Swift Company's slaughterhouse, where millions of hogs, cattle, and sheep were butchered every year. There, he saw animal carcasses being cut up piece by piece as they moved along overhead trolleys, with each butcher performing a specific task before sliding the carcass onward. Upon his return to Detroit, Klann told Martin that his trip to the slaughterhouse had given him an idea with big potential for Ford. From a process standpoint, he explained, there was no difference between taking things apart and putting things together. So just as Swift disassembled animals on a moving conveyor, couldn't Ford assemble things using the same, efficient method?

"If they can kill pigs and cows that way, we can build cars that way," Klann said.

"I don't believe it," Martin answered.

Klann was insistent. At its core, the analogy was very simple: Ford could build specialized conveyor belts to move components along a moving assembly line and have each person perform a specialized task, just as the butchers did. He had already worked at foundries where workers used conveyor belts to move sand, and at breweries where they used them to move grain. Cars would be no different.

"They made it work down in Chicago," Klann said. "Why can't we put them in here for pushing the job along the same way?"

"Yes, but sand is sand and grain is grain. It is all the same thing,"

Martin protested. "Here you've got something else. You've got this and that and pistons and rods."

Klann, convinced of his analogy, insisted that the process was identical. "It is the same thing," he said. "What difference does it make what you are going to handle as long as you put it together? When it moves along, you put it on and that's all."

"It's a simple thing, isn't it?" Martin said, starting to see the light. "Can you make it work?"

"If they can do it, we can do it," Klann answered.

"Well, see what you can do," Martin said.

So over the next several months, Klann and a few others at Ford began prototyping the world's first moving assembly line—not to put cars together, at first, but to test the concept by assembling engine components, and then entire Model T engines. The project got off to a terrible start. On the second day, a cylinder block fell from the line and snapped a man's femur, just above the knee. Word of the gruesome accident quickly reached management, and late that afternoon, Ford's vice president and general manager, James Couzens, came out to see what was happening with this so-called Goldberg job—a reference to the overly complicated would-be machines made famous by cartoonist Rube Goldberg.

An angry Couzens, one of Ford's original investors, threatened to fire Klann on the spot. "If you are going to just break legs," he said, "let's shut this thing off." Reluctantly, Klann ordered a halt. Then, in an effort to save his job, he spent the next hour walking Couzens through the innovative process and explaining all of its potential efficiencies. At stake was not just Klann's best idea but his very livelihood. Gradually, grudgingly, Couzens cooled off. Finally, he made a decision.

"Break all of their legs," he said.

The next morning, with new safety measures in place, Klann's assembly line started moving again. By the end of winter, Klann and his team had set up moving assembly lines for other major components, only to discover a new problem: The production lines were now so efficient that they produced parts and engines faster than workers could assemble them into cars.

Despite lingering management skepticism, Klann and his cohorts on the shop floor were keen to take the idea to what seemed its logical conclusion—to put together an entire car using their new method of moving assembly. To start, they wrote down a list of all the necessary parts and began to physically sequence the actual work on a series of wooden sawhorses, chalking up a concrete floor with large X's to mark the way through Ford's new factory at Highland Park. Their idea was to lay down rails of some sort, then pull the chassis along using a rope as workers added parts from adjacent bins or—in the case of heavy components—used hoists to set them in place.

In just a few weeks, they had laid down railroad tracks and set up a large, hand-cranked windlass at one end. As the cars got heavier with the addition of each big component, successively stronger ropes— some nearly as thick as a man's wrist—kept breaking from the strain. One executive who dropped by would laugh at their efforts; others just ignored them. Few recognized that what they were witnessing was the birth of a second Industrial Revolution.

Finally, over the summer, Klann and his team began building a mechanical conveyor that stretched six hundred feet. And then, on the first of December 1913—less than a year after Klann's epiphany in Chicago—a team working the moving line assembled a complete Model T in just over ten hours, more than two hours faster than the car's assembly using the traditional, stationary method.

Klann and his team kept refining their equipment and modifying how they staffed the line. By the end of the month, building each car took only two hours and forty minutes. By the spring of 1914, with continuous modifications to the line, that time had been slashed to about ninety minutes per car.

Lopping eleven hours off the production time for each car represented a quantum leap in efficiency and triggered a profound series of consequences. Most immediately, it enabled Ford to make more cars in a lot less time, using less labor per car, for less money. In 1914, the moving assembly line's second full year of operation, some 13,000 Ford employees manufactured 260,720 cars. To put this number in perspective, all of the other car companies put together employed five times as many employees, yet only beat Ford's total output by about 10 percent.

Ford's advantage—which had flowed directly from Klann's analogy between butchering hogs and building cars—enabled the company to quickly and steadily cut the price of the Model T from $575 in 1912, which was unaffordable for most Americans, down to $360. This put a car, previously a luxury item that only the well-to-do could afford, well within the financial reach of millions of working families. Eventually, with improvements to the line, the Model T's price would fall even further, to $280. While falling prices cut into the profit margin on every car, they drove up sales and revenue and allowed Ford—at the time just one among many competing automakers—to more than double its market share from 22 to 48 percent in only three years.

In 1914, as lower prices increased demand and revenues began to soar, Ford announced that it would begin paying its workers five dollars per day—double the prevailing factory wage. Offering this staggering leap in pay wasn't an entirely altruistic decision. Rather, it was a win-win approach designed to attract and retain enough people to work the new, monotonous assembly lines where they did the same specialized task over and over again.

The five-dollar day offered another benefit to company and workers, too: In concert with the Model T's falling price, the new, higher wage enabled Ford's own employees to buy the product they built, which boosted the company's sales and profits even further. "I'm going to democratize the automobile," Henry Ford had proclaimed in 1909. "When I'm through, everybody will be able to afford one, and about everybody will have one." He wasn't far off. By the time the last Model T rolled off the assembly line in 1927, Ford had sold 15 million cars, firmly established the automobile in American life, fueled the rise of America's expanding middle class, and revolutionized mass production in virtually every industry.

GIVING CREDIT WHERE CREDIT'S DUE

As the owner of the company and an early champion of time management studies in manufacturing, Henry Ford himself was quickly given the credit for creating the moving assembly line. "Save ten steps a day for each of twelve thousand employees," he later wrote, "and you will have saved fifty miles of wasted motion and misspent energy." Ironically, though, records suggest that Ford himself hadn't been keen on Klann's assembly line concept—not initially, at least.

"Mr. Ford didn't like it at first," recalled Richard Kroll, who supervised the company's experimental department from 1905 until 1917. "He went on a trip somewhere, and while he was on that trip, they put that line in." And while a few others within the organization tried to claim credit for the idea after its benefits became apparent, only Klann was able to offer a plausible, detailed account of its actual genesis. Even Ford's 1922 autobiography *My Life and Work* (which doesn't mention Klann at all) is vague about the creative origin of the moving assembly line, except to say "the idea came in a general way from the overhead trolley that the Chicago packers use in dressing beef."

In retrospect, the moving assembly line may seem like an obvious idea—too obvious for anyone to claim paternity. But the record suggests that it wasn't obvious to anyone but Bill Klann. If it had been, others would certainly have put it into motion first, including the Swift Company, which was making millions from the industrial disassembly of livestock. Similarly, other automakers with greater capital than Ford and facing similar production bottlenecks would likely have gotten the line rolling first, had they conceived the idea. But they didn't.

Rather, it was Klann, enriched by his eclectic background in manufacturing, brewing, foundry work, and conveyors, who first saw through the superficial differences between slaughtering animals and assembling cars. There, at the heart of both processes, lay an underlying structural analogy waiting to be exploited. This analogy, and Klann's determination to put his novel idea to work, ultimately unlocked trillions of dollars of growth in virtually every industry, and transformed the modern world. Hired at seventeen and a half cents per hour, Klann had earned his keep.

"OBVIOUS" DEPENDS ON 20/20 HINDSIGHT

In retrospect, it is tempting to view the printing press, the heliocentric solar system, natural selection, powered flight, and the moving assembly line as "obvious" innovations. But hindsight is always 20/20. Were these developments so obvious, others would surely have conceived them first. The fact that Asian scribes stepped back from the brink of a practical printing press; that Darwin's contemporary and competitor, Alfred Russel Wallace, was slow to recognize the significance of his own ideas on natural selection; that centuries of would-be aviators could not envision powered flight without wing flapping; and that Gustavus Swift, flush with capital and a hog disassembly line in full swing, failed to invent the moving assembly line, all show that such innovations were anything but obvious.

Not surprisingly, what is "obvious" or not is often a matter of dispute—especially after the fact. In 1787, when the drafters of the US Constitution identified the principles by which their nascent democracy would be governed, they enumerated the various legislative powers of the Congress. One of these included what has come to be called the copyright clause, which empowers Congress "to promote the Progress of Science and useful Arts, by securing for limited Times to Authors and Inventors the exclusive Right to their respective Writings and Discoveries."

The goal of that clause and the legislation that followed was to balance the legitimate interest that creators and inventors have in profiting from their creativity with the public's interest in healthy market competition. To achieve this balance, current law dictates that, among other requirements for obtaining a patent, an invention must not just be useful but also novel and nonobvious. That is, it must be "sufficiently different from what has been used or described before that it may be said to be nonobvious to a person having ordinary skill" in the field under consideration. What this effectively means is that many patent cases are decided on the basis of analogy, as judges must determine the degree to which Invention B is meaningfully different from Invention A and its various competitors.

The eminent jurist Learned Hand—an aptly named federal judge—acknowledged the challenge of this endeavor in 1946 when deciding a case involving small improvements to a refrigerator motor. "In appraising an inventor's contribution to the art," Hand wrote, ". . . the most reliable test is to look at the situation before and after it appears. Substantially all inventions are for the combination of old elements; what counts is the selection, out of all their possible permutations, of that new combination which will be serviceable. No objective standard is practicable.

"Courts, made up of laymen as they must be," Hand continued, "are likely either to underrate, or to overrate, the difficulties in making new and profitable discoveries in fields with which they cannot be familiar; and, so far as it is available, they had best appraise the originality involved by the circumstances which preceded, attended and succeeded the appearance of the invention." In other words, all discoveries owe some sort of debt to the adjacent possible.

STRETCHING REALITY

A recent series of patent cases involving Apple illustrates this enduring challenge. In one case, the US Patent and Trademark Office rejected, and then reversed itself, on the originality of the iPhone's so-called rubber band effect. In this feature, the virtual edge of a device's touch screen appears to stretch when one "scrolls" beyond the limits of a given list's content, then rebounds to normal position upon release. The feature, officially called inertial scrolling, was reportedly one of the features whose elegance convinced Jobs to proceed with the iPhone.

The digital illusion feels intuitively familiar and obvious, at least to anyone who has ever stretched a rubber band, worn clothes with an elastic waistband, or unrolled a poster only to have it recoil to its original form. Apple's brilliance, in part, lies in translating such familiar tactile experiences into a virtual, smaller, digital version that mimics the original. In short, it creates digital analogies that look the same, and seem to act the same, as their physical counterparts.

Apple's virtual page turn, through which users "turn a page" by swiping their finger across the screen in a motion analogous to turning a traditional paper page, was patented in 2012. But is this method of turning "pages" obvious, or is it not? Certainly the experience feels obvious, but actually delivering it—creating the digital illusion—is highly technical.

The European legal equivalent of obviousness is called a "lack of inventive step." This subtle phrase, which itself exploits an analogy—a physical step—is considered by some a more descriptive and accurate way of framing the challenge, because it acknowledges the inherently iterative nature of invention. Research suggests that, apart from accidental discoveries, those who achieve breakthroughs generally glimpse what's possible and pursue inventive next steps through analogy.

In a decades-long project at Rutgers University, scholars of the inventor Thomas Edison have been organizing and studying his voluminous personal papers—3.5 million pages of notes, sketches, diagrams, letters, and other documents relating to his experiments, inventions, and patents. What this archival project has revealed is that Edison's genius flowed largely from his ability to reason from analogy—drawing insights from one field or invention and applying them to another. Edison's early designs for a motion-picture machine, for example, featured a rotating cylinder covered in a spiral of sequential images. Records indicate that it was clearly based on the rotating cylinders and spiral grooves of his phonograph machine, designed a decade earlier.

"It was perhaps this trait more than any flashes of brilliance or cries of 'Eureka' that accounted for his great inventiveness," writes William Broad, a science reporter for *The New York Times*. "It is now thought that this hidden ability is what transformed one successful invention into another, eventually producing the phonograph, the incandescent light bulb, systems of electric power generation and motion pictures."

In a 1905 article entitled "The Modern Profession of Inventing," a journalist named French Strother asked Edison what qualities are essential for an inventor. Edison cited three.

Be Persistent

"In working out an invention, the most important quality is persistence," Edison said. "Nearly every man who develops a new idea works it up to a point where it looks impossible, and then he gets discouraged. That's not the place to get discouraged, that's the place to get interested."

In developing the phonograph record, Edison's team tried all kinds of wax mixtures—even inventing some of their own—but to no avail. Then an assistant suggested testing a prototype made of soap. While still inadequate, it was an improvement, which led to tests on every type of soap available. "I had seven men scouring India, China, Africa, everywhere, for new vegetable bases for new soaps," Edison said. "After five years we got what we wanted, and worked out the records that are in use today. They are made of soap—too hard to wash with and unlike any in use, but soap just the same."

Cultivate Your Imagination

"The second quality of an inventor," Edison noted, "is imagination, because invention is a leap of the imagination from what is known to what has never been before." Put another way, we can only conceive, understand, or explain something new in terms of what we already know. That's why imagination requires a willingness to recombine and reconfigure what we know, or at least what we think we know, and do so without inhibition.

Look for Analogies

"The third essential," he said, "is a logical mind that sees analogies." Disputing an apparent suggestion from Strother that a mathematical mind might be more important, Edison became heated. "No! No! Not mathematical. No man of a mathematical habit of mind ever invented anything that amounted to much. He hasn't the imagination to do it. He sticks too close to the rules, and to the things he is mathematically sure he knows, to create anything new. I don't know anything about mathematics; I can't even do proportion. But I can hire all the good mathematicians I need for $15 a week."

Edison certainly underestimated the creativity of great mathematicians; the same year the famous inventor was interviewed by Strother, Albert Einstein published his Special Theory of Relativity. And it's no coincidence that Einstein was an outstanding analogical thinker. "There is no logical way to the discovery of these elemental laws," Einstein would later write. "There is only the way of intuition, which is helped by a feeling for the order lying behind the appearance. . . ."

Edison was correct in linking persistence, imagination, invention, and analogy. Because more often than not, it is the persistent search for useful analogies—often subconscious and only sometimes expressed through language—that fuels the imaginative, inventive leap from what is known to something novel and useful. Such leaps of imagination are a type of shortcut. And while few such leaps lead anywhere we want to linger for long, the ones that do are often enlightening. As such, it seems only fitting that today, the most widely recognized symbol for a sudden insight or great idea is Edison's most famous invention—the lightbulb.

ANALOGY AND THE RISE OF R&D

In 1876, Edison opened a laboratory in Menlo Park, New Jersey, that historians now consider the world's first modern industrial research lab. Later, he would move his lab to different sites, but at its peak the facility employed more than a hundred assistants with a wide range of talents and expertise. It is hard to overstate the impact that Edison's approach had on the pace of technological progress. Not just on his own team, which had both broader and deeper sources of knowledge to draw upon, but on other large growing industrial concerns, which soon adopted his approach and assembled their own "inventions departments."

By the turn of the twentieth century, General Electric—the direct descendant of an Edison company—had 20,000 employees, a part-time "inventions department" of 300 men, and an annual R&D budget of $2.5 million. These innovators generated enough ideas to keep 15 patent attorneys and a team of clerks busy filing 40 patent applications per month. Still going strong more than a century later, GE now employs more than 300,000 people, operates a global R&D department of 2,800 scientists and technicians, spends $4.3 billion annually on research, and submits an estimated 200 patent applications per month. Appropriately, its blog is called *Edison's Desk*.

Notably, several of the companies that had inventions departments in 1905 (including the National Cash Register Company and Bell Telephone) hired their inventors not just from technical or scientific fields but from other backgrounds, too. "They come from all businesses and professions," a contemporaneous account reported. "One is an ex-newspaperman from the Middle West. Another was a grocery-man in a small town in California. Another was once known as 'The Lone Fisherman of Cape Cod.' "

While recruiting a fisherman or a grocer into an industrial R&D lab may seem counterintuitive in today's technological age, research suggests that heterogeneous teams actually produce better results. Kevin Dunbar is a psychologist who, in the late 1990s, observed eight university microbiology and immunology labs to study the way scientists think. Over time, several commonalities emerged among the most effective labs. Among them were two of special relevance. First, the most successful labs were those that made more frequent use of analogy, a practice that allowed them to leap to promising approaches or solutions relatively quickly rather than slowly and methodically searching through many possibilities.

Second, when a team of researchers was united in pursuit of common goals, those who collaborated with others of different professional backgrounds were more successful than those who worked in homogeneous labs, because more diverse labs could draw upon more diverse tributaries of knowledge and experience. In essence, they had richer sources from which to draw useful analogies. In a curious coda, though, Dunbar's study found that many scientists tend to undervalue analogy's catalytic role and even forget the analogies that led them to significant breakthroughs.

ANALOGY, BIOMIMICRY, AND THE ACCELERATION OF PROGRESS

Sometimes the most useful analogies are hidden in plain sight. One day in 1941, the Swiss engineer George de Mestral, out walking his dog, returned home with his wool socks covered in tiny, itchy burrs. In trying to pull the burrs off, de Mestral grew curious about their stubborn grip and put one of his socks under a microscope. Peering through the eyepiece and bringing the lens into focus, he was amazed to see that the burrs were covered in what looked like tiny hooks, firmly snagged amid the tangle of woolen loops protruding from his sock's fuzzy yarn. The burr's grip was clearly an evolutionary adaptation that helped its parent plant propagate itself. By hitching a ride on passing animals, each burr—a seed—gained wider geographical distribution. This distribution of countless burrs increased the species' likelihood of survival.

But de Mestral saw something else in the burr's tenacious grip—the potential for a new type of closure. Intrigued, he began experimenting to see if he could reproduce an analogous hook-and-loop closure in the lab. It proved a tough challenge, requiring almost fifteen years of trial and error before he was able to mass-produce a practical, synthetic imitation of nature's original. But when he did eventually launch what he called Velcro—a name derived from *velvet* and *crochet*—users were soon hooked.

In a similar spirit, researchers at Speedo studied how water flows over sharkskin and used what they learned to help develop the company's LZR swimsuit. Exceptionally fast swimmers, sharks are covered in tiny teethlike bumps called dermal denticles. The distribution of these denticles help a shark manage the flow of water over its body more efficiently, reducing both drag and the energy needed to swim faster. Shortfin mako sharks, believed to be the fastest of all sharks, have been clocked swimming forty-six miles per hour. To put this into perspective, the fastest human swimmers can barely top five miles per hour.

Applying these insights, Speedo's full-body LZR suits compressed certain parts of the human torso and used specially designed fabric whose drag, like sharkskin, varied depending on its location on the body.

It worked extremely well. In the summer of 2008, 98 percent of all swimmers who medaled at the Beijing Olympics, including Michael Phelps, did so wearing the special suit. Officials later determined that the suit conferred such an advantage on swimmers who wore it that they banned its use in future competitions.

Undeterred, Speedo applied these lessons from the LZR to its next-generation Fastskin suit. According to Speedo, the new suits reduce drag by more than 16 percent, which can lower a swimmer's oxygen consumption by up to 11 percent. "It's like miles per gallon in a car," Speedo research manager Joe Santry told *Scientific American*. "You can swim at the same speed, but use less fuel. It allows a swimmer to go harder for longer."

Still other researchers are studying the aerodynamics of owl feathers to learn how the birds fly so quietly, in hopes of applying what they learn to reduce aircraft noise—a problem that plagues cities as air travel continues to increase. Unlike most other birds of prey, such as eagles and hawks, many owls hunt at night, in silence. That is, rather than dive steeply from high altitude to grab their prey based on keen eyesight, nocturnal owls glide silently at low altitude—listening acutely to locate their next meal—before swooping in to strike. Believed to be the quietest of all fliers, owls have evolved over the past 60 million years to develop special feathers that break up, dampen, and absorb the sound waves created as wind passes over their wings.

Seeking to understand how such acoustical properties might be mimicked in aircraft design, NASA's Quiet Aircraft Technology Project has been exploring how to create "feathered" noise-dampening surfaces without increasing drag as aircraft reach high speeds. Possibilities include retractable fringes at a wing's trailing edge, or landing gear covered—like an owl's legs—in a velvety coating.

All of these examples of biomimicry have one thing in common: the exploitation of analogy to take advantage of the countless experiments that nature has already performed—through hundreds of millions of years of natural selection—to optimize and update the adaptations of every organism, plant, and animal on Earth. In a sense, scientists are recognizing the potentially tremendous value of natural innovations. The challenge is determining which ones are misleading, as wing flapping in human flight proved to be, and which ones offer true potential for practical use.

With a growing understanding of genetics, biologists can manipulate the process of genetic selection in a laboratory setting. Such deliberate manipulation of genetic material, primarily for agricultural and medical research, is itself the direct analogical descendant of Darwin's theory of natural selection, but accelerated and directed instead of slow and random. And while it is easy to take this fundamental understanding of evolution for granted today, Darwin's brilliant insight is obvious only in retrospect. Inevitably, though, as the world changes, people become accustomed to the "new normal," which itself becomes the baseline for still newer analogies and breakthroughs.

PRESSING AHEAD

In the 1550s, Gutenberg's invention of the printing press made the production of written information affordable for the masses, dramatically altering the flow of ideas across Europe and eventually around the world. Similarly, in the 1990s, the invention of the World Wide Web once again changed the way people access and trade ideas. Within just a few years, it gave billions of people around the globe the power to easily exchange unmediated, unfiltered information of all types. This has given individuals and groups with Internet access the unprecedented ability to communicate virtually anything, anywhere, anytime—a revolution whose social, political, scientific, and commercial impacts are still gaining momentum nearly twenty years after the Web first captured the popular imagination.

Just as the invention of the printing press can be attributed to one man, the World Wide Web was the brainchild of one man, too: Tim Berners-Lee. When Berners-Lee began conceptualizing what eventually evolved into the Web, he was a young software consultant on contract at CERN, the European Particle Physics Laboratory, near

Geneva. In his memoir, *Weaving the Web: The Original Design and Ultimate Destiny of the World Wide Web*, Berners-Lee noted that there was no single "Eureka!" moment. Much as key conceptual analogies enabled invention of the printing press, several conceptual analogies inspired and shaped the Web.

As a large international laboratory, CERN is a hive of activity with a heterogeneous mix of thousands of scientists, technicians, cultures, languages, and technology. In 1980, when Berners-Lee was hired for a short stint to work on a programming project concerning one of the lab's particle accelerators, he wrote a computer program to help him keep track of all the connections between the scientists, technicians, their computers, and their current projects. He called his program Enquire, after a Victorian advice book called *Enquire Within Upon Everything* that had fascinated him during his boyhood. The book, as he remembered, "served as a portal to a world of information, everything from how to remove clothing stains to tips on investing money. Not a perfect analogy for the Web, but a primitive starting point."

As Berners-Lee recalls, he liked Enquire "because it stored information without using structures like matrices or trees. The human mind uses these organizing structures all the time, but can also break out of them and make intuitive leaps across the boundaries—those coveted random associations."

Once Berners-Lee discovered these organizational connections, Enquire enabled him to map them. But when his brief contract ended, Berners-Lee left CERN—and the floppy disk on which he had stored Enquire—behind. And by the time he returned to the lab as a staff member a few years later, that disk had been lost. Still intrigued by the tangled network of connections and relationships his program had revealed, he set out to re-create and enhance it.

Berners-Lee had come to recognize that in any large and complex organization, how people actually collaborate, trade ideas, and get work done often diverges from formal hierarchy and official processes.

Similarly, he understood that information isn't necessarily hierarchical in nature, nor as useful when structured that way. This was especially true at CERN, and Berners-Lee believed that the organization could benefit from what he called a linked information system that would reveal the true nature of its internal connections and how its people and their ideas were related to each other.

"In an extreme view, the world can be seen only as connections, nothing else," Berners-Lee wrote, adding that "a piece of information is really defined only by what it's related to, and how it's related." For example, while dictionaries define the meaning of words, each definition is itself composed of still more words. As such, every word's definition depends on other, related definitions for its meaning. "The structure is everything," he wrote.

Conceptually, the human brain functions in a similar way. "There are billions of neurons in our brains, but what are neurons? Just cells," Berners-Lee wrote. "The brain has no knowledge until connections are made between neurons. All that we know, all that we are, comes from the way our neurons are connected."

Informally, Berners-Lee tried to interest CERN's managers in his ideas but was met with indifference. So in 1989, he submitted a formal proposal for support in developing his linked information system. He suggested that it could greatly enhance access to information within CERN by mimicking the way people actually interacted—not through hierarchy, flowcharts, and linear progression, but through a tangled "web" of largely informal connections.

Senior managers, apparently content with the way things worked or perhaps preoccupied with physics experiments, essentially ignored the proposal. But Berners-Lee was undeterred and began thinking about an even grander vision—a global version of his program that could exploit the growing reach of the Internet to connect millions of users.

"Suppose all the information stored on computers everywhere were linked," he wrote. "Suppose I could program my computer to create a space in which anything could be linked to anything. All the bits of information in every computer at CERN, and on the planet, would be available to me and to anyone else. There would be a single global information space."

A sympathetic colleague suggested that Berners-Lee simply side-step his bosses by programming his idea as a test of a new computer, the NeXT, that CERN wanted to evaluate. So Berners-Lee started writing the necessary code and brainstorming names for his project that would reflect its novel structure. He considered "Mesh" and "Information Mesh" but dismissed both because *mesh* sounded too much like *mess*. Another idea was "the Information Mine," but the analogy was wrong: Mines are local, not global, and mining is a one-way transaction. The system he envisioned was about empowering people to not only get information out of the system but also to put information in.

And then another name came to mind—the World Wide Web. A web was a term used in mathematics and seemed to capture the interconnected, nonhierarchical structure of the system he envisioned. It also appeared in nature; the word *web*, in reference to a spider's web, dates from the thirteenth century. The name made sense. The root of *web* was the Old English word *webb*, which referred to woven fabric. And like a fabric, a web's strength doesn't necessarily come from the intrinsic strength of the strands from which it is woven but from the redundancy of its connections. That's in part why fishing nets, hammocks, and trapeze nets—like digital networks—are so strong. Even if some links fail, the overall load is distributed through multiple pathways, and the whole remains greater than the hole.

Some at CERN told Berners-Lee that the name World Wide Web would never catch on, in part because it yields a nine-syllable acronym, WWW. But of course, within a few short years, the Web Berners-Lee had championed had spread far beyond academia to spark a global revolution in communications, commerce, industry, politics, dating, and culture.

Despite its rapid adoption, or perhaps because of it, the Web drew some of the same early criticism as the printing press did in the fifteenth century. For example, when Gutenberg and his competitors set up presses around Europe, many scholars felt threatened by their sudden loss of control over access to ideas. They suggested that the proliferation of printed material would—due to easy access—lead to superficial scholarship and "make men less studious." Other professionals, such as scribes, correctly feared that the new technology would put them out of work.

Five hundred years later, similar critics warned that the Web would degrade the quality of knowledge to which people had access and undermine the quality of scholarship and people's capacity for rigorous thought. In some ways, they were right: There is an immense amount of misinformation on the Web, sites that sell term papers, and an ever-increasing amount of gossip and pornography. By some estimates, people will create more than five zettabytes of information in 2015 alone—a veritable sea of information, much of it outdated and worthless even before it is posted.

But at the same time, the Web has played a catalytic role in increasing intellectual collaboration around the world and is increasing both transparency and accountability among those who would plagiarize or make shoddy arguments in today's digital commons. The Web is also accelerating the pace of innovation, as it offers people hyperlinked shortcuts to related information and others interested in those same ideas.

Back in 1999, which in the tech world seems like eons ago, Berners-Lee mused at length about the Web's ongoing evolution. His thoughts at that time, like his original vision, have proven remarkably prescient. "The new Web must allow me to learn by crossing boundaries. It has to help me reorganize the links in my own brain so I can understand those in another person's. It has to enable me to keep the frameworks I already have, and relate them to new ones," he wrote. "When we fail, we will have to figure out whether one framework or another is broken, or whether we just aren't smart enough yet to relate them."

This is also the challenge of analogy—learning to recognize what common, abstract frameworks might undergird and link seemingly disparate concepts. The deeper or more complex a challenge is, the harder it becomes to generate an analogy that illuminates it in a meaningful way. But just because we haven't discovered a way to relate seemingly disparate areas of knowledge doesn't preclude the existence or potential utility of such relationships. Innovators are those who spot useful analogies before others do and figure out how to put them to work.

CHAPTER 4

....

MORNING IN AMERICA

How Analogies Persuade

Late into a gloomy afternoon in the year 561, a traveling Irish monk named Columcille hunched over an oaken table in the Monastery of Druim Finn, furiously copying a book by the light of a sputtering candle. This was no ordinary book, and Columcille, a guest of the monastery's abbot, knew he would have to work quickly or risk discovery.

Normally, the vaulted scriptorium in which he labored would have been crowded with other scribes, all copying church documents, perhaps even the Bible itself. But this day was different—the High King Diarmait mac Cerbaill was due to visit the following morning, and the monks were busy elsewhere, preparing the monastery for his arrival.

Columcille, a prominent scholar, missionary, and warrior of aristocratic descent, had always been entranced by books, especially holy books, and had devoted himself to copying them and spreading their ideas. Earlier that day, when his host, Abbot Finnen, had shown him this particular book—a recent gift from a French monastery—Columcille instantly recognized its power. The volume was an illuminated copy of an original in Rome that offered holy commentary, largely unknown in Ireland, on biblical psalms. To Columcille, the book was a message from God to keep spreading the faith among his countrymen, too many of whom were still beholden to the bearded, pagan druids. And yet, while Abbot Finnen shared his guest's Christian faith, he wasn't keen on sharing his precious book with the masses.

So Columcille set out to make a perfect copy, in secret, from which his own acolytes could later make more copies. And if his efforts to spread the holy word saved even one pagan from the hellfire of eternal damnation, the risk of discovery was worth almost any price.

As legend has it, Columcille was so focused on his work that he hardly heard, or simply ignored, the monastery's evening bell, which signaled that the holy brothers were to return to their cells for prayer and sleep. Late that night, a sleepless monk noticed a candle's glow through the scriptorium window. Concerned, he went to wake the abbot. But by the time they burst in to discover what their guest was doing, Columcille was just finishing the book's final lines. Setting down his quill, he gathered up the pages of his manuscript, bid his outraged host a terse good night, and returned to his cell to sleep.

The next morning, Columcille awoke to the noise of the High King Diarmait's entourage arriving at Druim Finn and was summoned to a royal audience. Abbot Finnen was there with the king, waiting. Furious, the abbot demanded that Columcille, who was holding his newly copied manuscript, hand it over.

Columcille refused. "I labored that the wisdom in your book might be made known to men who have longed to know it," he said.

Finnen was unmoved. "I would have them come here to read the book, and so have my monastery famous throughout all Ireland and the Western world," he said.

"That is not a worthy consideration," Columcille replied, "and I am glad I have this copy to take away with me."

"You have not that copy," snapped Finnen. "For that is the child-book of my parent-book, and it must remain here."

Columcille turned to King Diarmait, who had been silent throughout the dispute. "It is well that you are here, O King, for you give utterance to the laws of Ireland," he said. "Is it not right that the wisdom that is in this book should be made open to many people?"

Gravely, the king shook his head and returned to the abbot's analogy. "The parent-book is Finnen's, and the child-book should be Finnen's also: this is my judgment, and no other judgment is possible. You, Columcille, may not take away the copy you have made."

Incensed, Columcille handed over the copy—a battle lost, but certainly not the war. "It is not a worthy judgment, O King of Ireland," he said. "I shall appeal to you where you give judgment on high issues, in your Judgment Hall of Tara. For know, O King, that this is not a small issue between Finnen and myself, but one affecting generations to come."

On the appointed day, the pair arrived at the Castle of Tara, northwest of what is today Dublin, to argue the appeal before a large gathering of courtiers, druids, jurists, and churchmen. Finnen made his case first, repeating his argument that, as Columcille copied his book without permission, "The son of the book belongs to me."

Columcille then made his case. Counselors to Finnen, determined to undermine an insolent renegade—a clever thief, really—then proceeded to cross-examine him. But Columcille was their intellectual equal and questioned them in return. As the Irish historian Padraic Colum would later write, the arguments dragged on through the night. "The King's great candles were lighted and burned down, and still points were being mooted and confuted," he wrote. "It seemed that the matter was not as clear as so many people had thought."

The wick of the last great candle flickered out as dawn arrived, and Columcille, book in hand, stood at the center of the hall to make his closing argument. "Finnen's claim would fasten a worn-out law on us," he said. "Books are different things from other possessions, and any law that deals with them should recognize such difference. And we learned men who have received a new heritage of knowledge—what should we do but multiply and scatter such books that contain this knowledge?

"I maintain that Finnen's book is none the worse for my having copied it," he continued. "It was not wrong on my part to copy the book, seeing that there was no profit for me in my doing so, but only labor, and seeing that I had the desire to give profit to all the peoples of Ireland, and without doing any damage to Finnen or to his book."

Columcille's argument failed to sway the king, who chided him for his impudence. "We know naught of these new-fangled ways of talking about people's property," the king said. "Our learned communities have always described a book copied as a 'child-book' and a book copied from as a 'parent-book.' These very terms imply that a person who has claim upon the one has claim upon the other." Then, citing ancient precedent, the High King Diarmait issued his ruling: "To every cow its calf, to every book its child-book. The child-book belongs to Finnen."

The crowd, many of whom feared Columcille's challenge to the king's authority, cheered. The king had once again shown himself to be a wise ruler. A calf does belong to a cow. After all, offspring belong to their parents, and this book was clearly offspring—a direct descendant of the original. Property was property, and therefore Columcille was a thief, just as someone who steals a calf.

Columcille cursed and strode angrily from the hall. However persuasive Finnen's analogy had seemed to the king, it was wrong. Dead wrong. Yes, calves belonged to cows, in a sense. Or perhaps to the cowherd who tended them, or the master whom the cowherd served. And while cows produced calves, Finnen's book hadn't copied itself—he, Columcille had done the work.

Still, Finnen had somehow seized the high ground of familiarity simply by stating the parallel between cows and books. How were two cows like two books? By virtue of their two-ness? Was copying a book really akin to a cow giving birth? And if so, what did that make the original author—another cow? For that matter, since the book expressed the word of God, did that make God a cow, too?

To Columcille, the analogy just didn't make sense—logically or emotionally. All he had hoped to do by copying the book was to spread the word of God. But the king didn't seem to care. Abbot Finnen had been so clever to plant the parent-book, child-book analogy in the king's mind, back at Druim Finn. Built upon the idea of descent, it told a simple and satisfying story that provided the king with a simple and satisfying justification for his initial, impulsive decision. And once the king had decided that the argument was sound, he was unlikely to change his position—not without losing face.

In the end, without a persuasive counter-analogy, Columcille had found himself arguing from the quicksand of an abstraction—that ideas cannot be owned—and failed to win the day. Meanwhile, his accusers had impugned his honor, effectively branding him a thief, and the ruling in their favor was a humiliating defeat. As he walked from the Judgment Hall and toward the castle gate, Columcille fumed. How was this fool Diarmait even fit to rule as high king?

Within weeks, Columcille had rallied an army and gathered to do battle with the high king's forces. The victor, he declared, would own the book. According to Irish lore, the fighting was as bloody as it was decisive, and by day's end 3,001 soldiers lay dead, all but one of them the king's men. History's first copyright battle had been a total rout, and as Columcille reclaimed the illuminated manuscript that had sparked the entire conflict, his men dubbed it the Battle Book.

LAYING DOWN THE LAW

The way the high king reached and expressed his verdict may seem like a medieval anachronism, but it is not. His approach to decision making—reasoning by analogy—still plays an important role today in many of the world's legal systems, in which jurists compare the specifics of a given case with some statute, precedent, rule, or cultural standard, then make a decision based on that comparison.

Such a sweeping declaration of analogy's central role in legal decision making may spark an objection among stringent legal formalists, who often misconstrue "the Law"—especially that of Continental Europe—as an entirely rational, logical, and formal system of reasoning. Such formalists would argue that analogical reasoning is not only illogical by its very nature but also inconsistent and unreliable in the outcomes it generates.

That is often true—analogy can be illogical, inconsistent, and unreliable. But that's also true of human thought, generally. And while deductive and inductive reasoning based on factual evidence play a vital role in law, such formal approaches to reason are just bricks in the legal edifice; that which actually binds them is the mortar of analogy. According to Harvard Law School professor Lloyd Weinreb, author of *Legal Reason: The Use of Analogy in Legal Argument*, "Without the intervention of analogical arguments, legal rules and the rule of law itself would be only theoretical constructs."

The following example illustrates just how much jurists must rely on analogies to navigate murky legal waters. In the 1896 case *Adams v. New Jersey Steamboat Company*, judges had to decide whether a steamboat company should reimburse a passenger, Harry C. Adams, for the $160 that was stolen from his locked cabin aboard an overnight steamboat trip from New York City to Albany. Not surprisingly, Adams wanted his money. The steamboat company insisted that, as it had not acted with negligence, it was not liable for the passenger's loss. Adams sued and, at trial before a sympathetic New York City jury, won. Fearing a precedent whose cost could multiply well beyond $160, the steamboat company sought to have the opinion overturned.

Eventually, judges on the New York Court of Appeals were left to evaluate competing analogies and how they might apply in the case. In past cases, courts had found that railroads were not liable for thefts from the berths of their passengers in sleeping cars. However, innkeepers *were* liable for thefts from their establishment's bedrooms. So the question became: Is a steamboat more like a railroad providing transportation or an inn providing accommodation?

On the surface, steamboats and trains seem to have more in common. Both are forms of steam-powered transportation intended to carry passengers from A to B. And in contrast to an inn's primary purpose, sleeping aboard a steamboat or train is merely incidental to a specific journey's timing and the desires of a given passenger, not intrinsic to their primary function as transportation. From this perspective, steamboats and trains seem to be more alike than steamboats and inns, which would suggest that the steamboat operator should not be liable for thefts from a passenger's cabin.

In unpacking the case, though, the judges also looked at deeper aspects of the competing analogies and zeroed in on the qualitatively different relationships that travelers establish with railroads and inns, and their different expectations of security. A sleeping car's berths were, by their open nature, not very secure. As such, passengers who slept in one could reasonably expect that their personal effects would be at some elevated risk of theft. Further, they determined that the outside vendors who operated sleeping cars were neither innkeepers nor carriers under the common law, because no case had yet dealt with this "convenience of modern origin."

By contrast, common law had long since established that innkeepers were liable for protecting guests and their possessions. This higher standard of protection was established in large part to discourage fraud and plunder by unscrupulous innkeepers themselves. The court found that "a steamer carrying passengers on the water, and furnishing them with rooms and entertainment, is, for all practical purposes, a floating inn."

Therefore, unlike a railroad passenger, the traveler who books passage and a room on a steamboat establishes legal relations with the carrier that are akin to those between guest and innkeeper. The court ruled that "the two relationships, if not identical, bear such close analogy to each other that the same rule of responsibility should govern." In other words, the steamboat was an inn, and its operators owed Adams $160, regardless of whether they were negligent.

Without the use of analogy, the court would have had much greater difficulty in issuing a persuasive ruling or extending the common law to address the emerging conflicts of its day. In its approach, the New York Court of Appeals did just what the Supreme Court would do more than a century later in *Smith v. Maryland,* the case that established the analogy between fingerprints and DNA. While the two cases are completely different, the jurists involved did what jurists often do—make their most persuasive arguments via analogy.

THAT DOG DON'T HUNT

Some legal scholars argue that the judicial tradition of legal precedent, using principles derived from past rulings to inform and bind future rulings, is something different from analogy. Such arguments split hairs. To insist on the difference is like arguing that an Irish setter is an entirely different animal from an English setter, when both are still hunting dogs of similar physiology and temperament. In this sense, rulings based on precedent constitute analogical thinking in an intellectual straitjacket: a tacit agreement to consider only *certain* past analogs in judging present cases. The goal is noble, because it is only fair to judge like cases in a like manner. But one does not have to be a law professor to recognize that the outcome of any given case can turn on *which* precedent or precedents are deemed relevant. In other words, which elements of past cases are analogous to the dispute at hand, and therefore determinate? Is that steamboat chugging up the Hudson River overnight like a railroad or an inn, and which corresponding legal precedent shall govern?

Ultimately, jurists identify relevant precedents via analogical reasoning because they have no other choice. This is because no two cases or situations are ever 100 percent identical. At a very minimum, they take place at a different time or place. Given this reality, those who would make judgments derived from past judgments must sooner or later evaluate the particulars of a given case in relation to some chosen standard or goal. Without some standard or goal as context, people would have no way to make anything but totally random judgments. At some level, the only way we *can* think is through analogy. It is how we advance our understanding in every realm, especially in the law. As Lloyd Weinreb writes, "Analogical reasoning does not undermine the rule of law but rather sustains it." Without analogy, law would never advance to address the challenges of its time effectively.

· · · · ·

Words have no intrinsic meaning except that which people assign to them. Does the word *kaki* mean anything to you? Probably not. But to a speaker of Malay, it means "foot." And while we may think "foot" is a simple concept, how would one actually define it? Is it the lower extremity of any leg? The bottom of a staircase? A unit of measure? One end of a bed? And how does one foot a bill? Or get off on the wrong foot, metaphorically speaking? The reality of everyday interaction is that we necessarily shoehorn a lot of meaning into any given word or phrase that isn't wholly defined by that specific language but rather by its context and the imagination of those who encounter it. This is one cause of misunderstanding in the world, because different people often infer different meaning from the same words.

Even single words can contain archaic analogies whose original meaning has been subsumed into a broader, more abstract concept. Today we read meandering prose, listen to meandering speeches, or spend a lazy afternoon meandering through the streets of Paris. But originally, the word *meander* was a proper name for the Meander River in ancient Turkey, whose lazy, looping course to the sea was made famous by Ovid, the Roman poet.

Sometimes it doesn't take millennia, but only a few years, for meanings to evolve via analogy. When people line up at the multiplex to see the latest Hollywood blockbuster, most don't realize that the word *blockbuster* was coined in World War II to describe a powerful bomb that could destroy an entire city block. After the war, *block-buster* soon lost its destructive connotation and came to describe anything that was—to use another analogy—"a big hit." Today, we use these words as verbal shorthand to describe what we think of as simple actions or things, but those very descriptions are also subjective arguments.

DON'T CHOKE ON YOUR OWN WORDS

In 1987, President Ronald Reagan nominated appeals court judge Robert Bork to the Supreme Court. By any measure, Bork was an experienced jurist and legal scholar. In addition to teaching law at Yale and serving as a federal judge, he had also been solicitor general under President Richard Nixon. But to many observers, his scholarly writings, his actions as solicitor general during the Watergate investigation, and his rulings from the bench also revealed a man whose judicial philosophy was, in the words of Senator Joe Biden, "out of the mainstream."

Indeed, Bork had opposed federal civil rights legislation ending racial segregation, supported a state's authority to criminalize the purchase of contraception by married couples, opposed First Amendment protection of anything except explicitly political speech, and believed that the Fourteenth Amendment's equal protection clause—which prohibits states from denying any person within its jurisdiction equal protection of the law—did not necessarily provide judicial protection to women encountering gender discrimination.

Opposition to his proposed elevation to the Supreme Court was immediate. Less than an hour after Bork was nominated, Senator Ted Kennedy delivered a fiery speech on the Senate floor, warning that "Bork's rigid ideology will tip the scales of justice against the kind of country America is and ought to be." As Kennedy described it, "Robert Bork's America is a land in which women would be forced into back-alley abortions, blacks would sit at segregated lunch counters, rogue police could break down citizens' doors in midnight raids, schoolchildren could not be taught about evolution, writers and artists could be censored at the whim of government, and the doors of the federal courts would be shut on the fingers of millions of citizens for whom the judiciary is—and is often the only—protector of the individual rights that are at the heart of our democracy."

It was strong, evocative language, in part because of all the visual imagery his words summoned in people's imaginations, such as women being forced into dangerous alleys, lunch counters for "whites only," police battering their way into innocent people's homes, and courthouse doors crushing the fingers of people seeking justice. In talking about courthouse doors taking off people's fingers, Kennedy was speaking figuratively. But this use of metaphor was all the more powerful because it translated the denial of justice—an abstraction—into a more tangible pain that anyone could understand. According to Kennedy, were Bork elevated to the Supreme Court, petitioners might not be able to make their case at all, let alone receive a fair hearing.

Kennedy's speech was just the opening salvo in months of heated public debate over Bork's nomination, marked by aggressive advocacy on both sides. That September, in five days of testimony before the Senate Judiciary Committee, Bork performed poorly. Under sharp questioning, he remained calm and confident but came across as a humorless intellectual who lacked empathy for ordinary citizens, especially women, minorities, and the disadvantaged. As millions of Americans watched on TV, Bork variously defended his positions or suggested that many of his views had been misrepresented or had evolved, and that senators should not necessarily rely on them to predict how he might rule as a Supreme Court justice.

Toward the end of Bork's testimony, a sympathetic supporter, Senator Alan Simpson of Wyoming, tossed him the proverbial softball. "Why do you want to be an associate justice of the United States Supreme Court?"

"Senator, I guess the answer to that is that I have spent my life in the intellectual pursuits in the law," Bork answered. "And since I've been a judge, I particularly like the courtroom. I like the courtroom as an advocate and I like the courtroom as a judge. And I enjoy the give-and-take and the intellectual effort involved. It is just a life and that's of course the Court that has the most interesting cases and issues and I think it would be an intellectual feast just to be there and to read the briefs and discuss things with counsel and discuss things with my colleagues. . . ."

Bork wandered on for a few more sentences about "maintaining constitutional governance," but the damage was already done. Almost immediately, critics began chewing on his choice of analogy—"an intellectual feast"—as a perfect encapsulation of why he was so ill-suited for the job. Was there any mention of ordinary people in his statement? A commitment to rendering justice? A hint of humanity, perhaps, let alone empathy? Even an abstract belief in the enduring nobility of American democracy and the role of the Court in its fulfillment?

To the contrary. In the absence of any compelling reason except his love of courtroom debate, analogizing the work of a Supreme Court justice to an "intellectual feast" suggested an unsettling emotional disconnect from the fact that high court rulings were not just intellectual exercises concerning a governing document but rather decisions affecting the lives of millions. Compounding matters, the analogy "intellectual feast" evoked images of gluttony. One could almost see the berobed judge sitting behind a table laden with roasted fowl and haunches of meat, gnawing away on the bones of other people's conflicts, the juices dribbling down his scraggly beard. As the Pulitzer Prize–winning columnist Ellen Goodman would later write, the public could practically "hear him salivating over the chance to chew on their rights."

Though Bork's confirmation was by that point already in jeopardy, the "feast" analogy cooked his goose. The judiciary committee voted 9–5 against his nomination, and the full Senate followed suit,

58–42. The bitter confirmation battle led President Reagan to nominate the more moderate Douglas Ginsburg (who later withdrew from consideration after it was revealed he had smoked marijuana), followed by Anthony Kennedy, who was confirmed. The battle also spawned the slang verb *to bork*, now in the *Oxford English Dictionary*, meaning to "obstruct (someone, especially a candidate for public office) through systematic defamation or vilification."

HITTING A HOME RUN

The Bork confirmation battle changed the way future Supreme Court nominees prepared for confirmation hearings, and the way they responded to their inevitable grilling before skeptical senators. A good example of this was the 2005 confirmation hearing of Judge John Roberts, who had been nominated by President George W. Bush to become chief justice. Roberts, a conservative with an opaque record, sought to allay the fears of liberal senators who were concerned that another conservative justice might help overturn well-established precedents the Court had established in past decades.

"Judges and justices are servants of the law, not the other way around. Judges are like umpires," Roberts reassured them in his opening statement. "Umpires don't make the rules; they apply them. The role of an umpire and a judge is critical. They make sure everybody plays by the rules. But it is a limited role. Nobody ever went to a ball game to see the umpire.

"I have no agenda, but I do have a commitment," Roberts continued. "If I am confirmed, I will confront every case with an open mind. I will fully and fairly analyze the legal arguments that are presented. I will be open to the considered views of my colleagues on the bench. And I will decide every case based on the record, according to the rule of law, without fear or favor, to the best of my ability. And I will remember that it's my job to call balls and strikes and not to pitch or bat."

For a nominee seeking to soothe any worries that he might lead a radical philosophical shift on the Court, making a simple analogy between judge and umpire was disarming. With an extraordinary economy of words, it appealed to people's positive associations with baseball and evoked many legitimate parallels. In baseball as in law, both sides in a given contest get to make their case, and do so through a process that plays out under the watchful eye of an impartial arbiter who applies the relevant rules. And where do umpires direct their attention on every pitch? Right down the center, penalizing pitchers whose throws are too high, low, left, or right.

Subtly, the analogy also suggested other parallels that argued for his confirmation. More than any other American sport, baseball tips its hat to its own history and tradition. As such, it celebrates continuity over change. What could be more appropriate in a chief justice whose job it is to honor legal precedent? Just to make sure the senators got his point, Roberts had amplified the basic analogy in more than one way, specifically: *"Nobody ever went to a ball game to see the umpire"* and *"it's my job to call balls and strikes and not to pitch or bat."* Such statements reinforced the notion that observers could expect few surprises from him as a judge, let alone anything radical. He was, in short, a neutral arbiter, not a player in the contest itself.

The analogy was persuasive in another way, too. Just as an umpire could not be expected to call a game before it was played, a judicial nominee could not be expected to articulate anticipated judgments before hearing the specifics of an actual case. To insist on such hypothetical judgments would be to demand that Roberts demonstrate prejudicial bias—exactly the opposite quality that one seeks in a judge. Would the analogy save him from such inevitable hypotheticals during cross-examination? No, but it helped inoculate him when he then deflected such questions as inappropriate.

In a hearing that quickly devolved into long senatorial speeches, detailed discussions of specific cases, and the nuances of constitutional philosophy, the umpire analogy—short and easy to understand—was a catchy sound bite that played over and over in the media. Even Senator Biden, who opposed Roberts' confirmation, acknowledged the analogy's effectiveness on the second day of the hearings. He called it a home run—all the passengers and conductors on his train ride home to Delaware had been buzzing about it, Biden said.

But when Biden finished with his friendly banter, he proceeded to explain why the umpire analogy wasn't apt at all. As he noted, the strike zone is defined by a rule, and while an umpire has the authority to apply that rule, he or she does *not* have the authority to change the rule itself—or any rule of the game, for that matter.

By contrast, a Supreme Court justice can and does change rules if he or she can muster a majority vote from their colleagues on the bench. And in sustaining or overturning the status quo, the Court shapes the meaning of the laws that society must live by, and even the meaning of the Constitution itself. In fact, the legal precedents each court inevitably sets become very difficult to overturn and can affect millions of people for generations to come. From segregation to wiretapping to rules governing money in public elections, the Supreme Court is not a passive arbiter in American democracy but rather a major player. "All of the things that we debate about here and the Court debates that deserve 5–4 decisions, they're almost all on issues that are ennobling phrases in the Constitution, that the founders never set a strike zone for," Biden said. "You get to go back and decide."

Biden's argument was correct but came too late. Despite the umpire analogy's fundamental flaw, Roberts' assertion had already stuck in people's minds. For millions of Americans and for thirteen senators on the eighteen-member committee who voted to recommend that Roberts be confirmed, an umpire was a judge, and a judge was an umpire. And a few weeks later, just as the Major League Baseball playoffs were about to begin, the full Senate voted 78–22 to elevate Roberts to the Supreme Court as chief justice.

In this leadership role, Roberts has indeed led the court to change many rules of the game—from the way corporations can help finance political campaigns to expanding the limits of permissible search and seizure through secret national security courts. But what's most relevant here is what his anodyne statement "Judges are like umpires" reveals about analogy's broader persuasive power. A closer look at the statement and how it meets the five criteria of effective analogies will show just how such analogies work so effectively.

1. Use the Familiar to Explain the Less Familiar

As noted, the first job of a persuasive analogy is to use something familiar to explain something less familiar. In the broadest sense, Roberts used a familiar figure in baseball—an umpire—to explain the job of a Supreme Court justice. In a culture unfamiliar with baseball, the analogy would not have worked; in America, as the baseball playoffs approached, it was a perfect call. The analogy was so basic that it didn't even require listeners to know much about baseball. Almost anybody who has ever seen a game on TV would recognize the umpire standing behind home plate making judgment calls. Their word is final, too.

2. Highlight Similarities and Obscure Differences

The second job of a persuasive analogy is to highlight similarities and obscure differences. In any analogy, there are going to be similarities and differences between the objects of comparison. The key is determining which are most relevant. Roberts, a man of sharp intellect and deep legal experience, probably recognized the logical weakness at the core of his assertion that judges are like umpires: Umpires can't change the rules, but Supreme Court justices can—and do. In fact, that is core to their job. To an attentive and astute listener, all of the similarities between judges and umpires do not trump the overriding and disqualifying difference: A Supreme Court justice is a rule maker, and an umpire is not. But the way Roberts shone a spotlight on the similarities had many observers nodding "yes" before anyone realized the big difference he was simultaneously sidestepping, unmentioned, in the shadows of his argument. How did he do this?

Research suggests that in business negotiations, sellers tend to do better when they make the first offer. In this instance, Roberts is selling an idea: "Judges are like umpires." By asserting the equivalence between the two, he psychologically anchors this argument in the minds of listeners, and the burden of disproving it falls on those who doubt its accuracy.

In the case of selling a given analogy, this first-mover advantage can be especially advantageous. Research by Northwestern University psychology professor Dedre Gentner and her colleagues suggests that even the simple assertion of an analogy can create an "analogical insertion effect" through which a listener mistakes their own inferences from an analogy as presented facts, even when those inferences don't fit with their prior attitudes or beliefs. Calling this the resistance-is-futile hypothesis, the researchers write that the analogical insertion effect can shift people's thinking against their own will, even when those changes are emotionally unpalatable.

Having stated the fundamental likeness of judges and umpires, Roberts bolsters his argument with evidence: "Umpires don't make the rules; they apply them." That is certainly true—umpires don't make rules. He follows this with another truthful parallel: "The role of an umpire and a judge is critical." Yes, both are vital in their own respective domains. Then, to bolster his case further, he expands on a shared responsibility: "They make sure everybody plays by the rules." Yes, under ideal circumstances, that is true, too. But note what Roberts omits: He never says that *judges* don't make rules. By stating that a judge is like an umpire, and that umpires don't make rules, he primes the average listener to infer that judges don't make rules. And he camouflages this quick sleight-of-mind among a host of obvious similarities.

The beauty of Roberts' analogy is that everything he said was factually true. But the main point he succeeds in establishing—that he will not change the rules of the game—is patently false. Because while the roles of judges and umpires are alike in a general sense, they are entirely different in the role most relevant to the question at hand:

Would Roberts, if confirmed as Supreme Court chief justice, overturn precedent and create new rules of the game?

3. Identify Useful Abstractions

Like most politicians, senators tend to yield to public opinion—after all, their jobs depend on keeping their constituents relatively happy. Recognizing this, Roberts knew he needed to convince not just the senators on the Judiciary Committee to support him, but the broader public that elected them. As his professional qualifications were clearly in order, the only question remaining was whether he would serve as a fair and impartial judge, regardless of his conservative philosophy.

One could approach this in a number of ways—by citing cases and legal writing that indicated a balanced, nonideological approach, or with character witnesses, or by specifying what he thought about key precedents on controversial issues. For the most part, Roberts used his umpire analogy to sidestep the pitfalls of specificity, which would have inevitably alienated senators on either or both ends of the political spectrum. The analogy overcame this challenge by transmuting a judge into an umpire. Umpires are fair. Therefore Judge Roberts, like an umpire, must be fair.

But what is fair? Fair is a subjective abstraction—an arbitrary determination that depends on individual perspectives and cultural norms. But absent details of how Roberts might decide specific, hypothetical cases, "fair" took on the broadest of meanings to become the perfect, idealized abstraction.

4. Tell a Coherent Story

As humans, we generally dislike uncertainty. To address this dislike, we construct coherent stories to help us structure the constant flood of incoming data we encounter, and then infer meaning from those stories. Over time, such stories cohere into general models, often described as experience, that enable us to make more effective decisions. Even gamblers at the racetrack, who derive a thrill from betting, construct narratives to justify their wagers and, at least emotionally, reduce their sense of uncertainty. Often it's just a simple story—maybe that a horse named Thunder's Echo has run well on wet tracks recently, and since the day's forecast calls for rain, Thunder's Echo is obviously a good bet to win, place, or show in the ninth race at Saratoga.

How many other horses are running? Twelve. What other factors could come into play? Innumerable, many of them random. Does that matter? Not to the gambler who has constructed a useful story to predict how events will unfold. And in a sense, we are all gamblers to a certain extent because we need to make decisions in a world of incomplete, inaccurate, and inconsistent information. In an uncertain world, stories offer us emotional reassurance, and coherent stories offer more reassurance. And as the psychologist Daniel Kahneman notes, "It is the consistency of the information that matters for a good story, not its completeness. Indeed, you will often find that knowing little makes it easier to fit everything you know into a coherent pattern." As such, people are prone to exaggerate the coherence of what they encounter, often at the expense of accuracy.

Coherent stories are easier to grasp. And when stories are easier to grasp, listeners are more apt to accept both the storyteller and their story's conclusions as credible. Returning to the judges-are-like-umpires analogy, Roberts offered his audience a coherent story. Not a complete story, by any means, for he omitted the relevant and disqualifying difference between judges and umpires. But since his story was coherent, it was much more credible.

5. Resonate Emotionally

Analogies that involve emotions generally fall into two broad categories. The first includes analogies about emotion, such as: "Anger is a hungry furnace; one is wise not to stoke it." The second includes analogies that generate or evoke specific emotions, often surprising the listener, making them laugh or making a comparison that is deliberately positive or negative. While analogies that evoke emotion in listeners are not always so useful in pursuit of innovation, such manipulation often plays a critical role in persuasion.

Roberts' judge-as-umpire analogy falls into this second category, as it evokes the positive feelings generally associated with baseball, including a vague sense of fairness, a nostalgic reverence for tradition, and the emotional satisfaction of a transparent world whose rules are clear and outcomes final. For those evaluating the Supreme Court nominee, such emotions were the opposite of provocative; in a nation still exhausted from the divisive acrimony of the previous year's presidential election, they struck a reassuring note.

Emotions, once triggered, are like a genie released from a bottle—hard to recapture and cork. And given that emotion often trumps reason, this is one reason why analogies can be so hard to parry. That is, in addition to whatever intrinsic logical parallels analogies may reveal or assert, the most persuasive analogies also make an intuitive, emotional appeal that often transcends logic. And as noted earlier, the brain tends to work hard to defend its intuitions against logical counterarguments, even to the point of discarding evidence that contradicts its preferred conclusion. As Kahneman notes, "When people believe a conclusion is true, they are also very likely to believe arguments that appear to support it, even when those arguments are unsound."

An astute observer will note that the five elements of Roberts' analogy—using the familiar to explain something less familiar, highlighting similarities and obscuring differences, identifying useful abstractions, telling a coherent story, and tapping into resonant emotions—overlap to a certain degree. This is quite common. In fact, the most persuasive analogies exploit such overlaps because they not only amplify the effect of any given element but also complicate rapid deconstruction, especially in the heat of an argument.

A RISING TIDE LIFTS ALL BOATS

Whether one is evaluating the words of an erudite Supreme Court nominee or the most common of idiomatic expressions, deconstructing an analogy through its five basic criteria works equally well. Typically, when someone says "a rising tide lifts all boats," they are suggesting that the benefits of economic growth accrue to everyone, whether that person owns a yacht or the humblest of metaphorical rowboats.

First, the analogy works well in that it uses something familiar and visual—a tide lifting boats—to describe something unfamiliar and abstract—economic growth and the benefits that accompany it.

Second, it highlights similarities; just as a rising tide lifts all boats, a growing economy generally benefits everyone, over time, by generating more opportunities, more income, and more tax revenue for public works and other programs. But even as it highlights this similarity, the analogy obscures a major difference: While a rising tide lifts all boats *equally*, a rising economy lifts the economic fortunes of citizens *unequally*, often grossly so. As recent economic trends reveal, a rising tide lifts the yachts much faster than it does the rowboats, while still more people—struggling to stay afloat—are calling out for a life ring.

Third, the analogy identifies a useful abstraction: Economic growth is "up." And as the linguist George Lakoff notes, up is a fundamental spatial metaphor with generally positive connotations. Up is the equivalent of more, and more signals plenty. Up is good. In concert with the use of familiar imagery—a rising tide lifting boats—to explain the unfamiliar, the analogy's abstraction also enables the average listener to easily visualize and process otherwise vague macroeconomic concepts concerning the distribution of economic growth across a diverse population.

Fourth, "a rising tide lifts all boats" offers a simple, coherent story. It may be incomplete as applied to economics, and it may obscure important differences, but as far as it goes, the analogy is still coherent.

Fifth, the rising-tide analogy resonates emotionally. If up is good, then a rising tide is good, and the benefits of economic growth are good. After all, who doesn't prefer plenty to poverty?

WHEN COMPETING ANALOGIES GO "HEAD-TO-HEAD"

What happens when analogies compete with each other? Often, when analogies duel for dominance, our instinct is to try reconciling the two into a single coherent narrative—one based on the highest possible alignment of the ideas that comprise each analogy, and the associations and emotions they evoke.

Earlier, we examined contrasting descriptions of the Ford Edsel, a car praised by *The New York Times* but derided by the public. As noted, the *Times* critic had likened the car's horizontal taillights to "the graceful wingspread of a sea gull" and suggested that the car's vertical front grille lent it a "distinctive continental flair." Many more people, when they finally saw the car, thought that same grille looked like a toilet seat. The toilet seat description, a simple analogy, prevailed over "continental flair," in part because it was more visually specific and familiar and therefore easier to grasp. But the toilet seat analogy also offered the public a more useful abstraction and triggered stronger emotions.

Having easily dispensed with continental flair, the mind next pursues coherence by comparing the toilet-seat analogy with the seagull analogy, trying to decide which one best describes the nature of the car as a whole. At first glance, both analogies are visual, accurate, and easy to grasp. In form if not function, the car's grille does look like a toilet seat, while its prominent taillights are a clear visual analog of a gull in flight.

Both analogies trigger their own networks of associated ideas, images, and emotions—many of them subconscious. Depending on how strongly these resonate, the mind will categorize some elements of each as unimportant or irrelevant. Next, it will try to use what it has determined relevant to construct an argument in which the analogies do not actually compete with each other. If the mind can't reconcile the two, one will trump the other as more convincing. In the case of the Edsel, the toilet-seat analogy moved more people, and the market spoke.

HOBBLING ALONG ON THE CRUTCH OF CLICHÉ

What happens when opponents offer competing analogies and both are clichés, neither of which is particularly compelling?

In a 2013 debate over the Affordable Care Act, the Republican Senate minority leader Mitch McConnell of Kentucky argued that he did not think it was possible to fix the law's shortcomings. "Everything is interconnected, 2,700 pages of statute, 20,000 pages of regulations so far. *The only solution is to repeal it, root and branch.*"

Taking the opposite position, Max Baucus, a Democratic senator from Montana and one of the law's primary authors, said: "I'm not sure we're going to get to the point where it's time to open the bill and make some changes. *Once you start, it's Pandora's box.*"

One could argue the finer points of each one, but neither would emerge victorious. And that is largely because the senators' chosen analogies are so clichéd they've lost their power either to provide new insights or to evoke the strong emotions that could possibly dislodge someone from an entrenched position. Unfortunately, too much of the rhetoric we hear from Washington slips into cliché.

So too does much of the jargon and rhetoric in the business world. How many times have CEOs and managers told their teams to "keep their eye on the ball" and "swing for the fences" without "dropping the ball" or losing sight of "true north" while they "think outside the box"? Given that familiarity breeds contempt, or at least indifference, is it any surprise that such jargon does little to engage and motivate employees? In many ways, such clichés are like the two-liter bottle of Diet Coke that's been left out on the kitchen counter after a party, uncapped. Yes, it's still theoretically drinkable in the morning, but it doesn't have any fizz left.

GETTING AWAY WITH MURDER

Sometimes how analogies sound can have an impact on their effectiveness. In one study, a test population that listened to a series of rhyming aphorisms and their nonrhyming equivalents reported that the rhyming versions offered more insight. For example, "Little strokes will fell great oaks" resonates more than "Little strokes will fell big trees."

Many persuasive speakers exploit this power of rhyme. In 1995, defense attorney Johnnie Cochran used a rhyming analogy to great effect in persuading a jury to acquit O. J. Simpson of murder charges. Strong circumstantial evidence pointed to Simpson's guilt in the brutal stabbing deaths of his ex-wife, Nicole Brown Simpson, and her companion, Ron Goldman. Among other evidence connected with the murder, police had recovered two leather gloves of a type that had been given to the football star by his ex-wife—one at the murder scene, and its match near his estate. According to the prosecution's DNA analysis, the match showed evidence of blood from O.J. and both murder victims.

Prosecutors were so certain of the accused's guilt that they had him try on the gloves in the courtroom. Cochran, though, insisted that his client wear latex gloves for the fitting, purportedly to avoid further contamination of the evidence. And whether it was because he was wearing the latex gloves, or that the leather gloves and their cashmere lining were stiff with dried blood, or that they had shrunk in the freezer used to preserve evidence, the gloves didn't seem to fit well. Theatrically wiggling his fingers, Simpson struggled to pull the gloves on, as some in the courtroom heard him protest, "They're too small . . . they're too tight."

Months later, in his closing argument, Cochran turned the whole spectacle to his advantage, calling it "the defining moment of this trial, the day [District Attorney Christopher] Darden asked Mr. Simpson to try on those gloves, and the gloves didn't fit. Remember these words: If it doesn't fit, you must acquit."

Coming toward the end of a long and highly publicized trial infused with broader issues of race, systemic police bias, sloppy detective work, and prosecutorial incompetence, Cochran's instruction to the jury rested on a simple analogy: The fit of the gloves equaled the fit of the evidence overall. If the gloves didn't fit the defendant's hands well, the entirety of the prosecution's evidence didn't fit well either. By their nature, gloves are supposed to fit their owner's hands perfectly; anyone who has tried on a pair a size too small knows how uncomfortable and difficult it can be. Subtly but clearly, Cochran was arguing that the prosecution's case must "fit like a glove" to find O.J. guilty as charged. Because if he were indeed the murderer, shouldn't the murderer's extra-large gloves fit his hands?

Like other persuasive analogies, Cochran's met five key criteria. First, it used something familiar, gloves, to simplify and explain something less familiar—weeks of complex evidence, much of it based on disputed forensic science. Second, it highlighted similarities—if the gloves didn't fit, the overall evidence didn't fit—and obscured differences, namely the damning DNA on the gloves and the incriminating locations where the two were found. Third, it identified a useful abstraction, that the fit of the gloves equaled the fit of the evidence overall (which reinforced the previous point). Fourth, the analogy told a coherent story: If the gloves don't fit, you must acquit. Fifth, it resonated emotionally, offering the jury a plausible and therefore satisfying justification—reasonable doubt—to find O.J. not guilty and, by doing so, condemn a racially biased, corrupt, and incompetent Los Angeles Police Department.

On October 3, 1995, as tens of millions of Americans watched on TV, the jury entered the courtroom to deliver its verdict: not guilty. Looking back nearly two decades later, the one line that most people recall from the trial is Cochran's succinct, rhyming summary: "If the gloves don't fit, you must acquit." That's not quite what Cochran said. Still, that is what people inferred from his analogy. Such conflation of distinct ideas is both common and powerful, and is one reason that analogies can be so seductive even when their core arguments are dubious.

THEIR FINEST HOUR

Winston Churchill, the British prime minister and wartime leader, delivered some of the most compelling speeches of the twentieth century. One reason they were so effective was Churchill's frequent and powerful use of analogy.

In 1897, when he was just twenty-two and a soldier in India, Churchill carefully studied what made public speakers effective, and drafted an essay—never published in his lifetime—entitled "The Scaffolding of Rhetoric." In it, he noted that "there are certain features common to all the finest speeches in the English language. In painting partly mechanical arrangements of colour give pleasure to the eye. In music certain combinations of chords and discords are agreeable to the ear. And the art of oratory has also its 'values' and its 'thorough base.'" One key truss in this scaffolding of rhetoric, he noted, is the effective use of analogy.

Analogy, Churchill wrote, "appeals to the everyday knowledge of the hearer and invites him to decide the problems that have baffled his powers of reason." And while he acknowledged that argument by analogy "leads to conviction rather than to proof, and has often led to glaring error," Churchill still defended its use.

"In spite of the arguments of the cynic the influence exercised over the human mind by apt analogies is and has always been immense," he wrote. "Whether they translate an established truth into simple language or whether they adventurously aspire to reveal the unknown, they are among the most formidable weapons of the rhetorician. The effect upon the most cultivated audiences is electrical."

He then proceeded to cite a few recent examples: his own father's description of British rule in India as "a sheet of oil" spread over "a vast and profound ocean of humanity," and Lord Salisbury's description of frontier wars as "the surf that marks the edge and advance of the wave of civilization."

"It is impossible to imagine any form of argument that could keep the field in the face of these or similar analogies," Churchill wrote. Some four decades later, such rhetorical tools would prove critical in rallying his reeling nation against the Nazi onslaught and in persuading the United States to support Britain's desperate fight for survival.

By early June of 1940, the last British troops retreated from mainland Europe in a chaotic seaborne escape from Dunkirk. Belgium had fallen to the Germans, and France was about to surrender. On June 18, having assumed the prime minister's post just the previous month, Churchill stood before Parliament and laid out the stakes in a speech that, a few hours later, he delivered again to an estimated four million anxious citizens who had gathered around radios in their homes and neighborhood pubs, at factories and military airfields, in shipyards and schools. For the first time in centuries, perhaps since the Spanish Armada set sail to invade in 1588, England's freedom was in grave and immediate doubt.

"What General Weygand has called the Battle of France is over," Churchill explained toward the end of his speech. "I expect that the Battle of Britain is about to begin. Upon this battle depends the survival of Christian civilization. Upon it depends our own British life, and the long continuity of our institutions and our Empire. The whole might of the enemy must very soon be turned on us. Hitler knows that he will have to break us in this island or lose the war. If we can stand up to him, all Europe may be free and the life of the world may move forward into broad, sunlit uplands. But if we fail, then the whole world, including the United States, including all that we have known and cared for, will sink into the abyss of a new Dark Age made more sinister, and perhaps more protracted, by the lights of perverted science. Let us therefore brace ourselves to our duties and so bear ourselves that, if the British Empire and its Commonwealth last for a thousand years, men will still say, 'This was their finest hour.' "

The speech, one of several momentous wartime addresses, is widely considered to be his finest. For those listening on the radio, his striking visual analogies—to "move forward into broad, sunlit uplands" or "sink into the abyss of a new Dark Age" among them—captured the essence of the challenge at hand: an epic battle for the ages, one between light and darkness, good and evil, hope and despair. A closer examination of this core analogy suggests other contrasts, too: up versus down, rise versus sink, climb versus fall, top versus bottom. These contrasting dualities are fundamental human experiences that everyone has experienced from birth onward and that generally trigger positive and negative emotions, respectively.

In *Metaphors We Live By*, George Lakoff and Mark Johnson identify these as orientational metaphors. While their meaning can vary by culture, Westerners generally feel that *up* is *happy*, and *down* is *sad*. This is reflected in expressions such as:

"He's feeling *up* today."

"My spirits are *soaring*."

"His speech gave her a real *lift*."

Alternatively:

"My spirits *sank*."

"When he got fired, he *fell* into a *deep depression*."

"I'm feeling *low*."

These expressions are derived, Lakoff and Johnson argue, from physical reality: When we're sad or depressed, our shoulders slump and our posture often droops. When we're happy, as when our favorite football team kicks a field goal to win the game as time runs out, we jump to our feet.

Similarly, they note that *health* and *life* are *up*, while *sickness* and *death* are *down*. Again, this concept finds expression in everyday language:

"Olympic athletes are in *peak* shape."

"Jesus *rose* from the dead."

"After her cancer screening came back negative, she felt on *top* of the world."

Alternatively:

"After waiting for the bus in the rain, she came *down* with a cold."

"Despite the best medical care, his health continued to *sink*."

"He seemed just fine, until he *dropped* dead on the way to work one day."

Again, such language is derived from our physical experience, since serious illness generally forces one to lie down, and when we're dead, we can no longer stand. We associate *down* with being controlled—forced to knuckle *under*, he *fell* from power. We think of *up* as being in control—judges on the bench *oversee* a courtroom, while a great surgeon is *tops* in her field.

In the same vein, *up* is associated with virtue—the *upright* citizens of Athens raised sharpened swords to defend their *highest* ideals. *Down* is associated with depravity—too late, the Trojans realized that the Greeks' strange wooden horse had been a *lowdown* trick.

As Lakoff and Johnson note, "No metaphor can ever be compre-hended or even adequately represented independently of its experien-tial basis." Churchill's choice of words exploited this, subtly entwining the up-down analogy with an equally powerful light-dark analogy. In daylight we can see. When we can see, we tend to feel safer than when we can't see, which generally happens at night. Similarly, light reflects knowledge, and darkness, ignorance: During the *Enlightenment*, West-ern scholars relit the *lamp of knowledge* that had been extinguished during the *Dark Ages*. Finally, light represents life and goodness—we wake up to a new day of possibility—while darkness represents death and evil, an everlasting burial from which we never awake.

Given these reflexive, if subconscious, physical associations with its intrinsic up-down, light-dark metaphors, Churchill's analogy drew its bucket from a deep emotional well. As such, those listening didn't just know or believe—but rather felt—that everything Britain held dear was now at stake in an uncertain life-or-death struggle whose out-come would define Britain for the ages.

From a rhetorical standpoint, Churchill's analogy meets all five criteria of persuasive analogies. First, he uses listeners' familiarity with landscape, and the concepts of high versus low and light versus dark, to explain the less familiar terrain of geopolitics and war. Sec-ond, he highlights similarities, such as the fact that high ground is usu-ally associated with victory, and obscures differences such as the fact that the Sun shines on victor and vanquished alike. Third, he identi-fies useful abstractions, such as the struggle between rising and sink-ing, light and darkness, good and evil, life and death. Fourth, he offers a coherent narrative: If Britain wins this battle for its very existence, those who fight for it will be lauded for a thousand years. Fifth, he evokes resonant emotions appropriate to the moment, including fear, hope, determination, patriotism, and courage.

Churchill's speech had a profound effect, and not just on his fellow citizens listening throughout Britain. Across the Atlantic, the prime minister's widely reported words stirred the emotions of millions of

American voters whose congressional leaders, many of whom were isolationists, wanted no part in a war against Germany.

Of course, words alone would not stem the onslaught. Outnumbered and outgunned, Britain needed material help from the United States. In just one ten-day stretch in July, the Germans sank eleven British destroyers—a highly damaging loss of life, capital, and warfighting capacity. Later that summer and into the fall, the Luftwaffe unleashed its full fury over the skies of England, attacking with a thousand-plane advantage. With outstanding strategy, determination, and a courage born of sheer desperation, English and Allied pilots held them off.

Both formally and through private channels, Churchill repeatedly requested help from the United States. President Franklin Delano Roosevelt was sympathetic, and through creative executive orders, did what he could to help. Congress, however, refused his entreaties to accelerate the buildup of America's defense industries and to give, sell, lend, or lease American war materiel to the British.

THE POWER OF A GARDEN HOSE

As Christmas approached, the president grew increasingly concerned about the possibility of a Nazi victory and was convinced that the United States must help the British more forcefully or eventually face a direct attack itself. Speaking to reporters at the White House about why it made sense for America to stop worrying about legal paperwork associated with support for Britain, he urged Congress to take action, regardless of the cost.

"Now, what I am trying to do is to eliminate the dollar sign," FDR said. "That is something brand new in the thoughts of practically everybody in this room, I think—get rid of the silly, foolish old dollar sign." And then he drove his point home by ad-libbing an analogy: "Suppose my neighbor's home catches fire, and I have a length of garden hose four or five hundred feet away. If he can take my garden hose and connect it up with his hydrant, I may help him to put out his fire. Now, what do I do? I don't say to him before that operation, 'Neighbor, my garden hose cost me fifteen dollars; you have to pay me fifteen dollars for it.'

"What is the transaction that goes on? I don't want fifteen dollars—I want my garden hose back after the fire is over. All right. If it goes through the fire all right, intact, without any damage to it, he gives it back to me and thanks me very much for the use of it.

"But suppose it gets smashed up—holes in it—during the fire; we don't have to have too much formality about it, but I say to him, 'I was glad to lend you that hose; I see I can't use it anymore, it's all smashed up.' He says, 'How many feet of it were there?' I tell him, 'There were one hundred fifty feet of it.' He says, 'All right, I will replace it.' Now, if I get a nice garden hose back, I am in pretty good shape.

"In other words, if you lend certain munitions and get the munitions back at the end of the war, if they are intact and haven't been hurt—you are all right; if they have been damaged or have deteriorated or have been lost completely, it seems to me you come out pretty well if you have them replaced by the fellow to whom you have lent them."

This garden-hose analogy—at once simple, succinct, and intuitive in its logic—was widely reported, and proved critical in helping the public understand the nature of the crisis. Who wouldn't lend their hose to a neighbor whose house was on fire?

Two weeks later, the president followed up with a radio address to the nation, one of his so-called fireside chats that he used to bypass the filter of reporters and speak directly to the American people. In it, he made a general analogy between the economic crisis of 1933 and the military crisis at hand, and offered a series of specific analogies to support his argument for American aid to Great Britain.

"Tonight, in the presence of a world crisis, my mind goes back eight years to a night in the midst of a domestic crisis. It was a time when the wheels of American industry were grinding to a full stop, when the whole banking system of our country had ceased to function. I well remember that while I sat in my study in the White House, preparing to talk with the people of the United States, I had before my eyes the picture of all those Americans with whom I was talking. I saw the workmen in the mills, the mines, the factories; the girl behind the counter; the small shopkeeper; the farmer doing his spring plowing; the widows and the old men wondering about their life's savings. I tried to convey to the great mass of American people what the banking crisis meant to them in their daily lives.

"Tonight, I want to do the same thing, with the same people, in this new crisis which faces America. We met the issue of 1933 with courage and realism. We face this new crisis, this new threat to the security of our nation, with the same courage and realism. Never before since Jamestown and Plymouth Rock has our American civilization been in such danger as now. . . ."

Control of the Atlantic, he explained, was critical to control of the western hemisphere and an explicit US security priority since the administration of James Monroe. In the current context, a strong British navy served as a powerful bulwark against Nazi aggression in the Americas.

"Frankly and definitely there is danger ahead—danger against which we must prepare," he said. "But we well know that we cannot escape danger, or the fear of danger, by crawling into bed and pulling the covers over our heads. . . ."

He took aim at the American "appeasers" who preferred to negotiate with Germany rather than throw in their lot with Britain. "They call it a 'negotiated peace,'" FDR said dismissively. "Nonsense! Is it a negotiated peace if a gang of outlaws surrounds your community and on threat of extermination makes you pay tribute to save your own skins?

"The experience of the past two years has proven beyond doubt that no nation can appease the Nazis. No man can tame a tiger into a kitten by stroking it. There can be no appeasement with ruthlessness.

There can be no reasoning with an incendiary bomb. We know now that a nation can have peace with the Nazis only at the price of total surrender. . . .

"In a military sense Great Britain and the British Empire are today the spearhead of resistance to world conquest. And they are putting up a fight which will live forever in the story of human gallantry," Roosevelt said.

Then he returned to the economic-industrial analogy with which he had opened his remarks, to argue that the United States must immediately and dramatically increase the production of armaments and send them to its allies.

"American industrial genius, unmatched throughout all the world in the solution of production problems, has been called upon to bring its resources and its talents into action," he said. "We must be the great arsenal of democracy. For us this is an emergency as serious as war itself. We must apply ourselves to our task with the same resolution, the same sense of urgency, the same spirit of patriotism and sacrifice as we would show were we at war."

Dubbed the Arsenal of Democracy speech, the president's fireside chat had a dramatic impact on American public opinion; polling afterward found that, in a dramatic shift, some 60 percent of Americans now agreed with his position.

Rhetorically, the speech can be summarized in its progression of the following six italicized analogies. The first is that, just as America overcame the economic crisis of 1933, *"a time when the wheels of American industry were grinding to a full stop,"* the nation could also overcome the current military threat through an aggressive, nationally coordinated industrial effort.

The second analogy highlights the futility of ignoring clear and present dangers: *"We cannot escape danger, or the fear of danger, by crawling into bed and pulling the covers over our heads."*

The third analogy argues against those advocating appeasement under the guise of a negotiated peace: *"Is it a negotiated peace if a gang of outlaws surrounds your community and on threat of extermination makes you pay tribute to save your own skins?"*

The fourth analogy suggests that it would be impossible to appease Hitler anyway: *"The experience of the past two years has proven beyond doubt that no nation can appease the Nazis. No man can tame a tiger into a kitten by stroking it."*

The fifth analogy describes Britain's critical leadership role in the battle for freedom: *"In a military sense Great Britain and the British Empire are today the spearhead of resistance to world conquest."*

The sixth and final analogy is one of FDR's most famous: *"We must be the great arsenal of democracy."*

Through these six analogies, the president made his case for rearming the United States and aiding Britain. And by linking the two issues, he framed the debate such that the isolationists found themselves trapped: If they didn't favor rearming America, did they believe an unarmed America was safer? If America's failure to aid Britain led to its defeat, would that defeat make America safer? As FDR had said, those arguments made as much sense as pulling the covers over one's head and hoping Hitler would go away, or trying to tame a tiger into a kitten.

FDR's insistence on preparing for war was relentless. A week later, he delivered his now famous Four Freedoms speech, in which he pledged American support for the freedoms of democracy and attacked isolationists as dangerous and self-serving appeasers.

"As a nation, we may take pride in the fact that we are soft-hearted; but we cannot afford to be soft-headed," he said. "We must always be wary of those who with sounding brass and a tinkling cymbal preach the 'ism' of appeasement. We must especially beware of that small group of selfish men who would clip the wings of the American eagle in order to feather their own nests. . . .

"Freedom means the supremacy of human rights everywhere," FDR concluded. "Our support goes to those who struggle to gain those rights or keep them. Our strength is our unity of purpose. To that high concept there can be no end save victory."

While it took several more months, Congress eventually fell in line and approved what grew to become $50 billion in American "Lend-Lease" military aid to Great Britain and other American allies.

Can President Roosevelt's persuasiveness be attributed to analogy alone? Of course not. But the analogies in his speeches were each loaded arguments that translated global affairs into terms that everyday citizens could grasp, and in a way that engaged and marshaled their emotions to support deeper American engagement. His leadership proved prescient: Within the year, Japanese warplanes attacked the US Pacific Fleet at Pearl Harbor, and America was at war.

I HAVE A DREAM

On September 8, 1962, a group of civil rights volunteers held a voter registration meeting at the Mount Olive Baptist Church in Terrell County, Georgia. Later that night, arsonists—who had been torching black churches associated with the civil rights campaign in nearby Albany—burned it to the ground. By morning, little remained of the church but its concrete steps and modest bell, which lay on its side among the smoking debris.

At a service following the firebombing, Prathia Hall, a young leader in the Student Nonviolent Coordinating Committee—one of the civil rights groups working in Albany and throughout the South— joined others amid the ruins, to mourn and regroup. "I have a dream," she prayed aloud. "I have a dream." Soon the entire group was intoning Hall's phrase, including Dr. Martin Luther King Jr., who had been jailed for his civil rights work in Albany earlier that year, and who had joined the service in solidarity.

As a preacher, King knew and embraced such rhetoric. Prophetic dreams are woven throughout the Bible, and more than a year before the Mount Olive church bombing, King himself had given a commencement address at Lincoln University entitled "The American Dream," in which he had quoted the Declaration of Independence and explored its unfulfilled promise of equality for all men. "America is essentially a dream, a dream that is as yet unfulfilled," he told students at the historically black university in Pennsylvania.

"It is a dream of a land where men of all races, of all nationalities, and of all creeds can live together as brothers. The substance of the dream is expressed in these sublime words, words lifted to cosmic proportions: 'We hold these truths to be self-evident—that all men are created equal; that they are endowed by their Creator with certain inalienable rights; that among them are life, liberty, and the pursuit of happiness.' This is the dream."

But even in an America booming with prosperity, the American dream was stubbornly elusive for millions of American blacks whose race excluded them from even the most basic rights of citizenship, let alone economic opportunity. For African Americans, discrimination, disenfranchisement, segregation, and racial violence were facts of life. And as civil rights organizers filed lawsuits, mounted boycotts, staged sit-ins, launched Freedom Rides, and led voter-registration drives in the late 1950s and into the 1960s, a violent backlash intensified, often inflicted or conveniently ignored by local law enforcement.

In his 1963 inauguration speech as governor of Alabama, George Wallace stood on the steps of the state capitol and proudly proclaimed, "Segregation now, segregation tomorrow, segregation forever!" In May of that year, Birmingham police chief Eugene "Bull" Connor and his men attacked civil rights marchers, many of them children, with police dogs and fire hoses. The Reverend Will D. Campbell, a Freedom Rider who was active in the movement, described the experience: "If it hits you right, the pressure from a fire hose can break your back. I remember seeing adults and children hit and rolling along the sidewalk like pebbles at high tide." Watching on TV, the rest of the nation also saw those images and, shocked by the brutality, finally began to grasp the ugly reality of Jim Crow and feel the need for strong federal action.

Before Birmingham, only 4 percent of Americans considered civil rights to be the nation's most pressing issue; afterward, that figure rose to just over half. To bring pressure to bear on Congress and the Kennedy White House, which was wary of alienating Southern Democrats, civil rights leaders called for a national March on Washington for Jobs and Freedom. In the two months leading up to the August 28 march, Americans staged 758 civil rights demonstrations in nearly 200 towns and cities across the country. Nearly 15,000 were arrested. On June 12, just hours after President Kennedy called for passage of a civil rights act, in a nationally televised address, a white supremacist assassinated NAACP organizer Medgar Evers in the driveway of Evers' Mississippi home.

With tensions high and the outcome uncertain, marchers began streaming into Washington by the tens of thousands. The night before the march, King—after meeting with aides—sat in his hotel room, working on the speech he was to deliver. Working from a draft prepared by his staff entitled "Normalcy, Never Again," he finished around 4:00 A.M. Late the following afternoon, when he finally took the podium as the day's closing speaker, King looked from where he stood on the steps of the Lincoln Memorial, out across a sea of humanity that filled the National Mall as far as he could see.

"I am happy to join with you today in what will go down in history as the greatest demonstration for freedom in the history of our nation," he began, in his deep baritone. "Five score years ago, a great American, in whose symbolic shadow we stand today, signed the Emancipation Proclamation. This momentous decree came as a great beacon light of hope to millions of Negro slaves who had been seared in the flames of withering injustice. It came as a joyous daybreak to end the long night of their captivity. But one hundred years later, the Negro still is not free. . . ."

For the next ten minutes or so, King held the crowd with a mesmerizing string of metaphors, speaking of how, in writing the Constitution and the Declaration of Independence, the founders "were signing a promissory note to which every American was to fall heir. This note was a promise that all men, yes, black men as well as white men, would be guaranteed the inalienable rights of life, liberty, and the pursuit of happiness. It is obvious today that America has defaulted on this promissory note, insofar as her citizens of color are concerned. Instead of honoring this sacred obligation, America has given the Negro people a bad check, a check which has come back marked 'insufficient funds.'"

He spoke of the "fierce urgency of now" and pressed those before him to continue their determined but nonviolent struggle for justice. "I am not unmindful that some of you have come here out of great trials and tribulations. Some of you have come fresh from narrow jail cells. And some of you have come from areas where your quest for freedom left you battered by the storms of persecution and staggered by the winds of police brutality," he said.

Unearned suffering is redemptive, he explained, and urged those gathered to go back to the Southern states and the ghettos and cities of the North and continue their work, "knowing that somehow this situation can and will be changed."

Then something unexpected happened. As Clarence Jones, one of King's staff who had helped draft the speech recalled, the singer Mahalia Jackson shouted "Tell 'em about the 'dream,' Martin, tell 'em about the 'dream'!"

Until this point, King had been reading his speech. Now he pushed aside the remainder of his text, which included an exhortation to pressure Congress for civil rights legislation, and a short conclusion about climbing hills of hope. Watching King, Jones told the person next to him: "These people out there today don't know it yet, but they're about ready to go to church."

Indeed, they were; and for many, it was a religious experience as

King began to preach from the heart, drawing from the ideas and language he had been honing for the past decade. "I still have a dream. It is a dream deeply rooted in the American dream," he began. "I have a dream that one day this nation will rise up and live out the true meaning of its creed: 'We hold these truths to be self-evident, that all men are created equal.' I have a dream . . ."

The extended riff that followed was adapted from a similar "I have a dream" speech King had delivered before 25,000 people in Detroit two months earlier. This time, though, the phrase would end up defining not just the speech or even the march on Washington, but also the very promise of American democracy itself.

"I have a dream that one day even the state of Mississippi, a state sweltering with the heat of injustice, sweltering with the heat of oppression, will be transformed into an oasis of freedom and justice," he said.

"I have a dream that four little children will one day live in a nation where they will not be judged by the color of their skin but by the content of their character. I have a dream today!

"I have a dream that one day, down in Alabama, with its vicious racists, with its governor having his lips dripping with the words of interposition and nullification, one day right there in Alabama little black boys and black girls will be able to join hands with little white boys and white girls as sisters and brothers. . . .

"I have a dream that one day every valley shall be exalted, and every hill and mountain shall be made low, the rough places will be made plain, and the crooked places will be made straight; and the glory of the Lord shall be revealed and all flesh shall see it together," he said.

King's words drew from the book of Isaiah, which spoke of a righteous God and prophesied that the Israelites would experience a second Exodus, this time from slavery in Babylon. Their escape would mark a triumph of faith over despair and herald a return to a purified Jerusalem.

It wasn't just King's rich metaphors that made his speech so powerful, although he used more than fifty of them. Rather, it was the deeper analogy he asserted between the biblical struggle for freedom and the American struggle for freedom.

"This is our hope, and this is the faith that I go back to the South with," he continued, grounding the biblical allegory in the challenging realities of a violent, segregated America. "With this faith, we will be able to hew out of the mountain of despair a stone of hope. With this faith, we will be able to transform the jangling discords of our nation into a beautiful symphony of brotherhood. With this faith, we will be able to work together, to pray together, to struggle together, to go to jail together, to stand up for freedom together, knowing that we will be free one day."

King's words weren't primarily aimed at swaying government decision makers. Rather, they were aimed at the thousands of citizens who had been risking their lives to tear down the edifice of institutionalized racial injustice in towns and cities across the country, particularly in the South. At a time of violence and official intransigence, King had to persuade those in the movement to continue their dangerous struggle to secure the civil rights of all Americans, regardless of any personal danger.

At this point a quarter million people were on their feet cheering, and some sobbing, as millions more watched on TV. As King scholar Eric Sundquist would later write, King had "created a new national scripture."

"And this will be the day, this will be the day when all of God's children will be able to sing with new meaning," King said, as the crowd roared its approval: " 'My country 'tis of these, sweet land of liberty, of thee I sing. Land where my fathers died, land of the pilgrim's pride, from every mountainside, let freedom ring.'

"And if America is to be a great nation this must become true. So let freedom ring from the prodigious hilltops of New Hampshire. Let freedom ring from the mighty mountains of New York. . . . Let freedom ring from Stone Mountain of Georgia! Let freedom ring from

Lookout Mountain of Tennessee! Let freedom ring from every hill and molehill of Mississippi. From every mountainside, let freedom ring.

"And when this happens, when we allow freedom to ring, when we let it ring from every village and every hamlet, from every state and every city, we will be able to speed up that day when all of God's children, black men and white men, Jews and Gentiles, Protestants and Catholics, will be able to join hands and sing in the words of the old Negro spiritual: Free at last! Free at last! Thank God Almighty, we are free at last!"

King's speech, widely considered one of the finest in American history, didn't persuade George Wallace or Bull Connor or millions of others who clung to the prejudices of old Dixie. But it did capture official attention. As one FBI agent wrote in an August 30 memo: "I believe in the light of King's powerful demagogic speech yesterday [that] he stands head and shoulders over all other Negro leaders put together when it comes to influencing great masses of Negroes. We must mark him now, if we have not done so before, as the most dangerous Negro of the future in this Nation from the standpoint of communism, the Negro and national security."

Richard Lischer, a Duke University professor specializing in the rhetoric of preaching, wrote in *The Preacher King*, "From the beginning in 1955, King's leadership of the Movement was a calculated act of interpretation carried out in the mirror of the Bible's imagery, stories and characters: the morning star of freedom illumined the darkness of an ordinary Southern city. Baptist and Methodist Rotarians were assigned and grudgingly assumed the role of 'the pharaohs of the South.' A festive parade of thousands along a state highway symbolized the Exodus from Egypt. Blood-spattered Negroes enacted the mystery of unmerited suffering. All of it was presided over by the black Moses who was willing to die for his people."

As expressed by King that day, "I Have a Dream" offered America an almost biblical vision of itself that seemed to represent the moral fulfillment of the nation's original ideals, if only enough good people had the conscience, courage, and commitment to persevere.

Inspired, thousands of those who marched on Washington, or who tuned in to King's speech over the airwaves, fanned out once again to continue their struggle across the country. Many in the South would end up beaten and bloody, or locked in jail cells. Others ended up dead—shot or lynched or buried in the steaming dirt of an earthen dam. But as they fell, so did opposition to civil rights. As pressure mounted on Washington, President Johnson—seizing the moment after the assassination of President Kennedy—forced through the Civil Rights Act of 1964 and continued to press for change in the years that followed.

"There is no issue of states' rights or national rights. There is only the struggle for human rights," Johnson told Congress in 1965. "Because it's not just Negroes, but really it's all of us, who must overcome the crippling legacy of bigotry and injustice. We shall overcome."

King wasn't the first to champion civil rights in twentieth-century America, but as Lischer writes, he was "the first to name the struggle and to declare its meaning." For King, the movement was the living embodiment of the transcendent, righteous struggle for human freedom and dignity, as expressed in the Bible. And this struggle was not just for American blacks but for all oppressed people, everywhere.

While the fight against segregation was far from over, the deeper analogy King envisioned—a promised land of genuine equality—began to redefine the way many Americans thought about civil rights, including women's rights and more recently gay rights. As King himself told the assembled multitudes stretching past the reflecting pool on that sweltering afternoon of America's discontent, "1963 is not an end, but a new beginning." From a mountain of despair, King *had* somehow hewn a stone of hope, and America would never be the same again.

· · · · ·

In the spring of 1984, an advertising executive named Hal Riney was sitting at the bar at Reno Barsocchini's, a dimly lit watering hole on Battery Street in San Francisco. It was midday, and the place was half-filled with regulars who had little better to do than talk sports and get an early start on happy hour. But for Riney, whose office was upstairs, it was a place to get away and think.

A few weeks earlier, he had gotten a call from a colleague in New York, inviting him to join a small team of advertising executives who were working on the reelection campaign of President Reagan. Riney agreed to help. But after two days of briefings by pollsters and aides—an experience he described as "a total waste of time"—he repaired to his favorite bar to get some real work done.

For two hours he scribbled away, which aroused the curiosity of his fellow patrons. "I remember a guy sitting next to me, one of those guys who hangs around the bar," Riney would recall years later. "He says, 'What are you doing, Hal?' I said, 'Well, I'm writing the president's advertising.' And he thought that was bullshit and just snickered."

Two of the ads he wrote that day are considered classics, and both are built on the foundation of analogy. The first spot featured the dangerous bear representing the Soviet Union, discussed in Chapter 2. The second was the iconic "Morning in America," a commercial that made the economic case for Reagan's reelection.

"It's morning again in America," the script began. "Today, more men and women will go to work than ever before in our country's history. With interest rates at about half the record highs of 1980, nearly 2,000 families today will buy new homes, more than at any time in the past four years. This afternoon, 6,500 young men and women will be married. And with inflation at less than half of what it was just four years ago, they can look forward with confidence to the future. It's morning again in America. And, under the leadership of President Reagan, our country is prouder and stronger and better. Why would we ever want to return to where we were less than four short years ago?"

It sounds straightforward enough, even plain. But its message is deeper and more powerful than it seems. Note that the only repeated phrase is the analogy, "It's morning again in America." The ad, which Riney also narrated, showed a sequence of gauzy images, among them a fishing boat at dawn, a farmer atop his tractor at sunrise, a paperboy on his bicycle delivering the morning news, a man heading off to work, a family moving into a new home, the US Capitol at daybreak, and three successive images of the American flag at the dawn's early light, including children hoisting it outside of a log cabin, a firefighter raising it in front of his truck, and a smiling, elderly home owner raising it before his front porch. In Reagan's America, it's morning all day—at least, metaphorically speaking.

Perhaps more than any other of Reagan's ads or speeches, "Morning in America" conveyed the spirit of sunny optimism for which he was famous. And compared to the grim malaise of the Carter years, still fresh in people's memories, that optimism was appealing—especially as Reagan was running against Carter's vice president, Walter Mondale.

But there's another analogical subtext, too. In 1984, Reagan was approaching his seventy-fifth year and, if reelected, would be the oldest US president ever to serve. Throughout the campaign, pundits questioned whether he still had the health, stamina, and mental acuity for such a grueling job. The worries were legitimate; as his son Ron later recalled, his father was showing signs of Alzheimer's during the 1984 campaign, and the White House staff did everything they could to control his exposure to situations in which his deteriorating faculties might be exposed.

At several moments in the first debate against Mondale, Reagan seemed befuddled. To millions of those watching, some of his stammering, meandering, stop-and-start answers even bordered on incoherence. As newsman Bob Schieffer later recalled, "It immediately set off this round of speculation: has the old man lost it?" Sam Donaldson offered a similar assessment: "He'd turned seventy shortly after becoming president, it was four years later, he was getting on, and . . .

suddenly the age thing was right on the table. Could we trust this guy, who we like, with another four years?"

"Morning in America" wasn't developed in response to President Reagan's damaging October 7 debate performance; it was put together over the summer and had begun airing in September. But as a counter to the idea of a president who was approaching his own twilight, "Morning in America" helped inoculate him to a certain degree; if his advancing age was suddenly front and center, a heavy ad buy of "morning" suggested the promise of a bright new day.

In the second debate, on October 21, one of the journalists posing questions to the candidates raised the issue of Reagan's age directly. Noting that the president was the oldest in American history and had reportedly been "tired" during the previous debate, he asked the president if he harbored any doubt about whether he had the stamina to handle the modern equivalent of a Cuban Missile Crisis. Reagan was ready with a self-deprecating quip. "Not at all," he said. "I will not make age an issue in this campaign. I am not going to exploit, for political purposes, my opponent's youth and inexperience."

As the crowd roared, even Mondale started laughing. And in terms of the president's reelection campaign, at least, it *was* morning in America again. A little more than two weeks later, Reagan won in a landslide.

Twenty years later, Republican strategist Dan Schnur, who in 1984 was a young assistant on the Reagan campaign's ad team, reflected on Riney's work in an interview with the *San Francisco Chronicle*. "Riney has the ability to cloak a strong message inside of a softer approach," he said. "Most political advertising hits viewers over the head, while his work makes just as strong a point but in a less confrontational and a more soothing manner."

A BICYCLE FOR THE MIND

At the time that Riney was selling the country an old president, another charismatic persuader, Steve Jobs, was about to sell the country a new computer. This was a bigger challenge, because while hundreds of millions of Americans were accustomed to choosing a president, few were accustomed to using a computer—let alone buying one.

Four years earlier, when Apple was a small company of five hundred employees selling the Apple II computer, Jobs outlined the challenge at Apple's Insanely Great conference. In a talk that showed the same grand vision but little of the polish that the world would later come to expect of him, Jobs stood behind a lectern and told of "the best analogy I've ever heard." He cited a study reported in *Scientific American* that calculated the locomotive efficiency of various animals—from fish to mammals to birds—to determine which could travel from A to B with the least expenditure of energy.

"The condor won. The condor took the least amount of energy to get from here to there," Jobs told the audience. "And man didn't do so well; he came in with a rather unimpressive showing about a third of the way down the list. But fortunately, someone at *Scientific American* was insightful enough to test man with a bicycle. And man with a bicycle won—twice as good as the condor. All the way off the list. And what it showed was that man as a toolmaker has the ability to make a tool to amplify an inherent ability that he has. And that's exactly what we are doing here [at Apple]. It's exactly what we're doing here."

As Jobs described it, Apple was building a "bicycle for the mind"—a tool that could take people's minds anywhere they could possibly imagine and multiply its power.

"We're not making bicycles to be ridden between Palo Alto and San Francisco. OK?" Jobs said. "We're making bicycles. And yes, certain bicycles have certain generic attributes like, in general, ten-speeds are better to ride in mountains than one-speeds and other things like that. But in general what we're doing is building tools to amplify a human ability.

"You could say that the Industrial Revolution was basically an amplification of a human ability: sweat. We amplified human sweat. What we're working towards now is the ability to amplify another human ability, and we're just starting to get glimmerings of where it's going to go."

His audience didn't know it at the time, but when Jobs delivered that talk, it was just months after his eye-opening visit to the Xerox Palo Alto Research Center, where he had recognized Apple's future in a graphical user interface that made computing possible for anyone in the world, regardless of their technical prowess or abilities. Even as Jobs spoke, a select team at Apple was working on just such an interface for the Macintosh.

Apple's goal was to remove all the barriers to using a computer, Jobs said. "Once you overcome that, it's a phenomenal tool," he explained. "And the reason I think that Apple has a chance of solving that problem, versus a lot of other computer companies that we all know of that are much, much larger than we are now," Jobs added, "is that our whole company, our whole philosophical base, is founded on one principle. And that one principle is that there's something very special and very historically different that takes place when you have one computer and one person."

In a question-and-answer session following his talk, Jobs declined to speculate on pending products. But he offered another analogy. "Apple is eventually going to have a broader line of products," he said. "Let's look at automobiles. Compare a Volkswagen Rabbit, a dump truck, and a Mercedes-Benz, let's say. They all have transmissions, they all have engines, four wheels, seats. Basically they all perform the same basic function: transportation. The difference is emphasis. There's a difference in emphasis. And that's what we're going to look at doing—computers with a different emphasis."

Over the next several years, Jobs and a small team of engineers and designers worked with a fierce intensity to make good on his vision. As the machine took shape, he approached Apple's ad agency,

Chiat/Day, to develop a Super Bowl ad for the Mac. "I want a thunderclap," Jobs told the creative team. Chiat/Day delivered, scripting and shooting an arresting sixty-second spot that echoed George Orwell's totalitarian novel *1984*. Filmed largely in a grainy blue-gray, the ad depicted a female athlete in red shorts and a white tank top, sledgehammer in hand, sprinting from pursuing Thought Police through a grim yet futuristic factory. As an ominous Big Brother delivers a televised speech about "a garden of pure ideology where each worker may bloom, secure from the pests purveying contradictory truths," the determined athlete bursts into an auditorium filled with rows of obedient, brainwashed workers staring dully at the screen.

With the Thought Police closing in, the rebel athlete hurls her sledgehammer at the flickering, snarling image of the totalitarian dictator who, acid with rage and righteousness, is thundering, "We shall prevail!" When the hammer hits his image, the screen explodes in a flash of blinding light.

For millions of viewers familiar with both the famous novel and IBM's nickname, Big Blue, the ad's message was unmistakable. Big Blue was Big Brother, and any future under its dominance was grim. Apple would set people free. Just in case anyone missed this point, the ad concluded with a narrator's voice calmly reading the words that rose from the bottom of the viewer's frame: "On January 24, Apple Computer will introduce the Macintosh. And you'll see why 1984 won't be like *1984*."

Wary of offending people, Apple's board of directors was reluctant to run the unconventional, aggressive ad. And except for a simple drawing of the revolutionary Mac on the athlete's tank top, the ad didn't even show the product Apple hoped to sell. But the company eventually deferred to the ad's passionate advocates.

The dramatic spot, which aired after a touchdown during the third quarter of Super Bowl XVIII on January 22, riveted a national audience of ninety-six million people and made the evening news on all three networks. *Ad Age* later declared it the "greatest commercial of all time."

A week after the Super Bowl, pundits were still buzzing about the ad's implications. "The fantasy commercial parallels reality, for Macintosh is a dramatic and risky attempt to make a technological end run around behemoth competitor IBM," wrote *Newsweek*'s Michael Rogers, adding that "Apple grew out of a suburban garage and became one of the country's leading computer makers in less than six years, only to collide head-on with a $40 billion company in the most volatile marketplace of the 1980s. For key employees, the new battle with IBM is almost a holy war against Orwellian forces that seek to subvert Apple's cherished vision of the personal computer as a tool to save the world."

Stu Schreiberg, a television executive who later produced a CBS special on the fifty greatest commercials in TV history, described the ad as "artistically incredible." As he noted, "You never see the product." You never see it because you don't have to—the analogy does the work, harnessing the emotional power of one of the twentieth century's most influential novels to sell one of the twentieth century's most influential machines.

And influential it was, though not because it was the most powerful computer. In actuality, the first Mac was woefully underpowered and required a lot of inconvenient disk swapping. But its intuitive, inspired graphical user interface—complete with icons representing documents, folders, scissors, paste, and a trash can—quickly persuaded millions of Americans that they didn't have to be a nerd or a geek to use a computer.

Like other effective analogies, the Mac's interface met the five essential criteria. First, it used something familiar, a desktop, to explain something less familiar, a computer. Second, it used its familiar icons to highlight similarities between both types of "desktop" work while simultaneously obscuring the fundamental differences between the physical and electronic manipulation of information. Third, it established a "desktop" as an abstraction—a flat surface on which people could perform almost any sort of work. It didn't matter whether that desktop was horizontal or vertical, physical or electronic. Fourth, the "desktop" told a coherent story: If someone could use a desk, they could also use a Mac. Fifth, from the beginning of the design process, Jobs had insisted to his designers that the Mac seem emotionally "friendly"—a novel concept in the world of technology. As a consequence, the Mac's desktop interface was so simple and intuitive to use—just point and click—that it assuaged latent popular anxiety about using computers and persuaded people to give the machine a try. This was Steve Jobs' talent as a persuader, recognizing the power of a simple analogy—a desktop—to transform people's relationship with computers, and even their notions of what a computer was.

In 1996, years after being ousted from Apple and before he returned to save the company, Jobs gave an interview to *Wired*, in which he was asked why more products aren't made with the aesthetics of great design. "*Design* is a funny word," Jobs said. "Some people think design means how it looks. But of course, if you dig deeper, it's really how it works. The design of the Mac wasn't what it looked like, although that was part of it. Primarily, it was how it worked. To design something really well, you have to get it. You have to really 'grok' what it's all about. It takes a passionate commitment to really thoroughly understand something, chew it up, not just quickly swallow it. Most people don't take the time to do that."

The slang word *grok*, coined by the science fiction writer Robert Heinlein, has two definitions: It means to understand thoroughly and intuitively, and to communicate sympathetically. Likewise, persuasive analogies also do both; they are easy to grasp, and they communicate their main idea in a way that is sympathetic to their audience, intellectually and emotionally. At best, such analogies are anything but superficial, but rather reflect an intuitive, deep understanding of two ideas and how an audience might reconceive the relationship between them.

With the Mac and with all the Apple products that followed after

Jobs' return from exile, Jobs continually exploited the falling price of computing power. Not necessarily to perform the actual task a user might seek to accomplish, but rather to make the execution of that task—the interface—profoundly and intuitively simple, whether that was for the iPod, the iPhone, or the iPad.

One of the reasons Jobs was so persuasive in selling his vision was that he was so fluent with analogy in all its forms—verbal, visual, tactile, and conceptual. His innovative products and business models triumphed not just on the basis of their enabling technology—little of which he himself invented—but rather on the basis of how he gave them simple human expression. From a document on a "desktop" to a physical "home" button on a smooth iPhone, to the way we "scroll" through names and songs or turn "pages" with our fingertips, Jobs remade the familiar anew, and made the new familiar.

And were Columcille, the Irish monk whose passion for beautiful books led to the world's first copyright battle, somehow shown an iPad, he could probably master it with the simplest of instructions. Why? Because the glowing pages he would turn with his fingertip, and the fonts and motifs and images he might encounter upon them, are not so different from those he furiously copied by a candle's glow in that empty scriptorium more than fourteen centuries ago. And thanks to the Web, he could even look at images of his own clandestine handiwork, now digitized for posterity.

CONNECT THE DOTS

In 2005, Steve Jobs was invited to deliver the commencement address at Stanford University. Graduation speeches are among the most difficult speeches to write well. This isn't just because many who attend such ceremonies are distracted and eager to get past the last speech and on with life, or at least on to another graduation party. It's also because graduation speeches are supposed to be full of wisdom. Unfortunately, those who seek to dispense wisdom in a twenty-minute graduation speech usually end up flailing about in a gooey tar pit of platitudes.

In a refreshing departure from this tradition, Jobs simply told stories from his life. One of them was how, as a freshman at Reed College, he dropped out of school but hung around campus attending classes that interested him. One of them was calligraphy. "I learned about serif and san serif typefaces, about varying the amount of space between different letter combinations, about what makes great typography great. It was beautiful, historical, artistically subtle in a way that science can't capture, and I found it fascinating," he said. One such font, designed in 1936, was named Columcille. But as Jobs noted, "None of this had even a hope of any practical application in my life."

Until it did. Ten years later, when Apple began designing the Mac, Jobs insisted that it incorporate multiple, proportionally spaced fonts. And as he remarked, "If I had never dropped out, I would have never dropped in on this calligraphy class, and personal computers might not have the wonderful typography that they do. Of course it was impossible to connect the dots looking forward when I was in college. But it was very, very clear looking backwards ten years later.

"Again, you can't connect the dots looking forward; you can only connect them looking backwards," Jobs reiterated. "So you have to trust that the dots will somehow connect in your future. You have to trust in something—your gut, destiny, life, karma, whatever. This approach has never let me down, and it has made all the difference in my life."

Notably, Jobs summed up the search for purpose and meaning in terms of an analogy drawn from a dot-to-dot coloring book, in which pictures only emerge through a sequential revelation of patterns that aren't necessarily obvious from the outset. In short, it's the coherence we seek to identify within a set of data or experiences that allows us to infer greater meaning. Pointillist paintings such as those of Georges Seurat, and later the pixelated Pop Art of Roy Lichtenstein, demand a similar ability to connect the dots, visually. Interpretation of Big Data operates in a similar way, through statistics and graphic visualization.

It is this instinct to identify coherent patterns and infer meaning from them that enables us to persuade through analogy. The most persuasive people link conceptual "dots" in such a way that their audience suddenly grasps new connections and perceives deeper meanings—meanings that resonate as true, whether or not they really are. Of course, in a complicated world that is rife with disagreement, there will always be many tools to persuade people—logic, data, threats, money, sex, shame, violence, peer pressure, and appeals to duty and idealism, among others. All have their advantages and disadvantages, but few are as elegant or versatile as a powerful analogy.

CHAPTER 5

....

SEEING THE BIG PICTURE

How We Can Choose Better Analogies

Apollo Robbins is a professional pickpocket. Widely considered the best in the world, he works, to the good fortune of his marks, as an entertainer, primarily in Las Vegas. While he steals for a living, he always returns what he takes. Once, chatting with former president Jimmy Carter's Secret Service detail, he lifted the thirty-ninth president's itinerary and the lead agent's badge, wristwatch, and keys to the motorcade. "They were on guard," he concedes. "I just had to adjust the way they were thinking."

Robbins, fascinated with magic tricks from a young age, honed his craft working at the now defunct Caesar's Magical Empire. Dressed as a wizard, he entertained guests by returning the rings, watches, wallets, and other items they didn't even realize he'd just stolen from them. And practice made perfect. Over five years, he picked more than 81,000 pockets.

Part of his skill depends on this highly developed physical technique. When he works a crowd, he will "accidentally" brush past people, touch them innocuously, and scan them for opportunity. "What I'm doing is taking inventory and making sight maps and getting a feel for who these people are and what I'm going to do with them," he told *The New Yorker*. "I'm a jazz performer—I have to improvise with what I'm given."

The other part of his skill is psychological. If Robbins asks someone if their American Express card is still in the wallet in their back pocket, their mind leaps to the wallet in the back pocket—momentarily freezing their attention and freeing him to steal from their jacket. "It's all about the choreography of people's attention," he said. "Attention is like water. It flows. It's liquid. You create channels to divert it, and you hope that it flows the right way."

Robbins is clearly as fluid with analogy as he is with picking pockets. He credits this to his father, who was a Baptist preacher and often taught through parable. In a service for children, his father might bring a turtle and talk about the hard shells people try to maintain and how they need to let God's love inside. Pickpocketing and misleading analogies are in a sense the same, as the misleading analogy picks a listener's mental pocket.

And this is true whether someone else diverts our attention through a resonant but misleading analogy—"Judges are like umpires"—or we simply choose the wrong analogy all by ourselves. Years after the Wright brothers had succeeded in building their flying machine, Orville admitted that he and Wilbur had initially looked to birds for clues to flight, but to no avail. "Although we intently watched birds fly in a hope of learning something from them, I cannot think of anything that was first learned in that way," Wright said. "Learning the secret of flight from a bird was a good deal like learning the secret of magic from a magician. After you once know the trick and know what to look for, you see things that you did not notice when you did not know exactly what to look for."

So, what should people look for when it comes to analogy? How can people make better use of analogy and avoid its significant perils?

The first, necessary step is to recognize when we are actually encountering an analogy, good or bad.

LEARN TO SPOT ANALOGIES IN DISGUISE

Analogies are like guests arriving at a big Halloween party—they come in many costumes, including ads, legal arguments, marketing taglines, mathematical formulas, business strategies, political slogans, biblical parables, logos, euphemisms, proverbs, art, insults, and sports clichés, among others. Once we start paying close attention, we discover that analogies are as common in everyday life as trains in a train station, always coming and going. Even the phrase "paying close attention" is a subtle analogy, as the verb *paying* establishes the parallel between attention and money; both come in limited quantities we can spend only once.

In a 2005 study published in the *Harvard Business Review*, Giovanni Gavetti, now an associate professor of business administration at Dartmouth's Tuck School of Business, and Jan Rivkin, now chair of the Strategy unit at Harvard Business School, wrote, "Leaders tend to be so immersed in the specifics of strategy that they rarely stop to think how much of their reasoning is done by analogy." As a result, they miss pitfalls as well as potentially useful insights. By contrast, "Managers who pay attention to their own analogical thinking will make better strategic decisions and fewer mistakes."

BREAK IT DOWN

It is always worth deconstructing an analogy to reveal its strengths and weaknesses. To illustrate, let's examine the common argument that managing America's federal budget deficit is like managing a household budget. According to this argument, no household can spend more than it takes in year after year, so neither should the federal government. It is a simple and appealing analogy—at least superficially.

The similarities are obvious: Generally, households and the federal government have both revenue and expenses. And just as households can borrow via credit cards, mortgages, bank loans, and payday loans, governments can borrow by issuing debt through bonds, treasury notes, and other financial instruments. In both cases, when expenses exceed income, households and governments have several choices: cut back on expenses, increase revenues, borrow money, or some blend of all three.

Because many of those who champion this government-as-household analogy also tend to be ideologically opposed to increasing government revenue, they focus almost exclusively on cutting government expenses. At first glance, the analogy tells a coherent story that resonates with many people.

But on closer examination, the government-as-household analogy obscures some fundamental, disqualifying differences. Start with the fact that, even as people create new households, others are dissolving. Every day of the year, as people divorce or die, household assets are broken up and redistributed. When that happens, those households cease to exist. Unlike a household, the United States of America will *never* divide up and distribute its remaining assets and cease to exist—at least not without dissolving itself as a nation. That's because the United States of America has needs and interests that are not merely long-term in nature, but perpetual. As such, our national interest does and should transcend generations, whether that's spending $15 million for the Louisiana Purchase, borrowing roughly $200 billion to fight and win World War II, investing nearly $130 billion to build the Interstate Highway System, or, on a more modest scale, funding research through the National Institutes of Health to save future generations from cancer and other deadly diseases.

And the long-term nature of national interests are the rule, not the exception. It takes a constant, rolling investment to maintain a strong defense, a robust infrastructure, good schools, and a just society in which all citizens enjoy both opportunity and equal protection under law. Such long-term investments sometimes require the government to borrow money. And the fact is, since the ratification of the US Constitution in 1789, the United States has been in debt every year but one. Just where would the United States be today if the federal government had treated its budget as a household budget? Conceivably, the country might have foundered long ago. Certainly, we would not be the superpower we are today.

This is not an argument for unconstrained, runaway debt. The United States faces an approaching crisis of long-term debt, much of it driven by rising health care costs, which the nation must address. Yet the need to manage this debt highlights two other fundamental differences that reveal the household-budget analogy to be faulty. First, the federal government has the legal authority both to print money and to issue long-term debt—instruments that are backed by the full faith and credit of the nation. Second, given that the federal government controls the money supply, it can manipulate inflation to drive down the value of the dollar and, in the process, make its debts cheaper and faster to pay off. Households enjoy none of these powers.

Despite these differences, the government-as-household analogy still resonates with people. The reason? It swaps out a complex question for a simpler one. Instead of asking people to explain how 535 members of Congress, all representing competing interests, should bring the federal budget into sustainable balance over the coming decades, it asks them: How would your family balance its household budget? However inaccurate, this swap draws on the familiar to explain the unfamiliar. It identifies a useful and appealing abstraction: balance. And however incomplete, the analogy is coherent within the frame it establishes. Finally, it taps into our common, natural desire to be not just solvent but to have money in our pocket. After all, who likes being in debt?

Once these emotions have been triggered—emotions that favor conclusions over arguments—it becomes hard to rebut such conclusions with logic alone. Like the pickpocket who distracts his mark, this clever swap distracts public attention from the analogy's disqualifying flaws, as well as all the other pressing challenges the nation faces.

DON'T BE LAZY

One reason people are so susceptible to misleading but resonant analogies is the human tendency to jump to conclusions. As Daniel Kahneman notes in *Thinking Fast and Slow*, our normal state of mind is to make snap judgments; we trust or distrust strangers without knowing why, and we just "know" that a business is going to succeed or fail without even analyzing it. "Whether you state them or not," Kahneman writes, "you often have answers to questions that you do not completely understand, relying on evidence that you can neither explain nor defend."

Kahneman suggests a reason for this leap to judgment: When we confront questions that are intrinsically hard, or about which we have insufficient evidence to make a reasoned decision, we often just answer an easier question and let that answer suffice. This substitute question is called a heuristic question, from the same Greek root as *eureka*, meaning "I have found it."

Evidence indicates that we are especially prone to swap in easier questions when strong emotions are involved. In such cases, the conclusion we reach is almost more important than the argument that took us there, as long as the conclusion resonates with our biases. Drew Westen, the author of *The Political Brain*, notes that the analogies we find compelling depend not necessarily on the degree of actual correspondence between source and target but also on our goals and the emotions that "fuel" our goals. That's in part because we favor coherence—especially emotional coherence—over accuracy, and will go to great lengths to ignore or deny contradictory facts. Sadly, such confirmation bias often makes factual evidence irrelevant and undermines productive discourse.

BEWARE OF HYPERBOLE

Adolf Hitler described Jews as "a virus" and, in 1942, said the "battle in which we are engaged today is of the same sort as the battle waged, during the last century, by Pasteur and Koch. How many diseases have their origin in the Jewish virus!"

What does one typically do with a virus? Try to eradicate it. Hitler's abhorrent analogy was embraced by millions of Germans, Poles, and others in German-occupied Europe because it resonated with and inflamed their deep anti-Semitism. By describing Jews as a virus, Hitler empowered his audience to project their own irrational fears, economic frustrations, anger, and prejudice onto easy scapegoats (which in addition to Jews included gays, gypsies, and communists). Sadly, many of those who had the courage to speak out against Hitler's Final Solution were herded into the Nazi gas chambers, too.

Hitler's analogy was extreme in its impact, though hardly unique. Throughout history, malevolent leaders have drummed up similar ethnic, racial, religious, and political hatred through similar "plague" analogies. And that's why, except in actual cases of genocide, making analogies to Hitler is a bad idea. Not only do such analogies trivialize the horror of the Holocaust and other genocides, they discredit the speaker. Not that this stops the frequent Obama-Hitler analogies from the gun lobby and antiabortion activists. In 2013, when Senator Ted Cruz demanded that Obamacare be defunded, he couldn't resist comparing the acceptance of the health care plan to the appeasement of Hitler in the lead-up to World War II.

"If we go to the 1940s, Nazi Germany—look, we saw it in Britain," Cruz said during a twenty-one-hour speech. "Neville Chamberlain told the British people: Accept the Nazis. Yes, they will dominate the continent of Europe, but that is not our problem. Let's appease them. Why? Because [stopping their advance] can't be done. We cannot possibly stand against them. . . . So we get to Obamacare, and what do all of those voices say? It cannot be stopped. It can't be done. We cannot defund it."

The next day, B'nai B'rith International joined a chorus of voices across the political spectrum that slammed Cruz for his analogy between Nazi Germany and Obamacare. "Nazi comparisons are never acceptable. No matter how one feels about this issue, or any issue, invoking Nazi imagery trivializes and undermines the atrocities perpetrated by the Nazi machine," the organization said in a statement, and called on Cruz to apologize. Later, on NBC's *Meet the Press*, Cruz flatly denied that he made the comparison.

But the Nazi analogy wasn't the Texas senator's only overreach. Approaching the end of his marathon speech, Cruz made yet another World War II analogy that drew intense criticism. He said he didn't want to miss the opportunity "to thank the men and women who have endured this, this Bataan Death March," referring to his own talk-a-thon. To survivors of the infamous 1942 march, during which some 10,000 captured Filipino and American soldiers died en route to a Japanese POW camp, Cruz's analogy was galling.

After a week of withering criticism from veterans, he apologized for the analogy. "I was trying to say they (staff) endured a long period of suffering not of their choosing, but I understand that that comment caused offense and I apologize. That was not my intention to do so," Cruz said.

Intended or not, offensive hyperbole is one of the most common pitfalls of analogy. And it's certainly not limited to one party or the other. In 2006, Democratic congressman Steny Hoyer told a crowd that Maryland lieutenant governor Michael Steele, who was running for the Senate, "slavishly" supported the Republican Party. Steele, an African American, accused Hoyer of racism. Hoyer apologized for his use of the word, saying no offense was intended. In all likelihood, neither Hoyer nor Cruz intended to offend. But their careless choice of analogies boomeranged.

DON'T GET FRAMED!

Apollo Robbins the pickpocket has described his work as a form of "impression management." One technique he sometimes uses is to lean into a mark's face, which focuses their attention and frames their field of view—a diversion that simultaneously frees his nimble fingers to do their work out of view, undetected. But while his physical skills are extraordinary, he considers his mental and verbal skills to be even more important. "It's more about knowing the mind-set of the person you're dealing with and how they're perceiving the situation," he said. "And the more someone *thinks* they know, the easier it is to work them."

This idea of framing, as noted earlier, is also relevant when it comes to avoiding being misled or manipulated by a false analogy. As the linguist and author George Lakoff writes, an opponent's language "picks out a frame—and it won't be the frame you want."

The subtle but enduring influence of Adam Smith's "invisible hand" analogy highlights the extraordinary power of selective framing. In his seminal 1776 treatise *The Wealth of Nations*, a foundational document for many conservatives, Smith wrote that every person "labours to render the annual revenue of the society as great as he can. He generally, indeed, neither intends to promote the public interest, nor knows how much he is promoting it. By preferring the support of domestic rather to that of foreign industry, he intends only his own security; and by directing that industry in such a manner as its produce may be of greatest value, he intends only his own gain; and he is in this, as in many other cases, *led by an invisible hand* to promote an end which was no part of his intention. Nor is it always the worse for society that it was no part of his intention. By pursuing his own interest he frequently promotes that of the society more effectually than when he really intends to promote it. I have never known much good done by those who affected to trade for the public good [emphasis by author]."

By attributing the individual and collective impact of human decisions in a marketplace to an abstract, disembodied hand, this analogy implicitly absolves people who run corporations of any significant moral responsibility for their actions, no matter what toll their actions might impose on people, communities, the nation, or the planet. In essence, the invisible-hand analogy obscures the direct responsibility that key leaders bear for decisions that, individually and collectively, are often very damaging to the larger public interest.

As a result, the analogy offers philosophical cover to those who would pick the public's pocket. As the 2008 economic crisis demonstrated, accountability is all but nonexistent. Which of the primary decision makers in the public and private sectors whose actions precipitated the crisis, even those whose actions were illegal, have paid any significant personal penalty for the damage they caused? Not many. After all, it's hard to handcuff an invisible hand.

Analogies such as the "invisible hand" and "government-as-household" are planted deeply in our cultural consciousness. As such, they can be difficult to uproot. But they also highlight why it is critical to become more proactive and creative about the analogies we accept, reject, or employ in our personal and professional pursuits, so that we don't get framed from the get-go. Because over the long term, playing defense within an unfavorable frame isn't a winning strategy.

REMEMBER THAT ANALOGIES ARE MODELS

Scott Page is the Leonid Hurwicz Collegiate Professor of Complex Systems, Political Science, and Economics at the University of Michigan. In addition to serving as director of the university's Center for the Study of Complex Systems, Page teaches one of the nation's most popular Massive Open Online Courses, titled "Model Thinking." In it, he explores how understanding and applying models can help people make better decisions.

"In order to be an intelligent citizen of the world, I think you have to understand models," Page says. That's because models, in their many forms, help enable people to structure and process the flood of information they encounter, and make more informed decisions as a result. From hedge fund algorithms to climate-change models to online calculators for retirement income, good models help translate complex concepts and diffuse data into discrete and potentially useful ideas.

The urge to model is nothing new. Albert Einstein once noted that poets, painters, philosophers, and theoretical physicists all pursue a similar human impulse: to express what they see in nature and create "a simple and synoptic image of the surrounding world. . . .

"Even at the expense of completeness, we have to secure purity, clarity and accurate correspondence between the representation and the thing represented," Einstein wrote. He added that in physics, as research and knowledge advance, the physicist "is astonished to notice how sublime order emerges from what appeared to be chaos. And this cannot be traced back to the workings of his own mind but is due to a quality that is inherent in the world of perception. Leibniz expressed this quality well by calling it a pre-established harmony."

This preestablished harmony is what we often attempt to reveal through models, identifying deeper patterns that might not at first be apparent among the noise of data and myriad irrelevancies. It is also what we attempt to reveal through the models we call analogies. Because models are analogies, and analogies are models; some are expressed as mathematical equations, some are visual in nature, such as maps and diagrams, and some take verbal form.

Scott Page characterizes the distinction between analogies and models as blurry. "Most people make most decisions by drawing simple sorts of analogies," he said. "Formal models allow you to look through the logic in gory detail, and adjudicate between them." Remembering that analogies are models is important because it encourages people to take a more dispassionate, rigorous approach to evaluating any given analogy's accuracy and relevance.

EXPLORE MULTIPLE ANALOGIES

"Analogies should enhance thinking, not substitute for it," write Keith Holyoak and Paul Thagard, who are noted authorities on analogy and creativity. Too often, they argue, people fixate on one analogy to such a degree that they neglect deeper thought about challenges, opportunities, or potential solutions. Accordingly, it is important to explore a wide range of models that could reasonably apply in a given circumstance, because they might yield many unexpected possibilities and even help reframe the challenge itself.

Often, there is no right or wrong analogy, at least not objectively, because different analogies provide different insights into the same challenge. One question that has long perplexed physicists is the following: Is light a wave or a particle, or both? In 1861 and 1862, James Clerk Maxwell, a Scottish physicist, derived a series of four mathematical equations that included a description of light as an electromagnetic wave. In 1905, Einstein, who at that time was an unknown patent clerk, published a paper describing the propagation of light in terms of particles. Both are insightful descriptions, depending on the scale at which one examines the problem—and both have practical applications. Alone, neither one can fully explain the observed behavior of light.

To envision the unity of these alternative descriptions, consider the stop-and-go flow of traffic through congested streets. Such traffic, while composed of individual cars, moves in waves. Prolonged red lights create more intense crests of congestion, and green lights allow the crests to move on. For urban planners and drivers seeking to avoid traffic jams, both analogies—cars as particles, traffic as waves—offer potentially useful insights.

The success or failure of a business or industry can also flow from the multiple analogies that inform their structure and operations. A good example is how people conceptualize large data centers. These sprawling facilities often house thousands of computers that companies use to store and manage data—everything from online sales to virtual meetings to the flow of inventory and overseas supply chains.

One of the biggest things that data centers sell customers is electricity—lots of it, with a guarantee that it will never fail. Since customers depend on such fail-safe power to keep their servers running at all times, providers often sell them twice what they need as part of their lease, whether or not they use the backup supply. This effectively marks up the regulated price of electricity by 100 percent. But since data centers aren't recognized as "utilities," most regulators don't notice that these companies are actually in the electricity business.

Other analogies could apply, too. In addition to selling electricity, data centers are landlords that lease out real estate. Some are even seeking Internal Revenue Service approval to become Real Estate Investment Trusts, which could save them hundreds of millions in corporate taxes. So, is a data center a service provider, a utility, or a landlord? In a sense, asking what a data center "is" or "is like" brings to mind the 1896 case of *Adams v. New Jersey Steamboat*, which we reviewed earlier. In that instance, courts had to decide if a steamboat was more like a hotel or a train, each of which had distinct public obligations and liabilities.

Then as now, those with the most persuasive analogies generally compete with considerable advantage. That's why looking at any challenge or opportunity through multiple analogies is always advisable, even if many are later discarded as invalid or unhelpful. In short, don't fall in love with your first model before dating some others.

ZOOM IN, ZOOM OUT

The search for and application of fresh analogies, whether quantitative or qualitative, has throughout history been a vital catalyst for innovation, persuasion, and progress. The thinkers who first championed a heliocentric universe, imagined a printing press, articulated a plausible theory of evolution, envisioned the moving assembly line, invented the airplane, convinced America to fight fascism and embrace civil rights, made computers accessible, and created the hyperlinked Web all recognized and exploited the power of analogy to reveal new possibilities.

The evolutionary biologist E. O. Wilson once described analogy as "the key instrument of the creative imagination." As he notes, the cost of information is falling even as access to it increases. The challenge is how to synthesize it in a useful way. "We are drowning in information, while starving for wisdom. The world henceforth will be run by synthesizers, people able to put together the right information at the right time, think critically about it, and make important choices wisely."

Effective synthesis flows from the connections and overlaps we recognize, and the way in which we interweave information from distinct sources to generate something new. Steve Jobs once told *Wired* magazine that "when you ask creative people how they did something, they feel a little guilty because they didn't really *do* it, they just *saw* something. It seemed obvious to them after a while. That's because they were able to connect experiences they've had and synthesize new things. And the reason they were able to do that was that they've had more experiences or they have thought more about their experiences than other people." People who lack the experience or ability to see these connections and conceptual overlaps, Jobs said, "end up with very linear solutions without a broad perspective on the problem."

Jobs liked to say that Apple, as a company, stood at the intersection of science and the humanities. He was paraphrasing Edwin Land, the cofounder of Polaroid, who once said, "Industry is best at the intersection of science and art." A generation before Jobs invented a "bicycle for the mind" that empowered millions of people to exercise their creativity, Land had helped democratize photography by putting the instant Polaroid camera into the hands of countless amateur photographers. At the same time, Land and his company also worked to support and facilitate the work of acclaimed visual artists such as Ansel Adams, the photographer, and Chuck Close, the painter.

Both Adams and Close have been recognized for the genius of their work. But as different as their work is, it captures their subjects—often the face of a mountain or the face of a man, respectively—with a deliberate and focused realism. With Close's images, that realism depends on the distance from which one views his images. Approach closely, and the realism that only moments earlier verged on photographic breaks apart into distinct units of color, organized within a deliberate grid yet nonetheless abstract. Step away, and the big picture comes into focus again. Much like an Impressionist, Close relies on the viewer to connect the dots—pixelated color—that comprise broader patterns.

Close's fascination with such effects apparently dates to his boyhood in Tacoma, Washington. After school, he would use his grandmother's magnifying glass to examine the illustrations in the magazines that came to her house, such as *Collier's* and *The Saturday Evening Post*, zooming in and out to see how Norman Rockwell and others achieved their effects.

More than half a century later, viewers interact with Close's paintings in much the same way, managing the "zoom" with their feet. At once monumental in scale and unrelenting in detail, they challenge us to look at what we see more abstractly, to consider things in a new way, to break apart our preconceptions and put them back together again.

Each of the views we encounter are "true" in their own way but do not offer us the only truth or the whole truth. What we perceive depends on how narrowly or broadly we focus our attention. In a sense, this is also a central challenge of analogy—managing our relationship with disparate ideas at just the right distance or level of abstraction.

Maxwell, the nineteenth-century physicist, once observed that a pun reveals two truths within one expression, while an analogy reveals one truth within two expressions. To search for better analogies is to search for truth, however elusive or subjective that truth may be. Sometimes, that search requires us to step back. At other times, it means getting close. Always, it requires a leap. Because analogies, like puns, are intellectual hyperlinks that establish or reveal relationships between disparate ideas.

IMAGINATION IS MORE IMPORTANT THAN KNOWLEDGE

Sometimes, the more we know about a situation or relationship, the less able we are to consider it from a fresh perspective. That's why conventional wisdom, what people "know," can blind them to deeper truths and other possibilities. Einstein once said, "I am enough of the artist to draw freely on my imagination. Imagination is more important than knowledge. Knowledge is limited. Imagination encircles the world." This is not to argue that knowledge is a liability. Quite the opposite is true. The more diverse and rich sources of knowledge from which we can draw ideas and inspiration, the better. But how we categorize that knowledge—and how well we resist categorization—determines how freely our imagination can retrieve and apply that knowledge. "Growth comes through analogy," said Einstein, ". . . seeing how things connect, rather than only seeing how they might be different."

It is in this way that the best analogies are all transformative: They help us see novel connections and relationships—insights that can unlock unrealized potential. That potential can take many forms. Sometimes, it is the potential advantage or efficiency made possible through a new invention, process, or tactic. Sometimes, it is the potential for progress that becomes possible when people suddenly are struck with new insight and are motivated to take action.

Bill Klann, Ford's journeyman mechanic, made the mental leap from the disassembly of animals to the assembly of cars, overturning what every automaker (and every other manufacturer) "knew" about efficient mass production.

R. V. Jones, the British scientific intelligence officer, struggled unsuccessfully to make Allied bombers invisible to Nazi air defenses, before he thought of hiding sand on a beach. As noted earlier, a few intrepid pilots then created a virtual "beach" by dumping thousands of metallic strips into the night sky. The fluttering descent of these strips so overwhelmed the enemy's radar that it caused the Germans to launch interceptors toward what they believed to be waves of attacking bombers, even as the Allies' real bombers attacked elsewhere, relatively unchallenged.

In an entirely different arena, Martin Luther King Jr. used analogy to persuade enough Americans that the ancient Israelites' struggle for freedom was America's struggle, too. Overturning conventional wisdom, his analogy—and the tactics of nonviolent civil disobedience—helped rally thousands of citizens to show that true power did not flow from fire hoses, beatings, and police dogs. Rather, power flowed from the moral outrage that such tactics aroused in millions of Americans.

Again, all of these innovators used creative analogies to exploit potential that others didn't see, and to achieve goals that more conventional thinkers "knew" could not be realized.

PLANT NEW SEEDS OF POSSIBILITY

In 2005, the College Board, which administers the SAT, dropped its long-standing section on analogies and replaced it with an essay section designed to test students' analytical and writing skills. While millions of students might have been relieved, the change was also met with sharp criticism. "Intentionally misleading comparisons are becoming the dominant mode of public discourse," wrote Adam Cohen in *The New York Times*. "The ability to tell true analogies from false ones has never been more important." While every American should be able to write well, he argued, "we would be better off with a nation of analogists."

One might debate the either-or nature of that statement or the value of fill-in-the-blank analogy questions. But Cohen is justified in criticizing America's failure to equip students with the critical thinking skills necessary to evaluate everyday analogies. Unfortunately, in a society obsessed with boosting performance on standardized tests, American schools are training too many students to answer standard questions rather than question standard answers. Yet it's only when enough people question such conventional wisdom that humans, organizations, and nations evolve and progress. Making analogies is instinctual, but systematically evaluating them takes discipline and practice.

In 1929, Einstein told *The Saturday Evening Post*, "I believe in standardizing automobiles. I do not believe in standardizing human beings. Standardization is a great peril which threatens American culture."

As Einstein noted about the auto industry, standardization in technology, processes, and networks yields many great benefits. In his day, the moving assembly line, born in Ford's Highland Park auto plant, quickly became the standard in virtually every industry. This enabled a dramatic leap in efficiency and prosperity that fueled the rise of the American middle class. More recently, in the 1990s, it was a new, common standard of communication between computers that enabled the Web to flourish and spread around the globe, with all its extraordinary benefits.

But there is an intrinsic and enduring tension between standardization and individual creativity. Because eventually, with too much standardization of thought, conventional wisdom tends to become merely conventional. Einstein once suggested that conventional wisdom is the source of many problems, and is ill suited to resolving them. Only when people can free themselves from the shackles of such thinking do we achieve breakthroughs. And if history is any guide, the way creative thinkers and leaders see beyond conventional wisdom is usually through the conception, recognition, or articulation of a better analogy.

In *The Gardens of Democracy*, Eric Liu and Nick Hanauer write that "the failure of American politics to address and solve the great challenges of our time—climate change, debt and deficits, worsening schools, rising health care costs, the shriveling of the middle class—is not just a failure of will or nerve. It is equally a failure of ideas and understanding. And the failure to address these challenges isn't just a matter of politics, but of survival."

A big part of this failure, they argue, is because our thinking is constrained by an outmoded analogy that grew out of the Enlightenment and gathered steam in the Industrial Revolution. That is, that the world and democracy "are a series of mechanisms—clocks and gears, perpetual motion machines, balances and counterbalances." From this perspective, the economy is largely an efficient and self-correcting mechanism; even the word *regulation* is mechanical in its origin and suggests that the natural motive force of the machine is being held back.

Many engines, for example, incorporate what is called a governor—a mechanism that limits their speed to avoid danger. But what constitutes danger? It's often in the eye of the beholder, and the Web is full of self-help articles and videos showing how to disable such governors. In a broader arena, many on the political right crusade against virtually any form of government regulation because it unduly restrains the economic "engine" that, in a "free" market, could run much faster, too.

Unfortunately, within this overarching industrial analogy, people tend to become interchangeable economic and political cogs, which Liu and Hanauer summarize as "votes to be collected by political machines; consumers to be manipulated by marketing machines; employees to be plugged into industrial machines." The costs imposed by such a faulty analogy are becoming heavier and heavier. As billions of supposedly rational actors around the world pursue what they perceive to be their own self-interest, the global commons—the lands, oceans, and atmosphere—are being fast degraded, to the detriment of us all.

"Conventional wisdom," Liu and Hanauer write, "conflates self-interest with selfishness." But in a world of finite resources, a purely industrial approach to extraction and production—and the strip-mining of public confidence in democratic institutions—is a zero-sum game that privatizes gains and socializes costs.

In reality, though, we don't live in a machine. A better analogy, they argue, might be that of a garden. A garden is a dynamic and inter-twined set of ecosystems. Properly cared for, a garden will flourish. Neglected or overworked, it will never yield the harvest we seek or need. Broadly speaking, this garden is not comprised of natural systems and resources alone, but of social structures, economic systems, and political networks, too. A garden without gardeners quickly be-comes overtaken by weeds.

"To be a gardener is not to let nature take its course; it is to *tend*. It is to accept responsibility for nurturing the good growth and killing the bad," Liu and Hanauer write. "*Tending* and *regulating* thus signify the same work, but tending frames the work as presumptively neces-sary and beneficial rather than as something to be suffered." And since analogies must resonate emotionally if they are to be effective, this framing—tending versus regulating—is important to consider.

WE REAP WHAT WE SOW

We live in a complex world, and the more complex something is, the more analogies could reasonably apply and surprise us with useful in-sights. A garden is certainly not the only analogy with which one might replace the rattling industrial machinery of centuries past. But as we increase our understanding of the world's natural systems and our impact on them—and their impact on us—the garden analogy offers more explanatory power. Whatever the relative merits of competing analogies might be, however, it's important that we explore them thoroughly.

For better and worse, analogies offer us conceptual and emotional shortcuts. And while a good shortcut is a great thing, a bad one can lead us astray. That's why being complacent or intellectually lazy about the analogies we choose or accept inevitably exacts a toll. At best, the result of such complacency is mediocrity; at worst, disaster.

By contrast, when we think more rigorously about the analogies we encounter or employ, we become more able to challenge conventional wisdom and more creative in our problem solving. This in turn equips us to discover new, unexpected possibilities that just might be hiding in plain sight. Ultimately, people who become truly adept at analogy are better able to avoid costly missteps, free their imaginations, and persuade others more effectively.

In sum, the art of analogy is the art of cultivating and communicating ideas—revealing fresh connections and relationships between things that are not only useful and make intuitive sense, but also bear up under honest scrutiny. Because while all analogies obscure complexity and some reveal simplicity, only the very best approach truth.

The perfect analogy makes things as simple as possible, but no simpler.

ACKNOWLEDGMENTS

Like a building that bears the name of one architect, a book usually bears the name of one author. But neither would be possible without the expertise and hard work of many others. First among those who helped transform *Shortcut* from idea into reality is my friend and agent, Gillian MacKenzie. She is both smart and kind, and a lot of fun to work with. I am also grateful to the talented team at Gotham Books, including Megan Newman, Brian Tart, Gabrielle Campo, Monica Benalcazar, Stephen Brayda, Lisa Johnson, Andrea Santoro, and Beth Parker. Without their vision and commitment, and that of former Gotham publisher Bill Shinker, this book would not be in your hands today.

I also owe a debt of gratitude to the New York Public Library and especially to librarian Jay Barksdale, who once again granted me access to the Wertheim Study, overlooking Forty-Second Street. The library's grandeur always inspires me to read more, think harder, and write better, and its quietude helps me get that work done.

Given its scope, this book necessarily integrates the scholarship and insights of many others. As such, I am grateful to the many academics, scientists, and other experts from whose ideas I have drawn.

Most of their names appear alphabetically in the bibliography, but some were personally generous with their time and expertise. These include Douglas Hofstadter and Robert Goldstone at Indiana University, George Lakoff at UC Berkeley, Dedre Gentner at Northwestern University, Keith Holyoak at UCLA, Kenneth Kurtz at SUNY Binghamton, Daniela Schiller at Mt. Sinai Hospital, Scott Page at the University of Michigan, Mark Weiner and George Thomas at Rutgers University School of Law, Brandt Goldstein and Art Leonard at New York Law School, Rodger Citron at Touro Law School, Nancy Packer at Stanford University, former White House Communications Director Loretta Ucelli, former White House Press Secretary Jake Siewert, former Deputy Assistant to the President Adam Rosman, and the incomparable sleight-of-hand artist Apollo Robbins. I am very grateful to them all for sharing their knowledge as I worked to distill a complex topic into an accessible book.

I also thank Christian Overland, Nardina Mein, and Linda Skolarus at the Henry Ford in Dearborn, Michigan, for their invaluable assistance with my research into the origins of the moving assembly line. The Henry Ford's collection of oral histories about the Ford Motor Company's early years offered a revealing look behind the curtains of established history and reminded me once again how important and rewarding it is to track down original source documents.

In New York, my friend Merry Conway's personal library once more yielded its riches. Her shelves are full of obscure but fascinating books that always remind me how many smart, creative people do exceptional work in relative anonymity. I far exceeded any reasonable due date on the books I borrowed, and appreciate her patience and generosity.

Several colleagues from my time at the White House, on Capitol Hill, and at several Democratic National Conventions were generous in sharing their insights into analogy's use in politics, economics, law, and communication. Those not mentioned earlier in these acknowledgments include Terry Edmonds, Sam Afridi, Jeff Nussbaum, Sarada

Peri, Jonas Keiffer, Paul Orzulak, Josh Lahey, Michael Schlein, Alexandra Veitch, Adam Frankel, Eric Lesser, Allegra Bennett, Ryan Jacobs, Andy Barr, David Litt, Mike Flynn, Stephen Krupin, June Shih, Jeff Shesol, Zev Karlin-Neumann, Kelly Johnson, and Gil Duran.

Also due for special thanks are my friends and colleagues at ROI Communication, especially those who shared their thoughts on analogy in corporate communication, including Barbara Fagan-Smith, Tina Beth Rosenblum, Christy Lang, Michele Glover, Lori Fraser, Sheryl Lewis, Mike Lynberg, Tina Cox, and Sheri Austin. Former ROI colleagues John Robertson and Sarah Jensen Clayton were also insightful and enthusiastic.

There is also a smart crew of morning regulars at Jack's Coffee on Tenth Street in New York City who helped me throughout this project. Whether I was sharing my latest research, sounding out ideas, or exploring possible titles, they always offered useful feedback. These include Larry Shaps, Jack Mazzola, Tom Ruff, Gilbert Giron, Alan Grossman, Marcy Heisler, Ted Heller, Perry van der Meer, Ken Berlin, Sarah LaFleur, Tim Stock, Marie Tupot, Dina Weisberger, Susie Lopez, Tiffany Wagner, Laura Ianuli, Sarah Irvin, Hilary Sobel, John Nathan, David Barber, Enrique Enriquez, Doug King, Richard King, and Isabell Coffey. Sadly, longtime regulars Lorraine Wilbur and Joe Colombo are no longer with us, but they were always supportive of my writing, and I am grateful to have enjoyed their friendship. Meanwhile, my ebullient friend David Trotta and Jack's team of friendly baristas also played an essential, daily role in this book—greeting me with good cheer every morning and fueling me with the espresso that got my days off to a strong start.

Later on during my workdays, Eric Schade, Alfie Rustom, Andrew Sispoidis, and Morgan Avery Sispoidis—regulars at Café Minerva—served as valuable sounding boards. On many afternoons, Tom Ruff would stop by with his dog, Tank, whose exuberance and wagging tail always offered me a brief but welcome respite from the keyboard. Meanwhile, Roz Golchehreh, Blair Steckler, Ian Olson, Bill

Philbin, Patricia Cappelletti, and Minerva's kitchen crew generously allowed me to type away at their bar for hours on end. Occasionally, I worked at Bee's Knees, Think Coffee, and the Marlton Hotel, and am grateful for their hospitality, too.

The staff at my favorite independent bookstore, Three Lives and Company, also helped me a great deal in tracking down books and evaluating titles and cover designs. This team included proprietor Toby Cox as well as Carol Wald, Joyce McNamara, Troy Chatterton, Amanda Lydon, Dave Burnham, Miriam Chotiner-Gardner, Ryan Murphy, and Natalia Fadul. Every writer should be so lucky to have such an excellent bookstore so close to home.

As my manuscript neared completion, several people were very generous in reading rough drafts and marking them up. These readers, some of whom I've previously thanked for other contributions to the project, included Elisha Cooper, Charlie Chambers, Mark Weiner, Bill Bisanz, Heidi Kraus Politis, Ken Baer, Barbara Kancelbaum, Rodger Citron, and Brandt Goldstein—good friends who all happen to be exceptionally smart, too. Throughout the project, Elisha and Brandt were especially insightful in helping me hone my arguments and brainstorm about the title and cover design.

Others who helped me in various capacities include Joe Corn, Tim Stanley, Stacy Stern, Maurice Schoenberger, Devon Spurgeon, Debbie Bosanek, Peter Schweitzer, Noah Dorsky, Jordan Spielman, Amanda Spielman, Tamar Schoenberg, Sally Pollack, Kathy Pollack, Lawrence Pollack, Judy Pazol, Larry Pazol, Stephen Gaffney, Tom Pazol, Brad Blumenfeld, Andrew Scott, Patrick McDonough, Al Cain, Ken Weine, Drew Isaacs, Erin Martin, Frank Schaefer, Sarah Chambers, Bob Bozic, Ann Marsh, Fred Firestone, Jo Firestone, Harper Alexander, Fergus McCormick, Bill Lyon, Stephanie Weiner, Garth Goldstein, Bob Bozic, Pete Peterson, and Warren Buffett.

Nancy Packer, who was my best English professor at Stanford, once told me that writing is like anything else—if you practice, you'll get better. Over the years, several people gave me important opportunities to do that, including Susan Linnee at the Associated Press, Congressman David Bonior on Capitol Hill, and President Bill Clinton at the White House. As President Clinton once noted, "If you see a turtle on a fence post, you know it didn't get there on its own." I am grateful to them all for helping me grow as a writer and advance my career.

Twenty years ago, when I was a young foreign correspondent in Madrid, I found a generous mentor in Bill Montalbano, of the *Los Angeles Times*. He was a supremely talented writer and editor, and more than once saved my stories with just the right analogy. His gift for wringing the most from language and life still inspires me.

I also thank Allie Dorsky, whose love and encouragement sustained me from day to day through many long months of research and writing, and whose edits were excellent, too. Whether I had a good day writing or a bad one, she was consistently enthusiastic. "I'm not worried," she always said. "It's going to be great!"

Finally, I am immeasurably grateful to my parents, Henry and Lana Pollack. Growing up, they always encouraged my sister, Sara, and me to let our imaginations roam, to think of the good, and to see the world as full of opportunity. Even more important, they set fine examples with the ambition and spirit of their own endeavors. Coincidentally, they both happen to be talented speakers and deeply engaged in science and public affairs, and so were unusually qualified to critique this manuscript. My dad, especially, spent many hours marking it up with his red pen, pushing me to tighten my arguments. It was great fun working with both of them, and the book is much stronger for their edits. Most of all, though, I appreciate their love and enduring faith in me. I couldn't be a luckier son.

NOTES

This book is a work of nonfiction, the contents of which include original scholarship, author interviews, and material from more than 325 books, articles, studies, websites, ads, videos, illustrations, artworks, and other sources. To avoid distracting readers, I omitted footnotes from the text itself. However, the following notes, cited by chapter and sentence, identify the primary sources from which I drew key ideas, quotes, and other information appearing in this book.

CHAPTER 1: APPLES TO ORANGES

2   **As Leonard Mlodinow notes in *Subliminal*:** Leonard Mlodinow, *Subliminal: How Your Unconscious Mind Rules Your Behavior* (New York: Vintage Books, 2012), 34.

2   **This is because our senses send our brains roughly eleven million bits of information per second:** Ibid., 33.

2   **"So if your conscious mind were left to process all that incoming information":** Ibid.

3   **But while many other animals are adept at such comparison,**

evidence suggests: James Blevins and Juliette Blevins, eds., *Analogy in Grammar: Form and Acquisition* (New York: Oxford University Press, 2009), 1.

3 **As researchers have explored the function of analogy in human thought:** Douglas Hofstadter and Emmanuel Sander, *Surfaces and Essences: Analogy as the Fuel and Fire of Thinking* (New York: Basic Books, 2013), dust jacket.

3–4 **They argue that whether we're ordering food in a new restaurant:** Ibid., 23.

4 **"If one never trusted a single analogy, how could one understand anything":** Ibid.

4–5 **"And of course all situations *are* in fact new":** Ibid.

6 **In 1843, John Stuart Mill wrote that there is no word:** John Stuart Mill, *A System of Logic, Ratiocinative and Inductive: Being a Connected View of the Principles of Evidence and the Methods of Scientific Investigation*, 8th ed. (New York: Harper & Brothers, 1882), 227.

6 **The *Oxford English Dictionary* suggests he may be correct:** *Oxford English Dictionary*, 2nd ed. (Oxford: Clarendon Press, 1989), 432.

8 **As Princeton economist and historian Tim Leonard argues:** Tim Leonard, "How Metaphors Shape Our View of the Economy," *Marketplace*, August 6, 2012.

9 **By the age of four, most can understand abstract analogies:** Blevins and Blevins, *Analogy in Grammar*, 1.

9 **Starting as infants with our own mother:** Hofstadter and Sander, *Surfaces and Essences*, 35.

9 **And much of this ability correlates with a gradual, evolutionary increase:** Heather Pringle, "The Origins of Creativity," *Scientific American*, March 2013, 42.

9 **As this and other areas grew, there was more room:** Ibid.

10 **Given that the number of notches matches the number of phases of the moon:** David Darling, *The Universal Book of Mathematics: From Abracadabra to Zeno's Paradoxes* (Hoboken, NJ: John Wiley, 2004), 313.

10 **Bushmen use similar tally sticks as calendars:** Ibid., 182.

11 **In retrospect, their navigational achievements are especially impressive:** David Lewis, *We, the Navigators: The Ancient Art of Landfinding in the Pacific*, 2nd ed. (Honolulu: University of Hawaii Press, 1994), 16.

14 **"Simply identifying and arranging symbols in some language":** Benjamin K. Bergen, *Louder Than Words: The New Science of How the Mind Makes Meaning* (New York: Basic Books, 2012), 10.

14 **According to Bergen, one of the core aspects of human cognition is:** Ibid., 46.

14   **Others might envision a pig wearing a caped superhero outfit:** Ibid., 20.

15   **Bergen marshals significant new laboratory and neurological evidence to support the embodied simulation hypothesis:** Ibid., 13.

15   **Now, depending on your personal experience, some of these words may evoke:** Ibid., 15.

15   **Similarly, if you are told to think about the actual motions you make in opening your front door:** Ibid., 14.

16   **Building on the seminal work of linguist George Lakoff and philosopher Mark Johnson:** Ibid., 208–211.

17   **As Bergen sums it up, "Evolution has cobbled together a new machine":** Ibid., 253.

17   **Years later, Bruce Reynolds, the mastermind of what quickly became known as:** Bruce Weber, "Bruce Reynolds, Audacious Engineer of Great Train Robbery, Is Dead at 81," *New York Times*, March 1, 2013.

18   **In this case, based on our knowledge of the creativity, planning, and extraordinary skill:** Ibid.

19   **System 2 works more slowly, logically, and deliberately:** Daniel Kahneman, *Thinking, Fast and Slow* (New York: Farrar, Straus and Giroux, 2011), dust jacket.

20   **When we avoid hard thinking, we save mental energy:** Ibid., 43.

21   **The car, whose initial clay model reportedly drew a standing ovation:** Stephen Miller, "Edsel's Designer Took Flop in Stride," *Wall Street Journal*, March 4, 2013.

21   **Thanks to a masterful public relations campaign:** Peter Carlson, "The Flop Heard Round the World," *Washington Post*, September 4, 2007.

21–22 **Quickly, people began lampooning its front grille:** William Yardley, "Roy Brown Jr., Edsel Designer, Dies at 96," *New York Times*, March 6, 2013, B17.

23   **"When they did interviews and asked about Edsel":** Carlson, "Flop Heard Round the World."

23   **Edsel had never been a popular name in the United States:** www.behindthename.com/top/name/edsel.

23   **In a curious twist, some etymologists trace:** *Etymology Dictionary* online; www.etymonline.com/index.php?allowed_in_frame=0&search=pretzel.

24   **Soon, dealers were shipping the animals back:** Carlson, "Flop Heard Round the World."

25   **Nevertheless, he lamented:** Grant Segall, "Mr. Edsel," *Sun Sentinel*, March 12, 1985.

CHAPTER 2: THREE STRIKES AND YOU'RE OUT

28 **"Everything that every player does is accounted for":** Michael Mandelbaum, *The Meaning of Sports: Why Americans Watch Baseball, Football, and Basketball and What They See When They Do* (New York: Public Affairs, 2004), 56–57.

28 **Soon, people were being sentenced to life in prison:** Brent Staples, "California Horror Stories and the 3-Strikes Law," *New York Times*, November 24, 2012.

29 **The cost to taxpayers? As much as $75 billion:** Brian Mann, "The Drug Laws That Changed How We Punish," National Public Radio, February 14, 2013. www.npr.org/2013/02/14/171822608/the-drug-laws-that-changed-how-we-punish.

29 **Where do you hide a grain of sand? You put it on a beach:** R. V. Jones, *Reflections on Intelligence* (London: William Heinemann, 1989), 130.

30 **Debate raged among Britain's military leaders:** R. V. Jones, *Most Secret War: British Scientific Intelligence 1939–1945* (London: Penguin Books, 2009), 293.

30 **At a critical meeting to decide the matter, Prime Minister Winston Churchill listened:** Ibid., 297.

30 **Conversely, the Germans suffered horrific casualties:** Ibid., 302.

31 **According to the janitor, the frustrated German station commander:** Ibid., 305.

31 **The goal, he said, was to prevent Indochina and Southeast Asia from toppling:** Patrick O'Sullivan, "Dominoes or Dice: Geography and the Diffusion of Political Violence," *Journal of Conflict Studies* 16, no. 2 (1996).

32 **A few weeks after Eisenhower's seemingly offhanded explanation:** Frank Ninkovich, *Modernity and Power: A History of the Domino Theory in the Twentieth Century* (Chicago: University of Chicago Press, 1994), 223.

32 **Under successive presidents, the analogy's hold on the American imagination continued:** Stephen Daggett, Congressional Research Service Report for Congress (RS22926), July 24, 2008.

32 **And even as Vietnam's government remains nominally communist:** Abigail Haworth, "From War Babies to Billionaires: Vietnam's Wealthiest Women," *Observer*, March 23, 2013. www.guardian.co.uk/world/2013/mar/24/war-babies-billionaires-vietnam-women.

33 **By 1983, it was selling nearly three times the number of personal computers as Apple:** Walter Isaacson, *Steve Jobs* (New York: Simon & Schuster, 2011), 160.

33 **Driven by a determination to build something that he said would "make a dent in the universe":** Ibid., 92.

34 **"People know how to deal with a desktop intuitively":** Ibid., 127.

34 **According to one of the Xerox PARC engineers who first demonstrated:** Malcolm Gladwell, "Creation Myth," *New Yorker*, May 16, 2011, 44.

34 **It also retailed for a whopping $16,595:** Isaacson, *Steve Jobs*, 99.

35 **"You're ripping us off!" Jobs yelled:** Ibid., 178.

35 **The skinny, bespectacled Gates seemed unfazed by the tirade:** Ibid.

37 **As a consequence, the premise structures not just the way we talk about arguments:** George Lakoff and Mark Johnson, *Metaphors We Live By* (Chicago: University of Chicago Press, 1980), 5.

37 **"Your claims are *indefensible*":** Ibid., 4.

38 **Since those actions tend to reinforce the metaphor that inspired them:** Ibid., 156.

39 **According to the FBI, she merited inclusion on the list:** Christopher Maag, "New Push to Capture Woman in '73 Killing of State Trooper," *New York Times*, May 2, 2013.

40 **"As a direct result, it leads us to exaggerate the importance of places like Afghanistan":** Andrew J. Bacevich, Testimony before the Senate Foreign Relations Committee, Washington, DC, April 23, 2009. www.foreign.senate.gov/imo/media/doc/BacevichTestimony090423a1 .pdf.

41 **"For political reasons, the Obama administration may have banished the phrase":** Bacevich, Testimony.

41 **But he also noted that "America is at a crossroads":** Barack Obama, Speech on national security at the National Defense University in Washington, DC, May 23 2013. www.whitehouse.gov/the-press-office/2013/05 /23/remarks-president-national-defense-university.

42 **"Looking beyond Afghanistan," he added:** Ibid.

42 **"The president's speech today will be viewed by terrorists as a victory":** Saxby Chambliss, Republican senator from Georgia, Interview with CNN, May 23, 2013. www.cnn.com/2013/05/23/politics/obama -terror-speech

42 **In his insightful book *Words That Work: It's Not What You Say, It's What People Hear*, the political strategist Frank Luntz:** Frank Luntz, *Words That Work: It's Not What You Say, It's What People Hear* (New York: Hyperion Books, 2007), 41.

42 **As Michael Mandelbaum notes in *The Meaning of Sports*, "War involves the organized, deliberate use of force":** Mandelbaum, *Meaning of Sports*, 128.

44 **In a commercial society, all this talk of war tends to alienate female audiences:** Luntz, *Words That Work*, 41.

44 **"There's altogether too much allusion to 'battles' and 'charging'":** Ibid., 42.

44 **"Cola wars, beer wars, and burger wars are entertainment":** Ibid., 43.

44 **According to a 2009 report in *The Washington Post*:** Les Carpenter, "NFL Orders Retreat from War Metaphors," *Washington Post*, February 1, 2009. http://articles.washingtonpost.com/2009-02-01/sports/36917465_1_steve-sabol-nfl-films-wars.

45 **According to *Advertising Age*, 55 percent of American women report:** Kim Bates, "Super Bowl Confessionals: Women Want Humor and Sex Appeal in Ads," *Advertising* Age, January 29, 2013. http://adage.com/article/special-report-super-bowl/super-bowl-ad-confessionals-women/239465/.

49 **"Every word, like *elephant*, evokes a frame":** George Lakoff, *Don't Think of an Elephant: Know Your Values and Frame the Debate* (White River Junction, VT: Chelsea Green Publishing, 2004), 3.

49 **In the speech, Bush proclaimed that "America will never seek a permission slip":** George W. Bush, State of the Union Address, 2004. www.washingtonpost.com/wp-srv/politics/transcripts/bushtext_012004.html.

49 **Through structure mapping, we correlate the role of the United States to that of a young student:** Lakoff, *Don't Think of an Elephant*, 4.

52 **According to Kahneman, "Jumping to conclusions is efficient if":** Kahneman, *Thinking*, 79.

52 **And once we're in midair, flying through assumptions:** Ibid., 80.

52 **When we encounter a statement and seek to understand it, we evaluate it by first assuming it is true:** Ibid., 81.

52 **Studies suggest that most people seek out only information that confirms the beliefs they currently hold:** Ibid.

53 **He notes that we make judgments constrained by two influences that often compete with each other:** Drew Westen, *The Political Brain: The Role of Emotion in Deciding the Fate of the Nation* (New York: Public Affairs, 2007), 99.

53 **As Westen writes, "Our brains have a remarkable capacity to find their way":** Ibid., 100.

53 **In other words, we jump to conclusions, recruit arguments to support them, and then:** Kahneman, *Thinking*, 45.

53 **Ultimately, it is the consistency of the story, not its completeness, that helps:** Ibid., 87.

54 "The right of the people to be secure in their persons": United States Constitution, Amendment IV. www.archives.gov/exhibits/charters /bill_of_rights_transcript.html.

55 After countervailing reversals in two state courts put Maryland's DNA collection statute in limbo: Transcript of Oral Argument, p. 35, *Maryland v. King*, 133 S. Ct. 1958 (2013) (No. 12-207).

55 As Sir Edward Coke, a prominent jurist of the seventeenth century, argued: Samuel Arthur Bent, compiler, *Familiar Short Sayings of Great Men, with Historical and Explanatory Notes*, 6th ed. (Boston: Ticknor, 1887; Bartleby.com, 2012). www.bartleby.com/br/344.html.

56 Most arrestees, he added, are "repeat customers in the criminal justice system": Transcript of Oral Argument, pp. 14–15, *Maryland v. King*, 133 S. Ct. 1958 (2013) (No. 12-207).

56 Chief Justice John Roberts interrupted. "Yes, but that doesn't mean": Ibid., 15.

56 Under sharp questioning, Dreeben insisted that the two were in fact analogous: Ibid., 16.

56 Justice Elena Kagan interjected: "If this were like fingerprints, I think that": Ibid., 16–17.

56 Later, Justice Alito weighed in: "But why isn't this the fingerprinting of the twenty-first century? What is the difference?": Ibid., 35.

56 King's attorney, Kannon K. Shanmugam, said they were different on three counts: Ibid., 36–40.

57 "Maryland searched my client without a warrant, in order to investigate": Ibid., 29.

57 In a 5–4 decision that found conservative and liberal justices on both sides, the majority found that: *Maryland v. King*, 133 S. Ct. 1958 (2013).

57 The majority went on to note that "the most direct historical analogue": Ibid.

57 "Finger printing seems to be no more than an extension": Ibid.

58 Writing for the majority in *Maryland v. King*, Justice Anthony Kennedy concluded that: Ibid.

58 Justice Antonin Scalia, joined in dissent by Justices Ruth Bader Ginsburg, Sonia Sotomayor, and Kagan, excoriated: Ibid.

58 "Today's judgment will, to be sure, have the beneficial effect of solving more crimes": Ibid.

59 As Scalia wrote, "King was not identified by his association with the sample": Ibid.

60 As the late Supreme Court Justice Oliver Wendell Holmes Jr.

once noted: Frederick Schauer, *Thinking Like a Lawyer: A New Introduction to Legal Reasoning* (Cambridge, MA: Harvard University Press, 2009), 104.

61 **"It is tempting to think that with deductive reasoning, we can come up with truth":** Cass R. Sunstein, "On Analogical Reasoning," *Harvard Law Review* 106, no. 3 (January 1993): 777.

62 **But as Sunstein notes, "The process of reasoning by analogy is not science":** Ibid., 780.

62–63 **Tired of paying nearly $150 million annually to hold more than 3,000 nonviolent offenders:** Data from the State of California's Legislative Analyst's Office. www.lao.ca.gov/laoapp/laomenus/sections /crim_justice/6_cj_inmatecost.aspx?catid=3.

CHAPTER 3: THE MODEL T-BONE

65 **And in an insight that Gutenberg later described as "coming like a ray of light":** James Burke, *The Day the Universe Changed: How Galileo's Telescope Changed the Truth—and Other Events in History That Dramatically Altered Our Understanding of the World* (Boston: Back Bay Books, 1985), 303.

65 **While Chinese and Korean scribes had experimented with movable type:** Ibid., 112.

66 **When Johann Fust, one of Gutenberg's primary investors, first arrived in Paris:** Ibid., 113.

66 **But then as now, the marketplace prevailed:** Ibid.

67 **Even so, such explanations sometimes take time to win over broader audiences:** George Bernard Shaw, *Annajanska, the Bolshevik Empress* (1917). www.gutenberg.org/files/3485/3485-h/3485-h.htm.

68 **As Copernicus later wrote, "When a ship is floating calmly along":** Nicolaus Copernicus, *On the Revolutions of the Heavenly Spheres*, 1543, trans./comments Edward Rosen (Johns Hopkins University Press), Chapter 8. http://www.webexhibits.org/calendars/year-text-Copernicus .html.

69 **But the printing press, at the time still a relatively new technology:** Owen Gingerich, *The Book Nobody Read* (New York: Walker Publishing, 2004).

69 **Centuries later, the eminent mathematician George E. P. Box:** G. E. P. Box and N. R. Draper, *Empirical Model Building and Response Surfaces* (New York: John Wiley, 1987), 424.

71 **"My aim in this is to show that the celestial machine":** Gerald James Holton, *Thematic Origins of Scientific Thought: Kepler to Einstein* (Cambridge, MA: Harvard University Press, 1988), 56.

72 **Later, lamenting how long it took him to figure out these laws,**

Kepler summed up his work with another analogy: Dedre Gentner, Sarah Brem, Ron Ferguson, Philip Wolff, Arthur B. Markman, and Ken Forbus, "Analogy and Creativity in the Works of Johannes Kepler" in *Creative Thought: An Investigation of Conceptual Structures and Processes*, eds. Thomas B. Ward, Steven M. Smith, and Jyotsna Vaid (Washington, DC: American Psychological Association, 1997), 411.

72 **"He was a highly creative thinker, whose work spans and contributes to a period of immense change":** Ibid., 404.

73 **The eighteenth-century philosopher Immanuel Kant once noted that while mathematical analogies address a quantitative relationship:** Immanuel Kant, *Critique of Pure Reason*, trans. J. M. D. Meiklejohn, Electronic Classics Series (Hazelton: Pennsylvania State University–Hazelton, 2013), 144.

73 **In the preface to the 1787 edition of his book *Critique of Pure Reason*, he praises Copernicus:** Ibid., 14.

73 **As he describes it, the adjacent possible "is a kind of shadow future":** Steven Johnson, *Where Good Ideas Come From: The Natural History of Innovation* (New York: Riverhead Books, 2010), 31.

73 **While the number of basic components that can be recombined:** Ibid.

75 **Darwin himself took up pigeon breeding:** Janet Browne, *Charles Darwin: Voyaging*, vol. 1, *Charles Darwin: A Biography* (London: Pimlico, 1995), 523.

75 **In the book, Darwin describes a perpetual and ubiquitous struggle for existence:** Charles Darwin, *On the Origin of Species* (Alachua, FL: Bridge-Logos, 2009), 61.

77 **As Montgolfier, who was a diffident lawyer with a keen interest in science, mathematics, and engineering, watched the hot smoke:** T. A. Heppenheimer, *A Brief History of Flight* (New York: John Wiley, 2001), 4.

78 **Thrilled with his discovery, Montgolfier seized a quill and paper:** Ibid.

78 **As Benjamin Franklin, then an American emissary to France, wrote:** Ibid., 15.

79 **Born into a wealthy, aristocratic family in Yorkshire, George was already showing an interest in all things mechanical:** J. Laurence Pritchard, *Sir George Cayley: The Inventor of the Aeroplane* (London: Max Parrish, 1961), 22–23.

79 **Doodles in one of his schoolboy notebooks show a balloon with geared, crank-driven propellers:** Richard Dee, *The Man Who Discovered Flight: George Cayley and the First Airplane* (Toronto: McLelland & Stewart, 2007), 38.

79   Meanwhile, Cayley started experimenting with small whirli-gigs: Heppenheimer, *Brief History of Flight.*

79   But while Cayley was steadily working his way toward a better understanding of basic aerodynamic principles: Charles H. Gibbs-Smith, *Sir George Cayley's Aeronautics, 1796–1855* (London: Her Majesty's Stationery Office, 1962), 22–30.

80   And by 1809, when he penned a three-part article entitled "On Aerial Navigation," Cayley had identified the basic principles: Jay Spenser, *The Airplane: How Ideas Gave Us Wings* (New York: Smithsonian Books, 2008), 6–9.

80   Achieving practical, powered, heavier-than-air flight was just a matter of time: Ibid., 9.

80   The air, he analogized, was effectively "an uninterrupted, navigable ocean": Gibbs-Smith, *Sir George Cayley's Aeronautics,* 70.

80–81 And for the next several decades, he worked on aviation only intermittently: Spenser, *The Airplane,* 10.

81   When Cayley, then seventy-nine, rushed up to congratulate his test pilot: Gibbs-Smith, *Sir George Cayley's Aeronautics,* 178–179.

82   In the spring of 1899, Wilbur penned what would become one of the most famously prescient letters: Spenser, *The Airplane,* 32.

82   the Wright brothers' background in the bicycle business gave them a significant advantage: Ibid., 34–36.

83   As a consequence, most of the Wrights' competitors were obsessed with designing aircraft of such intrinsic stability: Ibid., 35.

84   Likening their daily setbacks and breakthroughs to the ups and downs of the stock market: Peter Jakab, *Visions of a Flying Machine: The Wright Brothers and the Process of Invention* (Washington, DC: Smithsonian Books, 1990), 203–204.

84   One nagging problem was their twelve-horsepower engine: Ibid., 205.

84   "Stock went up like a sky rocket, and is now at the highest figure": Ibid., 205–206.

84   Around ten thirty that morning, they positioned the asymmetrical, seven-hundred-pound biplane at one end of a sixty-foot wooden track: Ibid., 206.

85   Exhausted but exultant, they sent a telegram to their father: Ibid., 212.

87   Still, it would be steady work and, unlike the ice company with its bad checks: "The Reminiscences of Mr. W. C. Klann," interview September 1955, Owen W. Bombard interviews series, 1951–1961, Accession 65, The Henry Ford, Dearborn, MI, 4.

88   "If they can kill pigs and cows that way, we can build cars that
      way": Ibid., 22.

89   Klann, convinced of his analogy, insisted that the process was
      identical: Ibid., 82.

89   "It's a simple thing, isn't it?" Martin said: Ibid.

89   "If they can do it, we can do it," Klann answered: Ibid., 22.

89   Word of the gruesome accident quickly reached management:
      Ibid., 29.

89   An angry Couzens, one of Ford's original investors, threat-
      ened to fire Klann: Ibid.

89   "Break all of their legs," he said: Ibid., 29–30.

90   And then, on the first of December 1913—less than a year af-
      ter Klann's epiphany in Chicago: Ibid., 80.

90   By the spring of 1914, with continuous modifications to the
      line, that time had been slashed: Ibid.

91   In 1914, the moving assembly line's second full year of opera-
      tion: Daniel Gross, *Forbes Greatest Business Stories of All Time* (New
      York: John Wiley, 1996), 82–83.

91   While falling prices cut into the profit margin on every car,
      they drove up sales and revenue: "Mileposts 1912," Antique Auto-
      mobile Club of America online. http://local.aaca.org/bntc/mileposts/1912
      .htm.

91   "I'm going to democratize the automobile," Henry Ford had
      proclaimed: Gross, *Forbes Greatest Business Stories*, 81.

92   "Save ten steps a day for each of twelve thousand employees,"
      he later wrote: Henry Ford, *My Life and Work* (Garden City and New
      York: Doubleday, Page, 1922), 77.

92   "Mr. Ford didn't like it at first," recalled Richard Kroll: Richard
      Nye, *America's Assembly Line* (Cambridge, MA: MIT Press, 2013.), 20.

92   Even Ford's 1922 autobiography *My Life and Work* (which
      doesn't mention Klann at all): Ford, *My Life and Work*, 81.

93   One of these included what has come to be called the copy-
      right clause, which empowers Congress: United States Constitu-
      tion, Article 1, Section 8, Clause 8.

94   To achieve this balance, current law dictates that, among other
      requirements for obtaining a patent, an invention must: "Nov-
      elty and Non-Obviousness, Conditions for Obtaining a Patent," General
      Information Concerning Patents, United States Patent and Trademark Of-
      fice online. www.uspto.gov/patents/resources/general_info_concerning
      _patents.jsp#heading-5.

94   The eminent jurist Learned Hand—an aptly named federal

judge—acknowledged the challenge: *Safety Car Heating & Lighting Co. v. Gen. Elec. Co.*, 155 F.2d 937 (2d Cir. 1946).

94 **"Courts, made up of laymen as they must be," Hand continued:** Ibid.

95 **The feature, officially called inertial scrolling, was reportedly one of the features whose elegance convinced Jobs:** Philip Elmer-DeWitt, "Patent Office Tosses Out One of Steve Jobs' Favorite Inventions," *CNN Money*, October 23, 2012.

96 **Records indicate that it was clearly based on the rotating cylinders and spiral grooves of his phonograph:** William J. Broad, "Subtle Analogies Found at the Core of Edison's Genius," *New York Times*, March 12, 1985.

96 **"It was perhaps this trait more than any flashes of brilliance or cries of 'Eureka' that accounted for his great inventiveness," writes William Broad:** Ibid.

96 **"In working out an invention, the most important quality is persistence," Edison said:** French Strother, "The Modern Profession of Inventing," *The World's Work: A History of Our Time*, vol. X (May–October 1905) (New York: Doubleday, Page, 1905), 6,294–6,295.

96 **While still inadequate, it was an improvement, which led to tests on every type of soap:** Ibid.

97 **"The second quality of an inventor," Edison noted, "is imagination":** Ibid., 6,295.

97 **"The third essential," he said, "is a logical mind that sees analogies":** Ibid.

97 **"There is no logical way to the discovery of these elemental laws," Einstein would later write:** Max Planck, *Where Is Science Going?* Prologue by Albert Einstein (New York: W. W. Norton, 1932), 10.

98 **By the turn of the twentieth century, General Electric:** Strother, "Modern Profession of Inventing," 6,296.

98 **Still going strong more than a century later, GE now employs more than 300,000 people:** Global R&D Fact Sheet, General Electric online. www.ge.com/about-us/research/factsheet.

98 **"They come from all businesses and professions":** Strother, "Modern Profession of Inventing," 6,298.

99 **First, the most successful labs were those that made more frequent use of analogy:** Kevin Dunbar, "How Scientists Think in the Real World: Implications for Science Education," *Journal of Applied Developmental Psychology* 21, no. 1 (2000), 50.

99 **Second, when a team of researchers was united in pursuit of common goals:** Ibid.

100 **Shortfin mako sharks, believed to be the fastest of all sharks:**

ReefQuest Centre for Shark Research, http://www.elasmo-research.org
/education/shark_profiles/i_oxyrinchus.htm.

101 **According to Speedo, the new suits reduce drag:** Jim Morrison,
"How Speedo Created a Record-Breaking Swimsuit," *Scientific Ameri-can*, July 27, 2012.

101 **"It's like miles per gallon in a car," Speedo research manager
Joe Santry told:** Ibid.

101 **Believed to be the quietest of all fliers, owls have evolved:**
John Roach, "Owls' Silent Flight May Inspire Quiet Aircraft Tech," *National Geographic News*, December 17, 2004.

101 **Seeking to understand how such acoustical properties might
be mimicked in aircraft design:** Ibid.

103 **He called his program Enquire, after a Victorian advice
book:** Tim Berners-Lee and Mark Fischetti, *Weaving the Web: The
Original Design and Ultimate Destiny of the World Wide Web* (New York:
HarperBusiness, 2000), 1–2.

103 **The book, as he remembered, "served as a portal to a world
of information":** Ibid.

103 **The human mind uses these organizing structures all the
time:** Ibid., 10.

103 **Berners-Lee had come to recognize that in any large and
complex organization, how people actually collaborate,
trade ideas, and get work done often diverges:** Ibid., 221.

104 **"In an extreme view, the world can be seen only as connec-tions":** Ibid., 12.

104 **"The structure is everything," he wrote:** Ibid.

104 **Conceptually, the human brain functions in a similar way:** Ibid.

104 **"Suppose all the information stored on computers every-where were linked," he wrote:** Ibid., 4.

105 **He considered "Mesh" and "Information Mesh" but dis-missed both:** Ibid., 23.

105 **Some at CERN told Berners-Lee that the name World Wide
Web would never catch on:** Ibid., 3.

105–106 **Despite its rapid adoption, or perhaps because of it, the Web
drew some of the same early criticism as the printing press
did in the fifteenth century:** John P. Davies, *DOA: Education in the
Electronic Culture* (Lanham, MD: Scarecrow Press, 2003), 5.

106 **By some estimates, people will create more than five zetta-bytes of information:** Patrick Tucker, "Has Big Data Made Anonym-ity Impossible?" *MIT Technology Review*, May 7, 2013.

106 **"The new Web must allow me to learn by crossing boundar-ies":** Berners-Lee and Fischetti, *Weaving the Web*, 207.

CHAPTER 4: MORNING IN AMERICA

109   **As legend has it, Columcille was so focused on his work that he hardly heard, or simply ignored, the monastery's evening bell:** Padraic Colum, *The Legend of Saint Columba* (New York: Macmillan, 1935), 71–89.

109   **Columcille refused. "I labored that the wisdom in your book might be made known to men":** Ibid., 73.

110   **Columcille turned to King Diarmait, who had been silent throughout the dispute:** Ibid., 74.

110   **Incensed, Columcille handed over the copy—a battle lost, but certainly not the war:** Ibid.

111   **"I maintain that Finnen's book is none the worse for my having copied it," he continued:** Ibid., 80–81.

111   **Columcille's argument failed to sway the king, who chided him for his impudence:** Ibid.

111   **Then, citing ancient precedent, the High King Diarmait issued his ruling:** Ray Corrigan, "Columcille and the Battle of the Book: Technology, Law and Access to Knowledge in 6th Century Ireland," in GikII 2 Workshop on the intersections between law, technology, and popular culture, Prof. Lilian Edwards, University College London, September 19, 2007, 6.

113   **According to Harvard Law School professor Lloyd Weinreb:** Lloyd Weinreb, *Legal Reason: The Use of Analogy in Legal Argument* (New York: Cambridge University Press, 2005), 13.

114   **In unpacking the case, though, the judges also looked at deeper aspects of the competing analogies:** *Adams v. New Jersey Steamboat Co.*, 151 N.Y. 163, 45 N.E. 369 (1896).

114   **The court found that "a steamer carrying passengers on the water":** Ibid.

114   **The court ruled that "the two relationships, if not identical, bear such close analogy":** Ibid.

115   **Some legal scholars argue that the judicial tradition of legal precedent:** Frederick Schauer, "Why Precedent in Law (and Elsewhere) Is Not Totally (or Even Substantially) about Analogy (August 2007)," KSG Working Paper No. RWP07-036 (2007).

116   **As Lloyd Weinreb writes, "Analogical reasoning does not undermine the rule of law":** Weinreb, *Legal Reason*, viii.

116   **When people line up at the multiplex to see the latest Hollywood blockbuster, most don't realize:** Brian Bowdle and Dedre Gentner, "The Career of Metaphor," *Psychological Review* 112, no. 1 (January 2005): 209.

117   **Less than an hour after Bork was nominated, Senator Ted Kennedy delivered a fiery speech:** Ted Kennedy, Speech to the United States Senate, July 1, 1987.

118   **Under sharp questioning, he remained calm and confident, but came across as a humorless intellectual:** Nina Totenberg, "Robert Bork's Supreme Court Nomination 'Changed Everything, Maybe Forever,'" National Public Radio, December 19, 2012.

118   **Toward the end of Bork's testimony, a sympathetic supporter, Senator Alan Simpson of Wyoming, tossed him the proverbial softball:** "The Bork Hearings; An Intellectual Appetite" *New York Times*, September 20, 1987.

119   **"Senator, I guess the answer to that is that I have spent my life in the intellectual pursuits":** Ibid.

119   **As the Pulitzer Prize–winning columnist Ellen Goodman would later write, the public could practically "hear him salivating":** Ellen Goodman, "At Least Souter Has Passed the Bork Test," Philly.com, September 22, 1990.

120   **The battle also spawned the slang verb *to bork*:** *Oxford English Dictionary* online. http://oxforddictionaries.com/us/definition/american _english/bork.

120   **"Judges and justices are servants of the law, not the other way around. Judges are like umpires":** John Roberts, Opening statement of testimony in Senate Judiciary Committee confirmation hearing, Washington, DC, September 12, 2005. www.cnn.com/2005/POLITICS/09/12 /roberts.statement.

120   **"I have no agenda, but I do have a commitment," Roberts continued:** Ibid.

121   **Just to make sure the senators got his point, Roberts had amplified the basic analogy:** Ibid.

122   **"All of the things that we debate about here and the Court debates that deserve 5–4 decisions, they're almost all on issues that are ennobling phrases in the Constitution":** Joe Biden, Senate Judiciary Committee confirmation hearing for John Roberts, Washington, DC, September 13, 2005. www.washingtonpost.com/wp-dyn/content /article/2005/09/13/AR2005091300979.html.

124   **Research suggests that in business negotiations, sellers tend to do better when:** Adam D. Galinsky, "When to Make the First Offer in Negotiations," Working Knowledge for Business Leaders, Harvard Business School, August 9, 2004. http://hbswk.hbs.edu/archive/4302.html.

124   **Research by Northwestern University psychology professor Dedre Gentner and her colleagues suggests that even the simple assertion of an analogy can create:** David A. Perrott, Dedre

Gentner, and Galen V. Bodenhausen, "Resistance Is Futile: The Unwitting Insertion of Analogical Inferences in Memory," *Psychonomic Bulletin & Review* 12, no. 4 (2005): 696.

124   **Calling this the resistance-is-futile hypothesis, the researchers write:** Ibid., 699.

126   **And as the psychologist Daniel Kahneman notes, "It is the consistency of the information that matters for a good story, not its completeness":** Kahneman, *Thinking,* 87.

126   **As such, people are prone to exaggerate the coherence of what they encounter:** Ibid., 114.

127   **And as noted earlier, the brain tends to work hard to defend its intuitions against logical counterarguments:** Ibid., 103.

127   **As Kahneman notes, "When people believe a conclusion is true":** Ibid., 45.

130   **In a 2013 debate over the Affordable Care Act, the Republican Senate minority leader Mitch McConnell of Kentucky argued:** Jonathan Weisman and Robert Pear, "Partisan Gridlock Thwarts Effort to Alter Health Law," *New York Times,* May 26, 2013.

130   **Taking the opposite position, Max Baucus, a Democratic senator from Montana:** Ibid.

131   **In one study, a test population that listened to a series of rhyming aphorisms:** Kahneman, *Thinking,* 63.

131   **Theatrically wiggling his fingers, Simpson struggled to pull the gloves on:** " 'They're too small. . . . They're too Tight' . . . OJ," *Chicago Tribune,* June 27, 1995.

131–132 **Months later, in his closing argument, Cochran turned the whole spectacle to his advantage:** Johnny Cochran, "If it doesn't fit, you must acquit." www.youtube.com/watch?v=P_apIbmsUwU.

133   **In it, he noted that "there are certain features common to all the finest speeches in the English language":** Winston S. Churchill, "The Scaffolding of Rhetoric," unpublished essay, November 1897. www.winstonchurchill.org/images/pdfs/for_educators/the_scaffolding _of_rhetoric.pdf.

133   **Analogy, Churchill wrote, "appeals to the everyday knowledge of the hearer":** Ibid.

133   **And while he acknowledged that argument by analogy "leads to conviction rather than to proof":** Ibid.

133   **"In spite of the arguments of the cynic the influence exercised over the human mind by apt analogies is and has always been immense":** Ibid.

134   **He then proceeded to cite a few recent examples: his own father's description of British rule in India:** Ibid.

134   "It is impossible to imagine any form of argument that could keep the field in the face of these or similar analogies": Ibid.

134   "What General Weygand has called the Battle of France is over," Churchill explained: Winston S. Churchill, Address to the House of Commons of the Parliament, June 18, 1940, *The Penguin Book of Twentieth-Century Speeches*, ed. Brian MacArthur (New York: Penguin Books, 1992), 189.

135   While their meaning can vary by culture, Westerners generally feel that *up is happy*, and *down is sad*: Lakoff and Johnson, *Metaphors We Live By*, 15.

136   These expressions are derived, Lakoff and Johnson argue, from physical reality: Ibid., 14–15.

136   Similarly, they note that *health* and *life* are *up*, while *sickness* and *death* are down: Ibid., 15.

136   In the same vein, *up* is associated with virtue: Ibid., 15–16.

137   As Lakoff and Johnson note, "No metaphor can ever be comprehended or": Ibid., 19.

138   "Now, what I am trying to do is to eliminate the dollar sign": Franklin Delano Roosevelt, White House press conference, December 17, 1940. http://docs.fdrlibrary.marist.edu/odllpc2.html.

139   "In other words, if you lend certain munitions and get the munitions back at the end of the war": Ibid.

140   "The experience of the past two years has proven beyond doubt that no nation can appease the Nazis": Franklin Delano Roosevelt, "The Arsenal of Democracy" (Fireside Chat), *The Penguin Book of Twentieth-Century Speeches*, ed. Brian MacArthur (New York: Penguin Books, 1992), 195.

141   Dubbed the Arsenal of Democracy speech, the president's fireside chat had a dramatic impact: Ibid., 197.

142   "As a nation, we may take pride in the fact that we are soft-hearted; but we cannot afford to be soft-headed," he said: Ibid., 198.

142   "Freedom means the supremacy of human rights everywhere," FDR concluded: Ibid., 201.

143   By morning, little remained of the church but its concrete steps and modest bell: Civil Rights Digital Library, "WALB TV newsfilm of the burned ruins of African American churches in Terrell and Lee counties, Georgia, 1962 August and September." http://crdl.usg.edu/export/html/ugabma/walb/crdl_ugabma_walb_walb00067.html.

143   At a service following the firebombing, Prathia Hall, a young leader in the Student Nonviolent Coordinating Committee: Faith Holsaert et al., eds., *Hands on the Freedom Plow: Personal Accounts by Women in SNCC* (Urbana, Chicago, and Springfield: University of Illinois Press, 2010), 180.

143   **Soon the entire group was intoning Hall's phrase, including Dr. Martin Luther King Jr.:** Richard Lischer, *The Preacher King: Martin Luther King Jr. and the Word that Moved America* (New York and Oxford: Oxford University Press, 1995), 93–94.

143–144   **Prophetic dreams are woven throughout the Bible, and more than a year before the Mount Olive church bombing, King himself had given a commencement address at Lincoln University:** Martin Luther King Jr., "The American Dream," Commencement Address at Lincoln University, Lincoln University, PA, June 6, 1961.

144   **"It is a dream of a land where men of all races, of all nationalities, and of all creeds can live together as brothers":** Ibid.

144   **The Reverend Will D. Campbell, a Freedom Rider who was active in the movement, described the experience:** Robert D. McFadden, "Rev. Will D. Campbell, Maverick Minister in Civil Rights Era, Dies at 88," *New York Times*, June 4, 2013.

145   **Before Birmingham, only 4 percent of Americans considered civil rights to be the nation's most pressing issue:** Gary Younge, "1963: The Defining Year of the Civil Rights Movement," *Guardian*, May 6, 2013.

145   **In the two months leading up to the August 28 march, Americans staged 758 civil rights demonstrations:** Ibid.

148   **As King scholar Eric Sundquist would later write, King had "created a new national scripture":** Eric J. Sundquist, *King's Dream* (New Haven, CT: Yale University Press, 2009), 18.

149   **As one FBI agent wrote in an August 30 memo:** W. C. Sullivan, "Communist Party, USA, Negro Question," United States Government Memorandum, August 30, 1963. www.npr.org/assets/news/2013/mlk-fbi-memo.pdf.

149   **Richard Lischer, a Duke University professor specializing in the rhetoric of preaching, wrote in *The Preacher King*:** Lischer, *Preacher King*, 197.

150   **"There is no issue of states' rights or national rights":** Lyndon B. Johnson, "We Shall Overcome" address to US Congress, March 15, 1965. http://historymatters.gmu.edu/d/6336.

150   **King wasn't the first to champion civil rights in twentieth-century America, but:** Lischer, *Preacher King*, 198.

151   **For two hours he scribbled away, which aroused the curiosity of his fellow patrons:** George Raine, "Creating Reagan's Image: S.F. Ad Man Riney Helped Secure Him a Second Term," *San Francisco Chronicle*, June 9, 2004.

151   **"It's morning again in America," the script began:** "Prouder, Stronger, Better" video, The Living Room Candidate: Presidential Cam-

paign Commercials 1952–2012, Museum of the Moving Image online. www.livingroomcandidate.org/commercials/1984/prouder-stronger -better.

152 **Throughout the campaign, pundits questioned whether he still had the health, stamina, and mental acuity:** Paul Bedard, "Reagan Son Claims Dad Had Alzheimer's as President," *U.S. News and World Report,* January 14, 2011.

152 **As newsman Bob Schieffer later recalled, "It immediately set off this round of speculation":** www.biography.com/people /ronald-reagan-9453198/videos.

152 **Sam Donaldson offered a similar assessment:** Ibid.

153 **In the second debate, on October 21, one of the journalists posing questions:** Ronald Reagan and Walter Mondale, Second Presidential Debate, Kansas City, Missouri, October 21, 1984. www.presidency.ucsb .edu/ws/index.php?pid=39296.

153 **Twenty years later, Republican strategist Dan Schnur:** Raine, "Creating Reagan's Image."

154 **"The condor won":** Steve Jobs, Address at Insanely Great Conference, 1980. www.youtube.com/watch?v=lJKlc4m5D50.

155 **"You could say that the Industrial Revolution was basically an amplification of a human ability":** Ibid.

155 **Apple's goal was to remove all the barriers to using a computer:** Ibid.

155 **"Apple is eventually going to have a broader line of products," he said:** Ibid.

155–156 **As the machine took shape, he approached Apple's ad agency, Chiat/Day, to develop a Super Bowl ad:** Isaacson, *Steve Jobs,* 162.

156 **"I want a thunderclap," Jobs told the creative team:** Ibid.

156 **Wary of offending people, Apple's board of directors was reluctant:** Ibid., 164.

157 **"The fantasy commercial parallels reality, for Macintosh is a dramatic and risky attempt to make a technological end run":** Michael Rogers, "It's the Apple of His Eye," *Newsweek,* January 30, 1984.

157 **Stu Schreiberg, a television executive who later produced a CBS special on the fifty greatest commercials:** Stuart Elliott, "Advertising; a New Ranking of the '50 Best' Television Commercials Ever Made," *New York Times,* March 14, 1995.

158 **In 1996, years after being ousted from Apple and before he returned to save the company, Jobs gave an interview to** *Wired:* Gary Wolf, "Steve Jobs: The Next Insanely Great Thing," Interview with Steve Jobs, *Wired,* February 2006.

158 **"*Design* is a funny word," Jobs said:** Ibid.

158   The slang word *grok*, coined by the science fiction writer Robert Heinlein, has two definitions: Dictionary.com.

160   "I learned about serif and san serif typefaces": Steve Jobs, Commencement Address at Stanford University, Stanford, CA, June 12, 2005.

160   But as Jobs noted, "None of this had even a hope of any practical application in my life": Ibid.

160   And as he remarked, "If I had never dropped out, I would have never dropped in on this calligraphy class, and personal computers might not have the wonderful typography that they do": Ibid.

160   "Again, you can't connect the dots looking forward": Ibid.

160   "So you have to trust that the dots will somehow connect in your future": Ibid.

CHAPTER 5: SEEING THE BIG PICTURE

162   Once, chatting with former President Jimmy Carter's Secret Service detail, he lifted the thirty-ninth president's itinerary: Adam Green, "A Pickpocket's Tale: The Spectacular Thefts of Apollo Robbins," *New Yorker*, January 7, 2013: 38.

162   "They were on guard," he concedes: Apollo Robbins, Interview with John Pollack, November 1, 2013.

162   Dressed as a wizard, he entertained guests by returning the rings, watches, wallets, and other items they didn't even realize he'd just stolen: Green, "Pickpocket's Tale," 43.

162–163 When he works a crowd, he will "accidentally" brush past people: Ibid., 39.

163   "What I'm doing is taking inventory": Ibid.

163   If Robbins asks someone if their American Express card is still in the wallet in their back pocket: Robbins, Interview with Pollack.

163   "It's all about the choreography of people's attention": Green, "Pickpocket's Tale," 41.

163   In a service for children, his father might bring a turtle and talk about the hard shells people try to maintain: Robbins, Interview with Pollack.

163   Years after the Wright brothers had succeeded in building their flying machine, Orville admitted: Jakab, *Visions of a Flying Machine*, 52.

163   "Although we intently watched birds fly in a hope of learning something": Ibid.

163   "Learning the secret of flight from a bird was a good deal like learning the secret of magic from a magician": Ibid.

164   In a 2005 study published in the *Harvard Business Review*, Giovanni Gavetti: Giovanni Gavetti and Jan W. Rivkin, *Harvard Business Review* 83, no. 4 (April 2005): 54.

164   By contrast, "Managers who pay attention to their own analogical thinking will make better strategic decisions": Ibid.

165   As such, our national interest does and should transcend generations: Matt Phillips, "The Long Story of U.S. Debt, from 1790 to 2011, in One Little Chart," *Atlantic*, November 13, 2012. www.the atlantic.com/business/archive/2012/11/the-long-story-of-us-debt-from -1790-to-2011-in-1-little-chart/265185.

165   investing nearly $130 billion to build the Interstate Highway System: "What Did It Cost?" Interstate FAQ, US Department of Transportation, Federal Highway Administration online. http://www .fhwa.dot.gov/interstate/faq.htm#question6.

167   As Daniel Kahneman notes in *Thinking Fast and Slow*, our normal state of mind is to make snap judgments: Kahneman, *Thinking*, 97.

167   Kahneman suggests a reason for this leap to judgment: Ibid.

167   Evidence indicates that we are especially prone to swap in easier questions when strong emotions are involved: Ibid., 103.

167   Drew Westen, the author of *The Political Brain*, notes that the analogies we find compelling: Westen, *Political Brain*, 95.

168   Adolf Hitler described Jews as "a virus" and, in 1942, said: Michael Burleigh and Wolfgang Wippermann, *The Racial State: Germany 1933–1945* (New York: Cambridge University Press, 1991).

168   "If we go to the 1940s, Nazi Germany—look, we saw it in Britain," Cruz said: Ted Cruz, *Congressional Record*, September 24, 2013.

168–169 "So we get to Obamacare, and what do all of those voices say? It cannot be stopped": Ibid.

169   The next day, B'nai B'rith International joined a chorus of voices across the political spectrum that slammed Cruz for his analogy: Statement by B'nai B'rith International, September 25, 2013. www.bnaibrith.org/5/post/2013/09/sen-ted-cruzs-use-of-hitler-analogy -to-denigrate-affordable-care-act-is-unacceptable.html.

169   He said he didn't want to miss the opportunity "to thank the men and women who have endured this, this Bataan Death March": Catalina Camia, "Sen. Cruz Apologizes for Bataan Death March Remarks," *USA Today*, October 2, 2013.

169   **After a week of withering criticism from veterans, he apologized for the analogy:** Ibid.

169   **In 2006, Democratic congressman Steny Hoyer told a crowd that Maryland lieutenant governor Michael Steele:** Ted Barrett, "Democrat Apologizes for 'Slavish' Remark," CNN, October 17, 2006.

169   **Hoyer apologized for his use of the word:** Ibid.

170   **One technique he sometimes uses is to lean into a mark's face:** Robbins, Interview with Pollack.

170   **But while his physical skills are extraordinary, he considers his mental and verbal skills to be even more important:** Ibid.

170   **"It's more about knowing the mind-set of the person you're dealing with":** Ibid.

170   **"And the more someone *thinks* they know, the easier it is":** Ibid.

170   **As the linguist and author George Lakoff remarks, an opponent's language:** Lakoff, *Don't Think of an Elephant*, 3.

170   **In his seminal 1776 treatise *The Wealth of Nations*:** Adam Smith, *The Wealth of Nations* (Blacksburg, VA: Thrifty Books, 2009), 320.

171   **"In order to be an intelligent citizen of the world, I think you have to":** Scott E. Page, "Model Thinking," University of Michigan online course. www.coursera.org/course/modelthinking.

172   **Albert Einstein once noted that poets, painters, philosophers, and theoretical physicists all pursue a similar human impulse:** Planck, *Where Is Science Going?*, 11.

172   **"Even at the expense of completeness, we have to secure purity, clarity and accurate correspondence":** Ibid., 9.

172   **He added that in physics, as research and knowledge advance:** Ibid., 11.

172   **"Most people make most decisions by drawing simple sorts of analogies":** Scott E. Page, Interview with John Pollack, June 21, 2013.

173   **"Analogies should enhance thinking, not substitute for it":** Keith J. Holyoak and Paul Thagard, *Mental Leaps: Analogy in Creative Thought* (Cambridge, MA: MIT Press, 1995), 133.

173   **Too often, they argue, people fixate on one analogy:** Ibid.

174   **Since customers depend on such fail-safe power to keep their servers running:** James Glanz, "Landlords Double as Energy Brokers," *New York Times*, May 14, 2013.

174   **Some are even seeking Internal Revenue Service approval to become Real Estate Investment Trusts, which could save:** Ibid.

174   **That's why looking at any challenge or opportunity through multiple analogies is always advisable:** Page, Interview with Pollack.

175   **The evolutionary biologist E. O. Wilson once described analogy as:** Edward O. Wilson, *Biophilia* (Cambridge, MA: Harvard University Press, 1984), 66.

175   **"We are drowning in information, while starving for wisdom":** Edward O. Wilson, *Consilience* (New York: Vintage Books, 1998), 294.

175   **Steve Jobs once told *Wired* magazine that "when you ask creative people how they did something, they feel a little guilty":** Wolf, "Steve Jobs," Interview.

175   **People who lack the experience or ability to see these connections:** Ibid.

175–176   **He was paraphrasing Edwin Land, the cofounder of Polaroid:** Alan Earls and Nasrin Rohani, *Polaroid* (Charleston, SC: Arcadia Publishing, 2005), 20.

176   **After school, he would use his grandmother's magnifying glass to examine the illustrations in the magazines:** Christopher Finch, *Chuck Close: Life* (New York: Prestel Publishing, 2010), 45–46.

177   **Maxwell, the nineteenth-century physicist, once observed that a pun reveals two truths:** Lewis Campbell, *The Life of James Clerk Maxwell* (London: Macmillan, 1882), 235.

177   **Einstein once said, "I am enough of the artist to draw freely on my imagination":** George Sylvester Viereck, "What Life Means to Einstein," Interview with Albert Einstein, *Saturday Evening Post*, October 26, 1929, 117.

178   **"Intentionally misleading comparisons are becoming the dominant mode of public discourse":** Adam Cohen, "An SAT without Analogies Is Like: (A) A Confused Citizenry . . ." *New York Times*, March 13, 2005.

179   **In 1929, Einstein told *The Saturday Evening Post*, "I believe in standardizing automobiles":** Viereck, "What Life Means," 117.

180   **In *The Gardens of Democracy*, Eric Liu and Nick Hanauer write that "the failure of American politics to address and solve the great challenges of our time":** Eric Liu and Nick Hanauer. *The Gardens of Democracy: A New American Story of Citizenship, the Economy, and the Role of Government* (Seattle: Sasquatch Books, 2011), 5–6.

180   **A big part of this failure, they argue, is because our thinking is constrained:** Ibid., 10.

180   **From this perspective, the economy is largely an efficient and self-correcting mechanism:** Ibid., 10–11.

180   **Unfortunately, within this overarching industrial analogy, people tend to become interchangeable:** Ibid.

181   "Conventional wisdom," Liu and Hanauer write, "conflates self-interest with selfishness": Ibid., 24.

181   A better analogy, they argue, might be that of a garden: Ibid., 10–11.

181   "To be a gardener is not to let nature take its course; it is to *tend*": Ibid.

SELECTED BIBLIOGRAPHY

Adair, John. *The Art of Creative Thinking: How to Be Innovative and Develop Great Ideas.* Philadelphia: Kogan Page Publishing, 2009.

al Tawansy, Abul Fotouh Muhammad. *Ibn Khaldoun.* Cairo: Supreme Council for Islamic Affairs, 1967.

Alexander, Bevin. *How Great Generals Win.* New York: W. W. Norton, 1993.

Anttila, Raimo. *Analogy.* Trends in Linguistics: State-of-the-Art Reports 10. The Hague: de Gruyter Mouton Publishers, 1977.

Anttila, Raimo, and Warren A. Brewer. *Analogy: A Basic Bibliography.* Library and Information Sources in Linguistics 1. Amsterdam: John Benjamins Publishing, 1977.

Aristotle. *The Art of Rhetoric.* Translated by H. C. Lawson-Tancred. New York: Penguin Books, 2004.

Bachelder, Louise. *Abraham Lincoln Wisdom and Wit.* Mount Vernon, NY: Peter Pauper Press, 1965.

Baggini, Julian. *Should You Judge This Book by Its Cover?* Berkeley: Counterpoint, 2010.

Barabási, Albert-László. *Bursts: The Hidden Pattern Behind Everything We Do.* New York: Dutton, 2010.

Barnden, John A., and Keith J. Holyoak, eds. *Analogy, Metaphor, and Reminding.* Advances in Connectionist and Neural Computation Theory 3. Norwood, NJ: Ablex Publishing, 1994.

Bent, Samuel Arthur. *Familiar Short Sayings of Great Men, with Historical and Explanatory Notes.* Boston: Ticknor, 1887.

Bergen, Benjamin K. *Louder Than Words: The New Science of How the Mind Makes Meaning.* New York: Basic Books, 2012.

Berman, Joshua A. *Narrative Analogy in the Hebrew Bible: Battle Stories and Their Equivalent Non-Battle Narratives.* Supplements to Vetus Testamentum 103. Leiden, Holland, and Boston: Brill, 2004.

Berners-Lee, Tim, and Mark Fischetti. *Weaving the Web: The Original Design and Ultimate Destiny of the World Wide Web.* New York: HarperBusiness, 2000.

Blevins, James, and Juliette Blevins, eds. *Analogy in Grammar: Form and Acquisition.* New York: Oxford University Press, 2009.

Boorstin, Daniel J. *The Americans: The Democratic Experience.* New York: Random House, 1973.

Bowdle, Brian, and Dedre Gentner. "The Career of Metaphor." *Psychological Review* 112, no. 1 (Jan. 2005).

Box, G. E. P., and N. R. Draper. *Empirical Model Building and Response Surfaces.* New York: John Wiley, 1987.

Boycott, Rosie. *Batty, Bloomers and Boycott: A Little Etymology of Eponymous Words.* New York: Peter Bedrick Books, 1982.

Broad, William J. "Subtle Analogies Found at the Core of Edison's Genius." *The New York Times,* March 12, 1985.

Brockman, John. *This Explains Everything: Deep, Beautiful, and*

Elegant Theories of How the World Works. New York: Harper-Perennial, 2013.

Browne, Janet. *Charles Darwin: Voyaging.* Vol. 1 of *Charles Darwin: A Biography.* London: Pimlico, 1995.

Buffett, Warren. *Tap Dancing to Work.* Collected and expanded by Carol J. Loomis. New York: Portfolio/Penguin, 2012.

Burke, James. *The Day the Universe Changed: How Galileo's Telescope Changed the Truth—and Other Events in History That Dramatically Altered Our Understanding of the World.* Boston: Back Bay Books, 1985.

Burke, Kenneth. *The Philosophy of Literary Form: Studies in Symbolic Action.* 3rd ed. Los Angeles and London: University of California Press, 1973.

Burleigh, Michael, and Wolfgang Wippermann. *The Racial State: Germany 1933–1945.* New York: Cambridge University Press, 1991.

Bush, Vannevar. "As We May Think." *Atlantic,* July 1945.

Butler, Samuel. *The Note-Books of Samuel Butler.* Blackmask Online, 2002. www.munseys.com/diskone/nbsb.pdf.

Campbell, Joseph, with Bill Moyers. *The Power of Myth.* New York: Doubleday, 1988.

Campbell, Lewis. *The Life of James Clerk Maxwell.* London: Macmillan, 1882.

Caro, Robert. *The Passage of Power.* New York: Alfred A. Knopf, 2012.

Chan, Joel, Katherine Fu, Christian Schunn, Jonathan Cagan, Kristen Wood, and Kenneth Kotovsky. "On the Benefits and Pitfalls of Analogies for Innovative Design: Ideation Performance Based on Analogical Distance, Commonness, and Modality of Examples." *Journal of Mechanical Design* 133 (Aug. 2011).

Chase, Stuart. *Guides to Straight Thinking.* New York: Harper & Brothers, 1956.

Churchill, Winston S. "The Scaffolding of Rhetoric." Unpublished essay, November 1897. www.winstonchurchill.org/images/pdfs/for_educators /the_scaffolding_of_rhetoric.pdf.

Cialdini, Robert B. *Influence: The Psychology of Persuasion.* New York: Collins Business, 2007.

Colum, Padraic. *The Legend of Saint Columba.* New York: Macmillan, 1935.

Constitution of the United States of America.

Cook, Jeff Scott. *The Elements of Speechwriting and Public Speaking.* New York: Macmillan, 1989.

Copernicus, Nicolaus. *On the Revolutions of the Heavenly Spheres,* 1543. Trans./Comments by Edward Rosen. Johns Hopkins University Press. http://www.webexhibits.org/calendars/year-text-Copernicus .html.

Crystal, David. *The Cambridge Encyclopedia of the English Language.* New York: Cambridge University Press, 1995.

————.*How Language Works.* New York: Overlook Press, 2005.

Csikszentmihalyi, Mihaly. *Creativity: Flow and the Psychology of Discovery and Invention.* New York: HarperCollins, 1996.

Daleski, H. M. *Dickens and the Art of Analogy.* London: Faber and Faber, 1970.

Darling, David. *The Universal Book of Mathematics: From Abracadabra to Zeno's Paradoxes.* Hoboken, NJ: John Wiley, 2004.

Darwin, Charles. *On the Origin of Species.* Alachua, FL: Bridge-Logos, 2009.

Davies, John P. *DOA: Education in the Electronic Culture.* Lanham, MD: Scarecrow Press, 2003.

Day, Samuel B., and Dedre Gentner. "Nonintentional Analogical Inference in Text Comprehension." *Memory and Cognition* 35, no. 1 (2007): 39-49.

Day, Samuel B., and Robert L. Goldstone. "Analogical Transfer from a Simulated Physical System." *Journal of Experimental Psychology: Learning, Memory, and Cognition* 37, no. 3 (2011): 551-567.

de Boinod, Adam Jacot. *The Meaning of Tingo and Other Extraordinary Words from around the World.* New York: Penguin Books, 2005.

Dee, Richard. *The Man Who Discovered Flight: George Cayley and the First Airplane.* Toronto: McLelland & Stewart, 2007.

Donald, David Herbert. *Lincoln.* New York: Simon & Schuster, 1995.

Dyson, James, and Giles Coren. *Against the Odds: An Autobiography.* London and New York: Texere, 2001.

Earls, Alan, and Nasrin Rohani. *Polaroid.* Charleston, SC: Arcadia Publishing, 2005.

Easley, David, and Jon Kleinberg. *Networks, Crowds, and Markets: Reasoning About a Highly Connected World.* New York: Cambridge University Press, 2010.

Einstein, Albert. *Essays in Science.* New York: Philosophical Library, 1934.

———. *The World as I See It.* New York: Philosophical Library, 1949.

Eisenberg, Melvin Aron. *The Nature of the Common Law.* Cambridge, MA: Harvard University Press, 1988.

Estrin, Judy. *Closing the Innovation Gap: Reigniting the Spark of Creativity in a Global Economy.* New York: McGraw-Hill, 2009.

Finch, Christopher. *Chuck Close: Life.* New York: Prestel Publishing, 2010.

Fischer, Roger Steven. *A Natural History of Language.* London: Reaktion Books, 1999.

Ford, Henry. *My Life and Work*. Garden City, NY and New York: Doubleday, Page, 1922.

Fowler, Henry W. *A Dictionary of Modern English Usage*. Oxford: Clarendon Press, 1926.

Fugere, Brian, Chelsea Hardaway, and Jon Warshawsky. *Why Business People Speak Like Idiots: A Bullfighter's Guide*. New York: Free Press, 2005.

Fuller, R. Buckminster. *Nine Chains to the Moon*. Philadelphia: J. B. Lippincott, 1938.

Funk, Wilfred. *Word Origins and Their Romantic Stories*. New York: Grosset & Dunlap, 1950.

Garfield, Simon. *Just My Type: A Book About Fonts*. New York: Gotham Books, 2011.

Geary, James. *I Is an Other: The Secret Life of Metaphor and How It Shapes the Way We See the World*. New York: Harper, 2011.

———. *The World in a Phrase: A Brief History of the Aphorism*. New York: Bloomsbury, 2005.

Gelb, Michael J., and Sarah Miller Caldicott. *Innovate Like Edison: The Success System of America's Greatest Inventor*. New York: Dutton, 2007.

Gentner, Dedre, and Albert L. Stevens, eds. *Mental Models*. Hillsdale, NJ: Lawrence Erlbaum Associates, 1983.

Gentner, Dedre, and Arthur B. Markman. "Structure Mapping in Analogy and Similarity." *American Psychologist* (Jan. 1997).

Gentner, Dedre, Keith J. Holyoak, and Boicho N. Kokinov, eds. *The Analogical Mind: Perspectives from Cognitive Science*. Cambridge, MA, and London: MIT Press, 2001.

Gentner, Dedre, Sarah Brem, Ron Ferguson, Philip Wolff, Arthur B. Markman, and Ken Forbus. "Analogy and Creativity in the Works of

Johannes Kepler." In *Creative Thought: An Investigation of Conceptual Structures and Processes,* edited by Thomas B. Ward, Steven M. Smith, and Jyotsna Vaid. Washington, DC: American Psychological Association, 1997.

Gibbs-Smith, Charles H. *Sir George Cayley's Aeronautics, 1796–1855.* London: Her Majesty's Stationery Office, 1962.

Gillespie, James J., Leigh L. Thompson, Jeffrey Loewenstein, and Dedre Gentner. "Lessons from Analogical Reasoning in the Teaching of Negotiation." *Negotiation Journal* 15, no. 4 (1999): 363–371.

Gingerich, Owen. *The Book Nobody Read.* New York: Walker Publishing, 2004.

Gladwell, Malcolm. "Creation Myth." *The New Yorker,* May 16, 2011.

Goldstone, Robert L., David Landy, and Lionel C. Brunel. "Improving Perception to Make Distant Connections Closer." *Frontiers in Psychology 2* (2011): 385.

Goldstone, Robert L., and Uri Wilensky. "Promoting Transfer by Grounding Complex Systems Principles." *Journal of the Learning Sciences* 17 (2008): 4,465–4,516.

Gottheimer, Josh. *Ripples of Hope: Great American Civil Rights Speeches.* New York: Basic Civitas Books, 2003.

Gottschall, Jonathan. *The Storytelling Animal: How Stories Make Us Human.* New York: First Mariner Books, 2013.

Gray, Dave, Sunni Brown, and James Macanufo. *Gamestorming: A Playbook for Innovators, Rulebreakers, and Changemakers.* Sebastopol, CA: O'Reilly Media, 2010.

Green, Adam. "A Pickpocket's Tale: The Spectacular Thefts of Apollo Robbins." *The New Yorker,* January 7, 2013.

Gross, Daniel. *Forbes Greatest Business Stories of All Time.* New York: John Wiley, 1996.

Grothe, Mardy. *I Never Metaphor I Didn't Like: A Comprehensive Compilation of History's Greatest Analogies, Metaphors, and Similes.* New York: HarperCollins, 2008.

Haidt, Jonathan. *The Righteous Mind: Why Good People Are Divided by Politics and Religion.* New York: Pantheon Books, 2012.

Hawking, Stephen W. *A Brief History of Time.* New York: Bantam Books, 1988.

"HBR List: Breakthrough Ideas for 2009." *Harvard Business Review,* February 2009.

Heath, Chip, and Dan Heath. *Decisive: How to Make Better Choices in Life and Work.* New York: Crown Business, 2013.

———. *Made to Stick: Why Some Ideas Survive and Others Die.* New York: Random House, 2007.

Heinrichs, Jay. *Word Hero: A Fiendishly Clever Guide to Crafting the Lines that Get Laughs, Go Viral, and Live Forever.* New York: Three Rivers Press, 2011.

Hemingway, Ernest. *Ernest Hemingway on Writing.* Edited by Larry W. Phillips. New York: Scribner, 1984.

———. *The Short Stories of Ernest Hemingway.* New York: Scribner, 1966.

Heppenheimer, T. A. *A Brief History of Flight.* Hoboken, NJ: John Wiley, 2001.

Hofstadter, Douglas R. *Fluid Concepts and Creative Analogies: Computer Models of the Fundamental Mechanisms of Thought.* New York: Basic Books, 1995.

Hofstadter, Douglas, and Emmanuel Sander. *Surfaces and Essences: Analogy as the Fuel and Fire of Thinking.* New York: Basic Books, 2013.

Hofstadter, Richard. *Anti-Intellectualism in American Life.* New York: Vintage Books, 1963.

Holsaert, Faith S., Martha P. N. Noonan, Judy Richardson, Betty G. Robinson, Jean S. Young, and Dorothy M. Zellner, eds. *Hands on the Freedom Plow: Personal Accounts by Women in SNCC.* Urbana, Chicago, and Springfield: University of Illinois Press, 2010.

Holton, Gerald James. *Thematic Origins of Scientific Thought: Kepler to Einstein.* Cambridge, MA: Harvard University Press, 1988.

Holyoak, Keith J., and Paul Thagard. *Mental Leaps: Analogy in Creative Thought.* Cambridge, MA: MIT Press, 1995.

Humes, James C. *Speak Like Churchill, Stand Like Lincoln: 21 Powerful Secrets of History's Greatest Speakers.* New York: Three Rivers Press, 2002.

Hurson, Tim. *Think Better.* New York: McGraw-Hill, 2008.

Isaacson, Walter. *Steve Jobs.* New York: Simon & Schuster, 2011.

Israel, Paul. *Edison: A Life of Invention.* New York: John Wiley, 1998.

Jacobs, Frank. *Strange Maps: An Atlas of Cartographic Curiosities.* New York: Viking Studio, 2009.

Jakab, Peter. *Visions of a Flying Machine: The Wright Brothers and the Process of Invention.* Washington, DC: Smithsonian Books, 1990.

Jobs, Steve. Commencement Address at Stanford University. Stanford, CA, June 12, 2005.

Johnson, Mark. *The Meaning of the Body: Aesthetics of Human Understanding.* Chicago and London: University of Chicago Press, 2007.

Johnson, Steven. *Where Good Ideas Come From: The Natural History of Innovation.* New York: Riverhead Books, 2010.

Jones, R. V. *Most Secret War: British Scientific Intelligence 1939–1945.* London: Penguin Books, 2009.

———. *Reflections on Intelligence.* London: William Heinemann, 1989.

Kahneman, Daniel. *Thinking, Fast and Slow*. New York: Farrar, Straus and Giroux, 2011.

Kant, Immanuel. *Critique of Pure Reason*. Translated by J. M. D. Meiklejohn. Electronic Classics Series. Hazelton: Pennsylvania State University–Hazelton, 2013.

Keyes, Ralph. *Euphemania: Our Love Affair with Euphemisms*. New York: Little, Brown, 2010.

Khurana, Rakesh. *From Higher Aims to Hired Hands: The Social Transformation of American Business Schools and the Unfulfilled Promise of Management as a Profession*. Princeton, NJ: Princeton University Press, 2007.

King, Martin Luther, Jr. "The American Dream." Commencement Address at Lincoln University. Lincoln University, PA, June 6, 1961.

———. *The Autobiography of Martin Luther King, Jr.* Edited by Clayborne Carson. London: Abacus, 2000.

———. "I Have a Dream." Speech delivered at the March on Washington for Jobs and Freedom. Washington, DC, August 28, 1963.

Kirkpatrick, Betty. *Clichés: Over 1500 Phrases Explored and Explained*. New York: St. Martin's Griffin, 1996.

Koestler, Arthur. *The Act of Creation*. London: Hutchinson, 1964.

Koulopoulos, Thomas M. *The Innovation Zone: How Great Companies Re-Innovate for Amazing Success*. Mountain View, CA: Davies-Black Publishing, 2009.

Kövecses, Zoltán. *Emotion Concepts*. New York: Springer-Verlag, 1990.

———. *Metaphor: A Practical Introduction*. 2nd ed. Oxford and New York: Oxford University Press, 2010.

———. *Metaphor and Emotion: Language, Culture, and Body in Human Feeling*. Cambridge: Cambridge University Press, 2003.

Kraska-Szlenk, Iwona. *Analogy: The Relation between Lexicon and Grammar*. München, Germany: Lincom Europa, 2007.

Kuhn, Thomas S. *The Structure of Scientific Revolutions.* 3rd ed. Chicago: University of Chicago Press, 1996.

Kurzweil, Ray. *How to Create a Mind: The Secret of Human Thought Revealed.* New York: Viking, 2012.

Lakoff, George. *Don't Think of an Elephant: Know Your Values and Frame the Debate.* White River Junction, VT: Chelsea Green Publishing, 2004.

———. *The Political Mind: A Cognitive Scientist's Guide to Your Brain and Its Politics.* New York: Penguin Books, 2009.

Lakoff, George, and Mark Johnson. *Metaphors We Live By.* Chicago: University of Chicago Press, 1980.

———. *Philosophy in the Flesh: The Embodied Mind and Its Challenges to Western Thought.* New York: Basic Books, 1999.

Landels, J. G. *Engineering in the Ancient World.* Berkeley: University of California Press, 1978.

Lanham, Richard A. *A Handlist of Rhetorical Terms.* 2nd ed. Berkeley: University of California Press, 1991.

Law, Vivien, and Ineke Sluiter, eds. *Dionysius Thrax and the Techne Grammatike.* Münster, Germany: Nodus Publikationen, 1995.

Lawley, James, and Penny Tompkins. *Metaphors in Mind: Transformation through Symbolic Modelling.* London: Developing Company Press, 2000.

Leatherdale, W. H. *The Role of Analogy, Model, and Metaphor in Science.* New York: American Elsevier, 1974.

Leith, Sam. *Words Like Loaded Pistols: Rhetoric from Aristotle to Obama.* New York: Basic Books, 2012.

Lenneberg, Eric H. *The Biological Foundations of Language.* New York: John Wiley, 1967.

Leonard, Tim. "How Metaphors Shape Our View of the Economy." *Marketplace*, August 6, 2012.

Leuchtenberg, William E. *Franklin D. Roosevelt and the New Deal 1932–1940.* New York: Harper Torchbooks, 1963.

Lewis, David. *We, the Navigators: The Ancient Art of Landfinding in the Pacific.* 2nd ed. Honolulu: University of Hawaii Press, 1994.

Lightman, Alan. *The Discoveries: Great Breakthroughs in 20th-Century Science.* New York: Pantheon Books, 2005.

Lischer, Richard. *The Preacher King: Martin Luther King Jr. and the Word that Moved America.* New York and Oxford: Oxford University Press, 1995.

Liu, Eric, and Nick Hanauer. *The Gardens of Democracy: A New American Story of Citizenship, the Economy, and the Role of Government.* Seattle: Sasquatch Books, 2011.

Lloyd, G. E. R. *Polarity and Analogy: Two Types of Argumentation in Early Greek Thought.* London: Cambridge University Press, 1966.

Luntz, Frank. *Words That Work: It's Not What You Say, It's What People Hear.* New York: Hyperion Books, 2007.

MacArthur, Brian, ed. *The Penguin Book of Twentieth-Century Speeches.* New York: Penguin Books, 1992.

Macknik, Stephen L., and Susana Martinez-Conde, with Sandra Blakeslee. *Sleights of Mind: What the Neuroscience of Magic Reveals About Our Everyday Deceptions.* New York: Henry Holt, 2010.

Mandelbaum, Michael. *The Meaning of Sports: Why Americans Watch Baseball, Football, and Basketball and What They See When They Do.* New York: Public Affairs, 2004.

Maryland v. King, 133 S. Ct. 1958 (2013).

McArthur, Tom, ed. *The Oxford Companion to the English Language* Oxford: Oxford University Press, 1992.

McInerny, Ralph. *Studies in Analogy.* The Hague: Martinus Nijhoff, 1968.

McKee, Robert. *Story: Substance, Structure, Style, and the Principles of Screenwriting.* New York: HarperCollins, 1997.

Menaker, Daniel. *A Good Talk: The Story and Skill of Conversation.* New York: Twelve, 2010.

Menand, Louis. *The Metaphysical Club: A Story of Ideas in America.* New York: Farrar, Straus and Giroux, 2001.

Michalko, Michael. *Cracking Creativity: The Secrets of Creative Genius.* Berkeley: Ten Speed Press, 2001.

———. *Thinkertoys: A Handbook of Creative-Thinking Techniques.* 2nd ed. Berkeley: Ten Speed Press, 1991.

Mill, John Stuart. *A System of Logic, Ratiocinative and Inductive: Being a Connected View of the Principles of Evidence and the Methods of Scientific Investigation.* 8th ed. New York: Harper & Brothers, 1882.

Miller, Anne. *Metaphorically Selling: How to Use the Magic of Metaphors to Sell, Persuade, & Explain Anything to Anyone.* New York: Chiron Associates, 2004.

Mithen, Steven. *The Prehistory of the Mind: A Search for the Origins of Art, Religion and Science.* London: Thames and Hudson, 1996.

Mlodinow, Leonard. *Subliminal: How Your Unconscious Mind Rules Your Behavior.* New York: Vintage Books, 2012.

Nehaniv, Chrystopher L., ed. *Computation for Metaphors, Analogy and Agents.* Lecture Notes in Artificial Intelligence 1562. Berlin: Springer-Verlag, 1998.

Nerhot, Patrick, ed. *Legal Knowledge and Analogy: Fragments of Legal Epistemology, Hermeneutics and Linguistics.* Law and Philosophy Library, vol. 13. Dordrecht, Netherlands: Kluwer Academic Publishers, 1991.

Neustadt, Richard E., and Ernest R. May. *Thinking in Time: The Uses of History for Decision Makers.* New York: Free Press, 1986.

Ninkovich, Frank. *Modernity and Power: A History of the Domino Theory in the Twentieth Century.* Chicago: University of Chicago Press, 1994.

Nye, Richard. *America's Assembly Line.* Cambridge, MA: MIT Press, 2013.

Osterwalder, Alexander, and Yves Pigneur. *Business Model Generation: A Handbook for Visionaries, Game Changers, and Challengers.* Hoboken, NJ: John Wiley, 2010.

O'Sullivan, Patrick. "Dominoes or Dice: Geography and the Diffusion of Political Violence." *Journal of Conflict Studies* 16, no. 2 (1996).

Oxford English Dictionary. 2nd ed. Oxford: Clarendon Press, 1989.

Paine, Thomas. *The American Crisis.* New York: Barnes & Noble, 2010.

Partridge, Eric. *Name into Word: Proper Names That Have Become Common Property.* New York: Macmillan, 1950.

———. *Origins: A Short Etymological Dictionary of Modern English.* New York: Macmillan, 1958.

Pearce, Peter. *Structure in Nature Is a Strategy for Design.* Cambridge, MA: MIT Press, 1978.

Penn, Derek C., Keith J. Holyoak, and Daniel J. Povinelli. "Darwin's Mistake: Explaining the Discontinuity between Human and Nonhuman Minds." *Behavioral and Brain Sciences* 31, no. 2 (Apr. 2008): 109–113.

Petroski, Henry. *The Evolution of Useful Things.* New York: Vintage Books, 1994.

Pink, Daniel. *Drive: The Surprising Truth About What Motivates Us.* New York: Riverhead Books, 2009.

Pinker, Steven. *The Language Instinct.* New York: William Morrow, 1994.

———. *Words and Rules: The Ingredients of Language.* New York: Basic Books, 1999.

Planck, Max. *Where Is Science Going?* Prologue by Albert Einstein. New York: W. W. Norton, 1932.

Plato. *The Republic*. Mineola, NY: Dover Publications, 2000.

Pollack, Henry N. *Uncertain Science, Uncertain World*. New York: Cambridge University Press, 2003.

———. *A World without Ice*. New York: Avery, 2009.

Pollack, John. *Cork Boat*. New York: Pantheon Books, 2004.

———. *The Pun Also Rises: How the Humble Pun Revolutionized Language, Changed History, and Made Wordplay More Than Some Antics*. New York: Gotham Books, 2011.

Posner, Richard A. "Reasoning by Analogy." Review of *Legal Reason: The Use of Analogy in Legal Argument* by Lloyd L. Weinreb. *Cornell Law Review* 91, no. 761 (2006).

Pringle, Heather. "The Origins of Creativity." *Scientific American*, March 2013.

Pritchard, J. Laurence. *Sir George Cayley: The Inventor of the Aeroplane*. London: Max Parrish, 1961.

Radford, Edwin. *Unusual Words and How They Came About*. New York: Philosophical Library, 1946.

"Reminiscences of Mr. James O'Connor, The." Interview conducted February 1955. Owen W. Bombard interviews series, 1951–1961. Accession 65. The Henry Ford, Dearborn, MI.

"Reminiscences of Mr. W. C. Klann, The." Interview conducted September 1955. Owen W. Bombard interviews series, 1951–1961. Accession 65. The Henry Ford, Dearborn, MI.

Rousseau, Jean-Jacques. *The Social Contract*. New York: Penguin Books, 1968.

Runco, Mark A., and Steven R. Pritzker. *Encyclopedia of Creativity*. San Diego and London: Academic Press, 1999.

Sandel, Michael J. *What Money Can't Buy: The Moral Limits of Markets*. New York: Farrar, Straus and Giroux, 2012.

Sawyer, R. Keith. *Explaining Creativity: The Science of Human Innovation*. Oxford and New York: Oxford University Press, 2006.

———. *Zig Zag: The Surprising Path to Greater Creativity*. San Francisco: Jossey-Bass, 2013.

Schauer, Frederick. *Thinking Like a Lawyer: A New Introduction to Legal Reasoning*. Cambridge, MA: Harvard University Press, 2009.

Schlesinger, Robert. *White House Ghosts: Presidents and Their Speechwriters from FDR to George W. Bush*. New York: Simon & Schuster, 2008.

Schulz, Kathryn. *Being Wrong: Adventures in the Margin of Error*. New York: Ecco, 2010.

Severn, Bill. *Place Words*. New York: Ives Washburn, 1969.

Shenker-Osorio, Anat. *Don't Buy It: The Trouble with Talking Nonsense about the Economy*. New York: Public Affairs, 2012.

Shlain, Leonard. *Art & Physics: Parallel Visions in Space, Time & Light*. New York: Quill, 1991.

Sieden, Lloyd Steven. *Buckminster Fuller's Universe*. New York: Basic Books, 1989.

Silverstein, David, Philip Samuel, and Neil DeCarlo. *The Innovator's Toolkit: 50+ Techniques for Predictable and Sustainable Organic Growth*. Hoboken, NJ: John Wiley, 2009.

Smith, Adam. *The Wealth of Nations*. Blacksburg, VA: Thrifty Books, 2009.

Sorensen, Ted. *Counselor: A Life at the Edge of History*. New York: Harper, 2008.

Spence, Roy M., Jr., with Haley Rushing. *It's Not What You Sell, It's What You Stand For: Why Every Extraordinary Business Is Driven by Purpose*. New York: Portfolio/Penguin, 2009.

Spenser, Jay. *The Airplane: How Ideas Gave Us Wings.* New York: Smithsonian Books, 2008.

Steinmetz, Sol. *Semantic Antics: How and Why Words Change Meaning.* New York: Random House, 2008.

Strother, French. "The Modern Profession of Inventing." *The World's Work: A History of Our Time,* vol. X (May–October 1905) New York: Doubleday, Page, 1905: 6,289–6,298.

Strunk, William, Jr., and E. B. White. *The Elements of Style.* 3rd ed. New York: Macmillan, 1979.

Sundquist, Eric J. *King's Dream.* New Haven, CT: Yale University Press, 2009.

Sunstein, Cass R. "On Analogical Reasoning." *Harvard Law Review* 106, no. 3 (January 1993): 741–791.

Sun Tzu. *The Art of War.* New York: Quill, 1993.

Taleb, Nassim Nicholas. *The Black Swan: The Impact of the Highly Improbable.* New York: Random House, 2007.

Tobin, Jacqueline L., and Raymond G. Dobard. *Hidden in Plain View: A Secret Story of Quilts and the Underground Railroad.* New York: Doubleday, 1999.

Tufte, Edward R. *Visual Explanations: Images and Quantities, Evidence and Narrative.* Cheshire, CT: Graphics Press, 1997.

Vanderwerth, W. C. *Indian Oratory: Famous Speeches by Noted Indian Chieftains.* Norman, OK: University of Oklahoma Press, 1971.

Vaught, Carl G. *Metaphor, Analogy, and the Place of Places: Where Religion and Philosophy Meet.* Waco, TX: Baylor University Press, 2004.

Viereck, George Sylvester. "What Life Means to Einstein." *Saturday Evening Post,* October 26, 1929.

Wallace, David Foster. *Consider the Lobster and Other Essays.* New York: Back Bay Books, 2007.

Webster's Third New International Dictionary, Unabridged. Springfield, MA: Merriam-Webster, 1993.

Weinreb, Lloyd. *Legal Reason: The Use of Analogy in Legal Argument.* New York: Cambridge University Press, 2005.

Westen, Drew. *The Political Brain: The Role of Emotion in Deciding the Fate of the Nation.* New York: Public Affairs, 2007.

Widmer, Ted. *Listening In: The Secret White House Recordings of John F. Kennedy.* New York: Hyperion, 2012.

Wilson, Edward O. *Biophilia.* Cambridge, MA: Harvard University Press, 1984.

———. *Consilience.* New York: Vintage Books, 1998.

Wolf, Gary. "Steve Jobs: The Next Insanely Great Thing." *Wired*, February 2006.

Wormeli, Rick. *Metaphors & Analogies: Power Tools for Teaching Any Subject.* Portland, ME: Stenhouse Publishers, 2009.

INDEX

Printed in the United States
by Baker & Taylor Publisher Services